John Napper Worsfold

History of Haddlesey

Its Past and Present

John Napper Worsfold

History of Haddlesey
Its Past and Present

ISBN/EAN: 9783337181352

Printed in Europe, USA, Canada, Australia, Japan

Cover: Foto ©ninafisch / pixelio.de

More available books at **www.hansebooks.com**

HADDLESEY CHURCH, AS ENLARGED AND IMPROVED IN 1891.
Frontispiece.

WITH NOTICES OF MANY NEIGHBOURING PARISHES AND TOWNSHIPS,
INCLUDING BIRKIN, BRAYTON, BURN, CARLTON, COWICK, DRAX,
GATEFORTH, EGGBOROUGH, KELLINGTON, ROAL,
PONTEFRACT, SELBY, SNAITH, ETC., ETC.

BY

THE REV. J. N. WORSFOLD,

RECTOR OF HADDL......,
*Fellow of the Royal Statistical Society, London,
Membre Honoraire de la Société d'Histoire, Vaudoise, etc.*

'When joyful hearts with loyal glee from Cowick raised the call
That spread from Hathelsen's bright stream to echo from Sandhall.'

LONDON:
ELLIOT STOCK, 62, PATERNOSTER ROW, E.C.
1894.

PREFACE.

IN sending out this greatly enlarged and completely rewritten work, it is proper I should add a few words of preface, so that readers may know what they are to expect in the following pages. I beg to state, then, that my object has been to recover from the past whatever I could gather that would shed light on the character and doings of our ancestors, with a view of guiding, stimulating, and informing those who now live as to conduct which should make them desirous of adding to the credit and the prosperity of the community in which God's providence has placed them. What patriotism is as regards our native land as a whole, so is an honest and intelligent desire for the reputation and wellbeing of our parish as a smaller and yet integral part of the land, whose glory and greatness is one of the dearest wishes of every true-hearted and intelligent Englishman. Everyone seems more or less to lament the deterioration of rural life—the tendency to crowd into towns, and the unhappy forgetfulness of large numbers who have been drawing considerable revenues from agricultural communities, of the claims which these communities have on them for moral sympathy and material help in order to enable them to realize that moral and material standard of life and circumstance by which rural communities may not unfairly contrast with the greater attractions in some respects of urban populations. I venture to say that no amount of legislative change can ameliorate the condition of the inhabitants of our rural districts unless it be accompanied by a transformation of character. It is moral worth, and not political franchises, that will raise our rural population. Where we have high moral character, intelligence, industry, self-denial, and public spirit, there is nothing in our political institutions which forbids village life to be as happy in all its true essentials as that of the mightiest city in our land. Trusting that the facts recorded in this volume, and the principles laid down, may help to this end is the Author's fervent prayer.

I will not close this short preface without expressing more formally and precisely than I have been able to do in the body of the work my great obligations to many friends and helpers. Notably to Mr. H. Chetwynd-Stapylton, for many private contributions of literary matter, and the kind use of his illustrations of remains of the Templar preceptory at Hirst, the south doorway, pillar-head of doorway, Templar seal, and ground-plan of buildings. To Dr. Fairbanks, late of Doncaster, for the engraving of brass of William Fitzwilliam, Esq., and Elizabeth his wife, who lived at Haddlesey. To Mr. Hodges of Hexham for permission to use his excellent plate of the Darcy tomb in Selby Abbey. Also to Miss Emily Holt, for her kindness in furnishing me with many most valuable details of the movements of Edward II., and of leading soldiers and statesmen of his time. Also to Mr. W. S. Kershaw, the courteous librarian of Lambeth Palace Library, for his very valuable help in furnishing copies of documents connected with the period of the Commonwealth. Also to the Rev. Canon Raine, of York, for valuable and ready use of the Minster library. To Mr. W. Paley Baildon, for information relative to Stapleton and Fitzwilliam property. To Lady Beaumont, of Carlton

Towers, for kind use of the library there. And to the Hon. Mr. and Mrs. Bryan Stapleton, for help with regard to their family pedigree. To the indefatigable Honorary Secretary of the Yorks Archæological and Topographical Society, for use of documents. Neither must I forget earlier obligations to Mr. Wadham Powell and Mr. William Morrell; nor later ones to Miss Davison, of Haddlesey House, who most obligingly has allowed me access to her family papers, and also to reproduce a facsimile of an autograph letter of Oliver Cromwell addressed to the constables and head-boroughs of West Haddlesey.

P.S.—I may add that the profits of this work (if any) will be given to provide a long-standing want of a mission-room and Sunday-school for the hamlet of Hirst Courtney in this parish, with a population of 116 persons, distant two miles from the parish church, or to wipe out the deficit of £60 still needed in payment of outlay on parish church enlargement.

HADDLESEY RECTORY,
April, 1894.

CONTENTS.

PREFACE - - - - - - - - PAGE v

CHAPTER I.
TOPOGRAPHY AND EARLY HISTORY.

Parish extent—Boundaries - - - - - 1-4

CHAPTER II.
EARLY NAMES AND CHARTERS.

Ralph de Hastings — Henry de Laci's Charter — Henry de Vernoil's Charter — Henry de Lacy's Charter — Roger de Rohal — Adam of Newmarket — Lord John Bellaaqua — John de Curteney - - - - - - 5-23

CHAPTER III.
ORIGIN OF THE KNIGHT TEMPLARS.

Emperor Constantine and Empress Helena — Pilgrimages to Palestine — Relics — Peter of Amiens — Council of Clermont — Walter the Penniless — The crusading army and its operations - - - - - - - 24-35

CHAPTER IV.
TOWNSHIP OF HADDLESEY—EARLIEST HISTORIC RECORDS.

Miles Bassett at East and Midel Hamsy — Charter of Peter Dodde — Charter de Hath'say — Charters of Ralph Miller,

William de Euermu, Walter de Euermu; Alan, Prior of
Drax; Ralph, villain; Hugh, son of Walter; Roger, son
of Goodrich, etc.   -   -   -   -   -   -   36-47

CHAPTER V.

THE KNIGHT TEMPLARS: THEIR GROWTH AND DECAY.

Site of the preceptory—Inventories of property and goods, etc.,
belonging to the Order in this neighbourhood   -   - 48-72

CHAPTER VI.

THE KINGDOM OF GOD AND HOUSE OF PRAYER AT HADDLESEY.

Its founder and benefactors—Lists of first clergy and patrons, etc. 73-88

CHAPTER VII.

THE STAPLETON DYNASTY, WHICH EXTENDED FROM 1262 TO THE DEATH OF THOMAS STAPLETON, ABOUT 1380.

The first Baron Stapleton—Battle of Bannockburn, and its
effects   -   -   -   -   -   -   -   89-96

CHAPTER VIII.

EDWARD II. AT HADDLESEY.

Residence of Edward II. at Haddlesey—The King's table—An
itinerary of his journeys, with illustrative map—National
history of this date—Queen Isabella at Cawood—Siege of
Berwick—The Despensers, father and son—Rebellion of
Thomas, Duke of Lancaster—His own execution and that
of other peers at Pontefract—Sandhall—Hatfield Hall, etc. 99-115

CHAPTER IX.

TEMPLE HIRST UNDER THE DARCYS.

Rise and progress of the family—Their services in war—Rate
of wages in fourteenth century for artificers—Also rate of
wages for agricultural labourers, and prices of farm produce
in the sixteenth century—Fishing records for same date   116-119

CHAPTER X.

SECOND BARON MILES STAPLETON.

The foundation of the Order of the Garter—The plague in
England—Baron Stapleton, Sheriff of Yorkshire and

Escheator for the King in Yorkshire—Holds an inquiry at Selby—Has David Bruce, King of Scotland, in his charge—Differences with his tenants at Carlton—Makes his will, and requests that he may be buried in Drax Church—Disputes about property after his death, and law suits in the Court of Chancery and at York—'Parson of Hathelsay' mentioned - - - - - - 120-131

CHAPTER XI.

EST HATHELSAY.

Poll-tax returns—Reign of Richard II.—Est Hathelsay—West Hathelsay—The two Hyrstes—The development of the Hathelsay family—Their migration to South Duffield—Position in Hemingborough—Pedigree, etc. - 132-141

CHAPTER XII.

TEMPLE HIRST AND THE DARCYS (*continued*).

A glance at doings in Parliament in the reign of Edward III.—One of Yorkshire's noblest sons appears in the arena as a patriot and theologian—Is supported by the Court and some of the nobility, including John of Gaunt and many of the clergy—Knights Hospitallers try to deprive Lord Philip Darcy of Temple Hirst—The Darcy tomb in Selby Abbey—Thomas Lord Darcy's connexion with Cardinal Wolsey—Dissolution of the monasteries - - - 142-152

CHAPTER XIII.

THE PILGRIMAGE OF GRACE.

The Pilgrimage of Grace extends from Lincolnshire to Yorkshire—The two provinces of York and Canterbury and the sentiments of their inhabitants—Robert Aske chosen to head 'The Pilgrimage'—Earl Percy refuses to join—Aske captures Pontefract and Lord Darcy of Temple Hirst—Henceforth Temple Hirst is the headquarters of the rebels—Duke of Norfolk out-manœuvres Aske, though Darcy will not betray him—Why Darcy sympathized with Aske—Death on Tower Hill—Courts of law at Temple Hirst 153-171

CHAPTER XIV.

THE DARCYS AFTER THE PILGRIMAGE OF GRACE.

Lord George Darcy and his tomb in Brayton Church—Lord John Darcy, his public employments—'The Good Lord Darcy' and his four wives—Lady Isabel Darcy of Aston—Conyers, Lord Darcy, Earl of Holderness—Pedigree of the Darcys of Aston—Duke of Leeds - - 172-182

CHAPTER XV.

THE STAPLETONS OF CARLTON AND BARONS BEAUMONT.

Arms and Motto—Lady Elizabeth Stapleton—John Stapleton—Brian Stapleton and the wars in France—Carlton Chapel first mentioned—Sir William Gascoigne (son of the chief justice)—Battle of Towton—Creation of the barony of Beaumont—Sir Brian Stapleton at Flodden Field, etc.—Lady Mary Stapleton, who gives silver candlesticks to York Minster—The title of Lord Beaumont revived in the person of Miles Thomas Stapleton of Carlton—Later peers and members of this family - - - - 183-191

CHAPTER XVI.

THE FITZWILLIAMS AT EAST HADDLESEY.

Family details - - - - - - 192-3

CHAPTER XVII.

HADDLESEY CHURCH: ITS CLERGY AND ENDOWMENTS
(resumed from Chapter VI.).

Sir Oliver Cromwell and James I.—Confiscation of Church property—Two priests' lands—National and ecclesiastical changes—Cromwell's letter to constables and head borough of West Haddlesey—Parliamentary surveys affecting Birkin and Haddlesey—Earl of Rosebery—Haddlesey separated from Birkin and re-endowed—Rev. Thomas Pickard, clerk, becomes Rector of Haddlesey under the new scheme—The upset at the Restoration of Charles II. as regards both Haddlesey and Birkin - - 194-206

CHAPTER XVIII.

THE HOUSE OF ANCASTER.

The house of Ancaster connected with Haddlesey in the seventeenth century—Death of Earl Lindsay—The Dukes of Ancaster—Duke and Duchess of Suffolk—Craft and cruelty of Bishop Gardiner—Richard Bertie escapes his reach by flight to Holland -   -   -   -   -   207-218

CHAPTER XIX.

EAST HADDLESEY (*resumed*).

East Haddlesey representative families, including Bromleys, Sawyers, and Crawshaws—Haddlesey Churchyard : its tombstones—Original lines of poetry—Haddlesey canal   219-225

CHAPTER XX.

THE DAVISONS OF HADDLESEY HOUSE (ANCIENTLY BEGHBY HALL).

Leading families in West Haddlesey—The Davisons of Haddlesey House—Miss Davison—Hirst Courtney township of to day—Tithe and tithe-rent charge : the difference in their value—Enclosure of commons land—Temple Hirst township of to-day—Present owner of the Templar Preceptory—Earl Sheffield -   -   -   -   -   226-232

CHAPTER XXI.

FROM DARKNESS TO LIGHT.

Parish history from Chapter XVIII. resumed—Rectors of Birkin from the restoration of Charles II.—The Thornton family—The Rev. Thomas Wright refuses a bishopric—Archdeacon Hill as patron—Rector Alderson—The Rev. Valentine Green at Haddlesey—Rev. S. C. Baker as curate—A new bell, with a new and enlarged church—Three Wesleyan chapels—New order in Council comes into force at the death of the Rev. Valentine Green -   -   233-241

CHAPTER XXII.

FURTHER PAROCHIAL DEVELOPMENT.

PAGE

Further parish progress—Rectory House built, A.D. 1875—Schools—Church enlarged by the additional chancel, etc., A.D. 1878—New font, A.D. 1884—Churchyard enlarged, A.D. 1886—Tower added to the church, with other additions, in 1891—Record of increased number of services—List of baptisms, burials, marriages, confirmations—Postal facilities—Parish Councils Bill—Closing reflections and the author's desire - - - - - -   242-249

LIST OF ILLUSTRATIONS.

	PAGE
HADDLESEY CHURCH - - - - - *Frontispiece*	
SOUTH DOORWAY OF PRECEPTORY - - - -	22
REMAINS OF TEMPLAR PRECEPTORY, TEMPLE HIRST -	47
PILLAR HEAD OF SOUTH DOORWAY OF PRECEPTORY -	48
ROAL HALL - - - - - *To face p.*	60
GATEWAY TO ROAL HALL - - - - "	62
GROUND-PLAN OF PRECEPTORY - - - - -	66
TEMPLARS' SEAL - - - - - - -	72
SIR WM. FITZWILLIAM AND LADY, WHO DIED AT HADDLESEY, A.D. 1474 - - - - - -	84
MAP TO ILLUSTRATE THE ITINERARY OF EDWARD II. AT HADDLESEY AND GENERAL TOPOGRAPHICAL REFERENCES IN THIS WORK - - - - - -	98
ARMS OF THE HADDLESEY FAMILY - *Between pp.* 138-139	
THE TOMB OF JOHN LORD DARCY AND MEINILL (WHO DIED AT TEMPLE HIRST, A.D. 1414) IN SELBY ABBEY, BEFORE ITS RECENT MUTILATION - - -	145
TOMB OF LORD GEORGE DARCY, SON OF THOMAS, LORD DARCY, OF TEMPLE HIRST, IN BRAYTON CHURCH, BEFORE ITS RECENT ALTERATION - - - -	175
FACSIMILE OF LETTER OF OLIVER CROMWELL *To face p.*	206
ANCIENT HOUSE OF THE BROMLEYS - - - -	221
HADDLESEY HOUSE - - - - - -	228
HADDLESEY RECTORY - - - - - -	238
HADDLESEY NATIONAL SCHOOLS - - - -	240

CHAPTER I.

TOPOGRAPHY AND EARLY HISTORY.

' When joyful hearts, with loyal glee, from Cowick raised the call
That spread from Hathelsea's bright stream to echo from Sandhall.'

IN dealing with the subject of parish history, we must either begin with the remotest period to which history reaches in the past, or else, beginning from the standpoint of the present, work backwards into antiquity. This is what we propose to do in this work, and so we start by saying that Haddlesey is situated in the south-eastern corner, *i.e.*, the fertile valley, of the great county of York, and forms part of the Parliamentary district of Barkstone Ash Division of the West Riding; its nearest and post town is Selby, famous for its grand abbey, founded by William the Conqueror. Another town nine miles distant, and famous in English history, is Pontefract. The neighbourhood was formerly included in the extensive forest of Sherwood (Baine's ' Yorkshire '), noted as the scene of the exploits of the bold outlaw Robin Hood and his merrie men. The parish of Haddlesey is bounded on the north by Brayton, on the east by Drax and Carlton; on the south by Hensall and Kellington, and west by Birkin. The scenery is for the most part level, though relieved by the two elevations of Hambleton

Hough,[1] and Brayton Bargh[2] on the north. There are also several patches of woodland, which diversify the otherwise unbroken expanse of extensive cornfields and pasture-land. But the most distinctive of all the geographical features is the river Aire, called by an ancient historian (Leland)[3] a 'royal river.' Rising in the high lands of the extreme west of the county, it flows down from *Malham Cove*,[4] a limestone cliff of some three hundred

[1] From the Celtic *hoga*, meaning a heap.

[2] Spelt generally 'Barff,' a contraction of Barugh, meaning a gravel mound shot up through the clay by some convulsion of nature. A beacon was erected on the Barff in 1803, when England was threatened with invasion by Napoleon.

[3] Thoresby ('Ducatus Leodiensis'), quoting Camden, says it derives its name from *ara* (Celtic), meaning slow, heavy, or calm and bright, as the river Arar (Saone, in France), which Cæsar says moves so incredibly slow that you can scarcely tell its course by the eye: 'Fluvium est quod fertur incredibili lenitate, ita ut oculis in utram partem fluat judicari vix possit.' May this remind us of the waters of Shiloah, *qui vont doucement* (Isa. viii. 6)? This our Aire is said in a MS. Survey to be 'celeberimum' and 'præstantissimum fluvium in partibus Borealibus.' It issueth from the root of the mountain Pennigent. The learned Selden, in his commentary on the latter part of Drayton's 'Polybion,' wherein he advances northward from the Don to the river Aire, says:

> 'Now speak I of a flood who thinks there none should dare
> Once to compare with her, supposed by her descent
> The darling daughter born of lofty Penigent,
> Who, from her father's foot by Skipton Down doth scud,
> And leading thence to Leeds, that delicatest flood,
> Takes Calder, coming in by Wakefield,' etc.

The Aire was made navigable in 1699 by the exertions of William Milner, Esq., then Mayor of Leeds.

[4] Malham Cove is a very interesting place. It may be described as a magnificent amphitheatre of rock of very fine limestone. These rocks are 286 feet in height from the base to the central summit. The sides of the amphitheatre tower towards each other, and in the middle is the central rock that slopes backward, and from the bottom of the precipice is a swift current of clear water, which is the source of the river Aire, in the very backbone of England, for the rivers which rise

feet high, and pursues its way along the picturesque valley to which it gives name (Airedale) with its waters uncontaminated as far as Skipton, the first town on its banks. From Skipton it flows on by Keighley, and from thence to Leeds, a distance of thirty-five miles from its source. From Leeds it wends its way through fertile meadows to Castleford, at which place it is joined by the waters of the Calder, and with its stream thus augmented, it flows on through Haddlesey, vessels of considerable tonnage wafted on its bosom, until effecting a junction with the Ouse at Airmin, i.e., Airemouth (*aire* and *mun*, Swedish or Danish for mouth), from whence it joins the Humber and flows into the German Ocean. The channel of the Aire is very deep and circuitous in its course in many parts. Not unfrequently it overflows its banks, and by so doing greatly adds to the fertility of the land contiguous to its banks. Some of its irruptions have, however, been attended with less pleasant consequences, *e.g.*, in the year 1069 William the Conqueror was detained against his will three weeks at Castleford by the overflowing of this river; but the Great Flood, the memory of which will last for a very long period in the district, occurred on Saturday, November 17, 1866. A rainfall of a very unusual character caused the river to overflow its banks and lay West Haddlesey under water. From West Haddlesey it flowed into the canal, which connects the Aire with the town of Selby, and deluged the latter place to the depth of several feet, even extinguishing the retorts of the gasworks and spreading terror and distress on every side. The waters reached their greatest height at half-past ten o'clock on Sunday morning, but did not recede to any extent for the next four-and-twenty hours. Monday being Selby market day, a few people from the

---

on the eastern side flow into the German Ocean and those on the west into the Irish Sea.

neighbourhood with difficulty made their way to the town, bringing with them sad tales of disaster as regarded their own parishes. The places which suffered most appear to have been Selby, Snaith, Camblesforth, the two Hursts, the two Haddleseys, Gateforth, Burn, Cawood, and Ryther. It was not before Saturday afternoon that the water was drained away by means of deep channels cut communicating with the Ouse. But terrible as was this inundation, it was as nothing compared to that which happened through the extraordinary rains of October 14 and 15, 1892. On this latter occasion some two-thirds of this parish was under water, in some places to the depth of seven or eight feet, causing a very large destruction of newly-stacked corn, as well as some hundreds of cattle.

But turning to the more normal character of the river, we would observe that large quantities of valuable fish, including salmon, have been found within its waters. Of late years, however, the pollution caused by the inflow of poisonous sewage from some of the manufacturing towns on its banks has been most destructive to this valuable article of human food, as well as rendering the water unfit for drinking purposes—indeed, a cause of much discomfort, not to say disease.[1]

[1] This great nuisance will, however, be remedied by the efforts of our sanitary authorities, strengthened by recent legislation, and the noble stream become again a thing of beauty and a channel of blessing to those who dwell on its banks.

CHAPTER II.

EARLY NAMES AND CHARTERS.

BUT we must proceed to consider the history of Haddlesey, a subject not so barren of interest as some might suppose, especially to persons of an antiquarian taste. The district is one of those which were the last to acknowledge the power of the Norman invader, and retains many Saxon words in use up to the present time; for instance, low-lying pasture-land is called an 'Ing'; a wood is termed a 'Hag'; a close a 'Garth'; to carry is spoken of as 'leading.' But the very name of the place is intensely and significantly Saxon. Haddlesey is a corruption of Athelsey, which was compounded of 'Atheling,' the name of the last Saxon prince, and 'ey' an island or river[1] (there is a stream on the south side of the parish still called the Ey). The name was then first corrupted to Hathelsey as in documents above five hundred years old, and subsequently to Addlesey, and lastly to Haddlesey. There are many places in England the names of which are traceable to a similar etymology, and which have experienced similar corruption, *e.g.*, the

---

[1] So Sheppey, in Kent, was formerly written 'Sceapeye'; *i.e.*, island of sheep—R. de Hoveden. While I still adhere to the above as the most probable derivation of Haddlesey, yet I am willing to confess that more recent study of the topographical character of the place impresses me with the *plausibility*, to say the least, of Mr. Wheater's

village of Addle, from John de Adela, near Leeds; Adlingfleet, properly Athelingflete, on the Ouse; also in the county of Surrey Addlestone, and in the city of London itself Addlestreet, Aldermanbury, and the island of Athelney, Somerset, which is a corruption of Athelingey, or island of nobles.

Another circumstance which gives an interest to this parish arises from the fact of the Knight Templars having had one of their earliest and most important establishments within its boundaries, the foundation of Temple Hirst being antecedent to either of its greater sisters Newsam or Ribstane. The original founder was Ralph de Hastings. There is great difficulty in tracing this family, although its members seem to have played a very conspicuous and honourable part in the transactions of

---

speculations as given in the *Leeds Mercury*, some years ago. Mr. Wheater says: 'Hathelsey is but a corruption of the words which in Saxon speech mean "the beautiful water," the beauty of the scene being enhanced by the rays of the eastern sun shimmering on the waters between the foliage of the woods, where timber and pasture intermingled. . . . Longfellow must have seen such a Hathelsay in the great land of the West, a thousand years later, when he speaks of the "shining big-sea-water":

> '"Dark behind it rose the forest,
> Rose the black and gloomy pine-trees,
> Rose the firs with cones upon them;
> Bright before it beat the water,
> Beat the clear and sunny water,
> Beat the shining big-sea-water."'

To endorse this view, we may imagine that some hundreds of acres of land alongside of the old 'ey' (as now called) and the shire fleet as denominated in the charter of Henry Vernoil, were in Saxon times permanently covered with water, surrounded on the higher ground to the north by wood—*i.e.*, hyrstland—from which pasture-ground for the early settlers was found by essarting—*i.e.*, clearing out a space in the woods. In this way Haddlesey would be truly, as very occasionally written, 'Hathel*sea*'; and these conclusions all harmonize with the signification of the river Aire.

their day. Henry de Hastings was one of the prisoners taken on the barons' side by Prince Edward at the battle of Evesham. Perhaps because Edward I. had robbed the Templar treasury of £10,000 in 1262. It is important, however, to remember that Richard Hastings was head of the Templars in London in 1154, and was employed by the King, Henry II., in various important negotiations; among others, that of the betrothal of the French Princess Margaret to Prince Henry of England. Certain castles in France were held by the Templars pending the celebration of the nuptials. By hurrying on the marriage (though both the engaged parties were infants 'crying in the cradle'), the English King obtained *immediate* possession of the French fortresses, to the great annoyance of the King of France. The Templars who took part in this marriage and were custodiants of the castles were Robert de Pirou[1] (afterwards Master of the Preceptory at Temple Hirst), Tostes St. Omer, and Richard Hastings (see Roger Hoveden and Addison, 'Knight Templars'). The above Richard Hastings was the friend and confidant of Thomas à Becket. During the disputes between à Becket and the King, we are told that the Archbishop withdrew from the council chamber, where all his brethren were assembled, and went to consult with Richard de Hastings, the Prior of the Temple at London, who threw himself on his knees before him, and with many tears besought him to give his adherence to the statutes of the Council of Clarendon.

To return to the person of Ralph de Hastings, it is reasonable to suppose that he may have been at the date of the foundation of the Templar preceptory at Hirst mesne lord of Birkin, this place being an isolated nook

---

[1] The family are supposed to have been lords of Lessay, near Carrenlan, on the west coast of Normandy, opposite Jersey, and the founder of its famous abbey, William de Pirou, was steward of Henry I.

connected ecclesiastically with Snaith, though some writers think that it was part of the parish of Brayton in Saxon times. Whether so or not, the area extending east and west from Carlton to Haddlesey, and south and north from Kellington to Burn and Barlow, was one great hyrst or wood, and Ralph de Hastings, whose ancestral home was at Fenwick (Hugh Hastings is said to hold lands at Fenwick, Snaith, etc., A.D. 1540), seems to have approached Hurst from the south side of the Aire (perhaps from Potterlawe, of which we shall have more to say later on). His charter of donation is lost, but we have that of Henry Laci, the superior lord, confirming it, as follows :

THE CHARTER OF HENRY DE LACI IN CONFIRMATION OF THE GRANT OF HURST BY RALPH DE HASTINGS.

'To the archbishops and bishops, and all the sons of the holy Church both present and to come, Henry de Laci giveth greeting and faithful salutations in Christ. Be it known unto you that I, for the health of my soul and for the health of the soul of my father and of the soul of my mother and of the souls of my relations and my ancestors, have granted to the brethren of the temple of Solomon that gift which Radulph de Hastings made them of my land of Hurst. Wherefore I will that they hold that land with all its appurtenances in such wise that they hold no alms in England better and more freely, and as their charter, which they hold of Radulph, witnesses. And this charter was made in the presence of brother Richard de Hastings (Preceptor at Hurst) at Bruges—the witnesses being: Radulph, the son of Nicolas, his steward; Roger de Tilli, probably a relative of Ralph de Tilli, one of the Templars at the siege of Acre; Adam, the son of Peter (de Birkin, 1190); Roger, the son of Turstan;

Matthew de Maluvir[1] (later on Malauverer and Mallory); Robert the chamberlain; Robert the baker; William de Vilers; Hugo the Abbot; William the cook; Alan the chamberlain.'

Otto de Tilli was a witness to the Kirkstall Abbey charter, and Ralph and Hugh de Tilli figure in later documents. William de Vilers also was a witness to the Kirkstall charter. A question has been raised as to the place where Henry de Laci executed this charter of confirmation. I cannot see why there should be any hesitation in accepting the word 'Bruges' as the name of the well-known city in Flanders. And the association is highly instructive from several points of view. First of all, it reminds us that in the twelfth and following centuries—indeed, up to the times when Fleming artificers settled in our eastern counties — England was the chief wool-producing country, and that Bruges was the great central mart for the world's commerce at that time. So that Englishmen were often at Bruges, and there transacted not only commercial but political and ecclesiastical engagements. The number of witnesses to De Laci's charter show they were such as could be only had at some place of common and convenient resort. That such a place was Bruges may be inferred from other circumstances; e.g., the grant by King John to hold a weekly fair at Wakefield (Doc. A, 384, Cat. Public Records) is given by the hand of the Provost of Beverley, and the Archdeacon of Wells at Bruges (Bruge) 15th of March, 5 King John. Further, in the reign of Edward III.,

---

[1] Maulever, meaning 'the bad hunter,' is not a complimentary epithet. The arms of the family are three greyhounds, and the story is that the founder, being about to loose his dogs for coursing, did it so badly that there was more likelihood of strangling the dogs than of catching the hare (Thoresby). John de Maulever was with Sir Miles Stapleton in France A.D. 1308, making preparations for the marriage of King Edward II. See Y. A. J., vol. viii., p. 92.

when the Pope tried to obtain the removal of the Statutes of Præmunire and Provisors, a conference was held at BRUGES, where the famous reformer, John Wycliffe, one of the King's chaplains, attended to represent the interests of England against the encroachments of the Papacy.

All the witnesses to the charter of Henry de Laci are more or less significant personages, but it is important to get some idea of Henry de Laci himself as the superior lord of Ralph de Hastings, and of others who were benefactors to the Templar Preceptory at Hirst. The founder of the family seems to have been ILBERT DE LACI, Lord of Bois l'Eveque in Normandy, created an English baron about the year 1072 for his services to William I. at the conquest of England.

His eldest son was ROBERT DE LACI, FITZ-ILBERT or DE PONTEFRACT. He succeeded his father about 1090, and founded the Priory of St. John of Jerusalem at Pontefract. He married Matilda, of whom we know but little. Their eldest son was ILBERT, who fought at the battle of Lincoln on behalf of King Stephen, and was one of the leaders at the Battle of the Standard, A.D. 1138. His third brother was HENRY DE LACI, with whom we have most to do. He seems to have founded Kirkstall Abbey in 1177, and confirms the grant which William de Villers (one of the signatories of his own charter confirming the grant to Temple Hirst) made to the newly-founded Preceptory of Temple Newsam after the suppression of the order so closely associated with Hirst.

ROBERT DE LACI, the only son of Henry, is one of the *witnesses* to the charter of his father confirming the gift of Henry Vernoil to Hirst; he also confirms the donations of his father to Kirkstall and other places at Pontefract Castle. He is succeeded by JOHN, Constable of Chester and Baron of Flamborough; and this latter by ROGER DE LACI, Baron of Halton and Constable of Chester. He died in 1212, and his gift of Bradley to

Fountains Abbey is witnessed by William Fitz-William, Adam de Novo Mercato, and Henry his brother.

We proceed, then, to quote the next considerable gift to the Preceptory at Hirst conveyed by the charter of Henry de Vernoil.

Henry de Vernoil's Charter.

'Let men present and to come know that I Henry de Vernoil have given and granted (and by this my charter and this my seal confirmed) to God, and the house of the Temple of Jerusalem, and to brother Robert de Pirou (who then held the house of Hirst), in pure and perpetual alms, freely and quit of all secular service, xxxiiii acres of land and the house of Randolph of Potterlaw, and pasture for one hundred sheep in the common pasturage of the town of Eggborough and my meadow that lies between the River Aire and the Shire Fleet free to have and to possess, for xii pence to be paid on the feast of Saint Martin. And for this grant the aforesaid brother Robert hath given to me of the charity of the house of the Temple vii marks of silver, and to Henry Hatecrist a half-mark, to free the land from pledge—the witnesses being: Bertram, Prior of Pontefract,[1] and the whole congregation, Jordan Foliot,[2] Adam the son of Peter (de Birkin), Thomas

---

[1] The order of Black or Dominican Friars was established in Pontefract about 1256 by Edmund de Lasey, the son of John de Lasey (Constable of Chester, and by his wife Earl of Lincoln). See article in *Leeds Mercury* and Holmes's 'Black Friars of Pontefract.'

[2] Jordan Foliot, one of the witnesses to this charter, was himself a benefactor to the preceptory at Hirst, having given to it forty acres of land situated at Fenwick, near Doncaster. He owned lands also at Firsby, in Lincolnshire. Gilbert Foliot was Bishop of Hereford from 1148 to 1163; Robert, from 1174 to 1186; Hugh, from 1219 to 1234. William Foliot, formerly Rector of Brayton, gave two acres in Brayton to Selby Abbey. See *Yorkshire Archæological Journal*, vol. viii., pp. 278, 279, for further particulars of the Foliots. He died June 5, 1258.

his brother, Otto de Tilly,[1] Henry de Waleis,[2] Malger de Stiverum, William de Beleue,[3] Samson the son of Henry, Henry the son of Jordan Foliot, Jordan de Ledestun, and Alexander and John and Roger de Ruhal, who have granted and confirmed these.'

HENRY DE LACY'S CHARTER, IN CONFIRMATION OF THE CHARTER OF HENRY DE VERNOIL.

'To all the sons of the holy Mother Church, both present and to come, Henry de Lacy giveth greeting. Be it known unto you that I have granted (and by this present charter confirmed) to God and the Blessed Mary and to the brethren of the Temple of Solomon all those lands which brother Robert de Pirou (Master of the Preceptory at Hirst) obtained of my fee in the territory of Eggborough[4] in meadows and fields and ploughed lands; namely, certain lands of the holding of Henry de Vernoil and of Alexander de Rohal and of John de Rohal and of Roger de Rohal, to have and to hold in free and perpetual alms in such wise as the charters of the subscribers on their behalf witness. Now, this charter was made at Easter, when the lord Henry did hasten upon

---

[1] Otto de Tilli. In notes on the Earl of Strafford's quarterings in *Yorkshire Archæological Journal*, vol. vi., p. 374, mention is made of Sir Henry de Neumarch (or Newmarket), who married Dionysia, daughter and heiress of Otho de Tilli.

[2] In the Pontefract Chartulary, under date April, 1248, mention is made of gifts by Richard Wallensis (or Waleis).—*Yorkshire Archæological Journal*, note, p. 533, Wapentake of Osgoldcross, by R. Holmes.

[3] William de Belewe = Bella aqua. Thos. and John Bellaqua, Kts., and Lady Alice Bellaqua are in the list of those buried at the priory of the Blackfriars of York. See above, vol. vi., pp. 415, 416.

[4] Judging from the fact that Poterlawe was in this territory, and the list of those paying poll-tax 2 Richard II.—*e.g.*, Henry Shyrwood, merchant, 6s. 8d., with seven servants; Margaret Shyrwood, innkeeper, five servants; with many others, including John Laverock and his wife, 4d., etc.—we may conclude that it was a considerable village in ancient times.

his journey to Jerusalem ; the witnesses being Robert de Lacy, his son and heir ; *Adam de Reinervil, seneschal ;*[1] William de Builli ;[2] Thomas the son of Peter ; Thomas de Reinervil.'

Endorsed ' HIRST.'

ROGER DE ROHAL'S CHARTER.

'To all the sons of holy Mother Church, both present and to come, Roger de Rohal giveth greeting. Be it known unto you, that I have given and granted (and by this my charter confirmed), to God and to Holy Mary, and in the hands of brother Robert de Pirou (Preceptor), and to the other brethren of the Temple of Solomon, Alan, my man, who was the son of a villain of Hirst, in pure and perpetual alms,[3] to have for ever, in freedom and quietness — the witnesses being William, chaplain of Kellington ; Alexander de Rohal ; William the steward ; Arengrimus ; Roger Arengrimus ;[4] William de Hirst, and many others.'

Endorsed ' HIRST.'

(Dodsworth MSS., folio 180.)

---

[1] This name occurs with Henry the Clerk of Kellington and others to a charter of 'Roger, son of Walter de Witewode, giving 2 bovates of his demesnes in Withewode to the monks of Pontefract ; dated on the second lent after Sept. 27th, 1172,' when Henry II. swore at Avranches to take the cross from the Christmas following.—*Archæological Journal*, vol. viii., p. 500, note.

[2] Of the family of the Counts of Eu in Normandy and owners of Tickhill Castle.

[3] This gift of a serf to charitable bodies seems to have been common, not only from the act of Henry de Vernoil above, but also from the fact recorded in Dugdale, that Nicholas de Stuteville gave Michael de Hamelscia, his villain, and all his progeny to the Dean and Chapter of St. Peter's, York.

[4] Aregrim and Arnegrim both appear in names of tenants *in capite*, time of Edward the Confessor, in Domesday Book.

THE CHARTER OF ADAM, THE SON OF LORD JOHN OF NEWMARKET.

'To all the sons of holy Mother Church to whom the present writing shall come, Adam, the son of Lord John of Newmarket, giveth greeting for ever in the Lord. Be it known unto all of you that we for the health of our soul, and of the souls of our ancestors and descendants, have given and granted (and by this present writing declared quit of us and our descendants for ever) to God and Blessed Mary and to the Master and Brethren of the Order of the Temple of Solomon of Jerusalem, Peter, the son of Hugo de Moseley, once our serf, with all his issue, born and unborn, and with all his goods and chattles, acquired and to be acquired, without any reserve. On condition, namely, that the aforesaid Peter and his heirs be free men of the aforesaid Master and Brothers of the Order of the Temple for ever, and that they have free administration in the ordering and disposing of their goods and chattles according to their will. And for this gift and for the having of his freedom the said Peter and his heirs will pay annually to the *Chapel of the Temple of Hirst* to light the altar of the Blessed Mary one penny on the day of her Assumption. To hold and have the said Peter and his heirs free and quit of all service of us and our heirs to the aforesaid brethren for ever. And that so neither we nor our heirs nor anyone through us shall be able at any time, in any way, to assert or establish any right or claim on the aforesaid Peter or on his issue or on his goods or chattles, as aforesaid, we have caused our seal to be affixed to this present writing'—The witnesses being Peter de Gypton, probably a member of the Priory of Pontefract (*Y. A. J.*, vol. xi., p. 29) ; William de Normanton ; William de Wadworth ; Thomas de Venella (of the little house), in Hirst ; Roger de Behal, in Hausey (*i.e.*, Haddlesey) ; Richard, the son of Alan de Hausey (Haddlesey) ; Galfrid de

Poterlawe, clerk; Hugo de Landrik, clerk, and others (Dodsworth MSS.).

The grantor of this charter is said (Baine's 'Yorkshire Past and Present') to have held three knights' fees under De Laci, Earl of Lincoln, and also two knights' fees of the honour of the Earl of Warren. His father, Lord John of Newmarket, and his sons, Adam and John, are in the list of those buried in the churchyard of the Blackfriars of Pontefract. But only the heart of Adam de Newmarket himself seems to have been deposited there (Holmes's 'The Blackfriars of Pontefract'). Adam de Newmarket was summoned to two Parliaments in the reign of Henry III., viz., in the years 1261 and 1265. He seems to have taken the side of the barons in their quarrel with Henry, and was taken prisoner at the siege of Northampton, A.D. 1264. In 1230 Adam de Newmarket founded the chapel of St. Nicholas, Cobcroft, in Darrington parish. Among the signatories to this charter is Roger de *Behal, in Hausey*. The italicised words open up material for inquiry. Where was 'Behal'? The word often occurs in the course of this history, sometimes written Beghly. Had it not been said to be 'in Hausey,' an expression frequently used in early records of Haddlesey, we might have concluded the allusion was to the township of Beaghal, in the parish of Kellington, but the appendage 'in Hausey' forbids any such conclusion.

'Galfrido, of Poterlawe, clerk,' is also noteworthy, first of all as reminding us of the fact that whilst all Templars were not ecclesiastics, yet that in the order were clergy, so that they could be supplied with all the offices of religion by members of the Templar brotherhood.

Again, Potterlawe is a place whose name often occurs in connection with the Templar preceptory at Hirst. I think the charter of Henry Vernoil makes it plain that Potterlawe was in the township of Eggborough, the site probably of what is now known as Sherwood Farm, and that after Henry de Vernoil's gift it was attached to the preceptory at Hirst as its grange, a very convenient arrangement for the brethren, in relation to their use of Kellington Church, made over to them by Henry de Lacy.

In the records of Selby Abbey and elsewhere, from the way in which Potterlawe is spoken of, it seems to have consisted of several cottages as well as 'the house of Randolph,' mentioned in Henry de Vernoil's charter. In 1343 it appeared that there were tenements in Potterlawe which the Abbot of Selby received from the Templars in exchange for tithes of Willoughton, Lincolnshire.

The etymology of Potterlawe, viz., *lawe* or *low*, a hill—as Taplow, Bucks, on the Chiltern Hills—well agrees with the site I assign to it, which is on rising ground.

The next chartered gift to Templars at Hirst is that of Lord John Bellaqua, the son of Lord Thomas. This is a family whose name often occurs in the history of this parish. His daughter Sibill was married to Sir Miles, Baron Stapleton, of Haddlesey.

THE CHARTER OF LORD JOHN, SON OF LORD THOMAS DE BELLAAQUA.

' To all the sons of holy Mother Church to whom this present writing cometh, the Lord John, the son of the Lord Thomas de Bellaaqua, giveth greeting in the Lord. Know ye that I, for the health of my soul and for the souls of all my ancestors and descendants, have given and granted (and by this my present charter confirmed) to God and the Blessed Mary, and to the Master and Brethren of the Order of the Temple of Solomon at Jerusalem, a piece of land in the south copse of my wood of Byrne, in trenches, wherein it is inclosed, lying to *the northward* of the said Brethren of Hyrst, extending to the west over against the trench which is called "the Haddlesey ditch." And this piece of land contains in itself six acres of land, with forty perches and twenty feet, and with free entrance and exit, and that the said piece shall be enclosed at the will of the said Brethren and at the convenience of the same Masters and Brethren for all days, to wit, henceforward to deal with it without any challenge or contradiction or hindrance on the part of me or my heirs. To hold and to have to the aforesaid Master and Brethren of the Order of the Temple of Solomon at Jerusalem of me and my heirs freely, quietly, completely, rightly and peaceably, whether there be more or less than six acres in the aforesaid piece of land, with all the appurtenances, liberties and easements appertaining to such a tenement, by payment to me and my heirs annually of two shillings (*solidi*), that is to say, the one half at Whitsuntide and the other half at the festival of St. Martin in the winter, for all other services and demands and aids and tallages, and for all manner of services and customs. And all the aforesaid piece, with its trenches, I, verily, the said John and my heirs, will warrant and acquit to the aforenamed Master and Brethren of the Order of the Temple of Solomon at Jerusalem, to hold it for their separate use for all the days of the world, and in consideration of the aforesaid service will on all occasions defend it, even against all men and women. In witness whereof I have confirmed this present writing with the protection of my seal—the witnesses being Henry de Heck, John de Gowdal, *William de Holm* (*i.e., Insula*) *Lord of Hyrst Courtenay*, Roger de Behal,[1] John Balkoc de Hausay (Haddlesey), Roger, the son of Hugo de Hausay (Haddlesey), Galfrid de Potterlawe, clerk, and others.'

Continuing the benefactions to Temple Hirst, I quote

[1] We have not the words 'in Hausey' repeated here, but doubtless, from later inquiries among the oldest inhabitants, this Behal is the place afterwards called Beghby, and represents the spot on which Haddlesey House now stands.

and translate from Dugdale's 'Monasticon,' vol. vi., part ii., p. 838. Sir[1] Robert de Stapleton gave the Templars there the town of Osmundthorpe, A.D. 1172. This place is said to have been the Villa Regia of the kings of Northumberland. Thoresby speaks of it in his time as one mile from Leeds, on the Wye Beck.

Page 839, Henry III., King of England, gave to the Templars a market in the town of Wetherby, in county of York . . . and also free warren in all lordships, manors and lands of his . . . and at Newsam, Wetherby, Ribstane, *Hurst*, Whiteley and Westerdale, in county of York.

Page 840, No. xxvii.: Some of the signatures of witnesses to a charter of Roger de Mowbray of all his land in Ketely, Isle of Axholme, viz., Allan, chaplain of the Temple; Peter, clerk; Robert de Dayville, and Hamon Beleu, *i.e.*, Bellaqua, are of interest to us.

Also some of the witnesses to No. xxxiii.: A charter of Hawise de Grantvill of a gift of a bovate of land in Skelton, and of a toft in Wynhill. To God and blessed Mary and brethren of the Order of Solomon's Temple *at Newsam*, viz., Lord Robert de Stapleton and Jordanus de Insula (especially).

But still more so No. xxxv., charter of John de Curteney of lands in EAST HIRST. This is from an autograph in the abbey of St. Mary's, York, and the translation is taken from an article in the *Leeds Mercury*.

'John de Curteney giveth greeting in the Lord to all seeing or hearing these letters. Be it known to all, that I, for the health of my own soul and of that of Emma my wife, and of those of my ancestors and survivors, have given, granted, and by this my present charter have confirmed to God and to blessed Mary and to the Brethren of the Order

---

[1] He held two knights' fees under Henry de Lacy. See *Yorkshire Archæological Journal*, Mr. Chetwynd-Stapylton's article on the Templars at Temple Hurst.

of the Temple, all the land in the territory of EAST HYRST according as the ditch of the said Brethren runs, and extends from the boundaries of Carlton up to the ploughland of Hyrst (*i.e.*, West Hyrst); and (as much is included in short and distinct speech) all the land in length and breadth in all ways and senses as the ditch of the aforesaid Brethren extends to and comprises: to have and to hold to the said Brethren of the Order of the Temple, all the said land, with all rights and easements which can be conveyed to them freely, quietly, perfectly, and peacefully; paying to me and my heirs annually ten shillings at two terms, namely, at Whitsuntide 5s. and at Martinmas in winter 5s., for every service and secular claim. Moreover I have given, granted, and quit-claimed to the same Brethren of the Order of the Temple, all common rights which I or my heirs or my men at Hyrst have or may have in the wood of the said Brethren of the Order of the Temple, that the said Brethren may enclose or clear their wood freely at will; to their greatest advantage, without any claim or hindrance (*calumpnia*) from me, my heirs or my men. And for this my concession, donation and quit-claim, the aforesaid Brethren of the Order of the Temple have granted and quit-claimed to me, my heirs and my men, all the common right which they or their men have or might have in my wood, so that I may enclose or clear my wood freely and to my greatest advantage without any claim from the aforesaid Brethren of the Order of the Temple or their men. And I and my heirs will guarantee, acquit and defend all the aforesaid land, for the aforesaid service, to the aforesaid Brethren, as it is provided. But as this my donation, concession, confirmation and quit-claim may continue for ever confirmed and unimpaired, I have corroborated this present writing with the impression of my seal.'

Witnesses: Lord Adam de Bellaqua, Henry de Beilaye, Jordanus de Insula, Simon de Rupe, Alan de Smitheton,

John, son of Elias,[1] Ralph de Rohale, and many others. These names are interesting from their association with other transactions of the Templars, but I only stay here to notice one, viz., that of Ralph de Rohale, who is mentioned as giving one-third of Brayton Church to the monks at Selby; see p. 221, Coucher book of Selby, charter of Ralph de Ruhale, cccxxxvi., witnessed by Hilard de Hecke, and others.

The above charter of John de Curteney's is supposed to have been given *ante* 1227, and was followed by a final concord in 1234. The document, No. xxxiv., is headed: '*A fine raised by John de Curteney and Emma his wife upon their lands in Est Hyrst*' [19 Hen. III.]. 'This is the final concord, made in the Court of our Lord the King at York, on the Tuesday next after the feast of St. Hilary, 19 Hen. III., in the presence of Robert Bertram, Robert de Ros, Adam of Newmarket, William York and Jollanus de Nevill, justices itinerant, and other faithful lords of the King then present; between brother Robert de Stanford, Master of the Order of the Temple in England, plaintiff, by Robert de Almanthorp, his attorney for gaining or losing; and John de Curteney and Emma his wife, defendants, of 60 acres of land, with their appurtenances in Est Hyrst, whence it was agreed between them in the same court, viz., that the said John and Emma recognised that the whole of the aforesaid land with its appurtenances was the right of the said Master and Brethren, as that which the said Master and Brethren have of the gift of the said John and Emma, to have and to hold of the said Master and his successors, and the said Brethren of the said John and Emma, *and the heirs of the said Emma*, for ever. In consideration of paying to them annually 10s. sterling at two terms of the year; one half at Whitsuntide and the other half at Martinmas for every service and claim. And the aforesaid John and

---

[1] Elias is said to have been Vicar of Whitkirk.

Emma *and her heirs* will warrant, defend and acquit to the said Master and his successors and the aforesaid Brethren, the whole of the aforesaid land with its appurtenances, for the aforesaid services against all men for ever. And, moreover, the said John and Emma remit and quit-claim for themselves and the heirs of the said Emma to the said Master and his successors and the aforesaid Brethren, all right and claim which they have in the common part of the wood of the Master and aforesaid Brethren of West Hyrst for ever, as in herbage and other things, so that the said Master and his successors and the aforesaid Brethren may enclose and clear of the same wood as much as they wish at their convenience without hindrance from the aforesaid John and Emma and *the heirs* of the said Emma for ever. And for this recognition, warrant, remission, quit-claim, fine and concord, the said Master remits and quit-claims for himself and his successors and aforesaid Brethren, to John and Emma and to the heirs of the said Emma, all right and claim they may have in the common part of the wood of the same John and Emma at Est Hyrst for ever, as well in herbages as other things, provided that the said John and Emma and *the heirs of the said Emma*[1] may enclose and clear as much of the same wood as they

---

[1] One feels that he would much like to know more about Emma, the wife of John de Curteney. Probably her husband was a Brayton man whose ancestral estate is said to have become the glebe land of the present vicarage. But for herself, evidently she was an heiress who brought the lands of 'Est Hyrst' to her husband, which were afterwards to be called by his name (Hirst Courtenay); and it is singular that East Hirst is the only township in Haddlesey parish which bears the name of a former proprietor. There is one other name connected with Est Hyrst as its 'lord,' and it is that of William de Holm (or Insula) as a signatory to the charter of Lord John Bellaaqua, and so I venture the conjecture that Emma, the wife of John de Curteney, was a daughter of the house of Insula, or de Lisle, as they were afterwards called.

wish at their convenience without hindrance from the said Master and his successors and the aforesaid Brethren for ever.'

Page 817: It is remarked 'that Temple Hurst in Yorkshire is in the Deanery of the Ainsty and Arch-

SOUTH DOORWAY OF PRECEPTORY.

deaconry of the West Riding,' showing that that Deanery was not only very extensive, but that it even exceeded the limits assigned to it by Canon Raine, who says, in his 'York,' that 'The Ainsty is the tract of country bounded by the rivers Wharfe and Nidd and Ouse.' In the case of Temple Hirst it reached the

Aire, possibly because the great forest which surrounded York seemed to continue its area up to the banks of the Aire in this parish.

In 'Kirkby's Inquest,' A.D. 1277, we read, 'Hirst Courtenay: John de Foxoles and his co-heirs hold there 2 carucates of land, for which they pay vs. & xd. as knight's fee.'

CHAPTER III.

ORIGIN OF THE KNIGHT TEMPLARS.

OUR former chapter concluded with the mention of the gifts made to Knight Templars and their establishment in that part of our parish which previous to their connection with it was called West Hirst, as the other township of the same name was called East Hirst, before the manor was possessed by John de Courtenay, who made it over to the Templars for a payment of 10s. yearly, as Sir Ralph de Hastings had previously done the other village—the word Hirst, I may explain, is a Saxon word signifying wood or grove, and so agrees with what we have previously said; hence in the New Forest, Hampshire, Lyndhurst (the chief place in the district) is called, and really is, a wood of *lime-trees*, Linherst of Doomsday. But I think it will be desirable to turn aside awhile from the condition and development of the Order in our own parish to an inquiry which cannot fail to suggest itself to a thoughtful mind, viz.:

THE ORIGIN OF THE MOVEMENT.

In doing this we have to return to the early days of Christianity, to the time when all the events connected with the Saviour's earthly life and the main facts associated with the world's redemption were fresh and real to human thought; when those words of mingled weakness and power, 'It is finished!' prolonged their echoing spell upon ears which themselves had listened or heard the repetition from the actual participators in the tragedies of the cross and the triumphs of the tomb.

Very early in the history of the Church did travellers brave many dangers, and make long journeys and absences from home and kindred ties, at great cost of money, to visit Bethlehem, Galilee, but especially Jerusalem and the site of the cross, the tomb of the Saviour, and the mount on which the feet of Jesus rested last before His farewell to earth, until He comes again in the clouds of glory to reign victoriously in that very city in which He was put to open shame and cruel death.

The Emperor Constantine (possibly a Yorkshire man), and his mother Helena, the Empress, erected churches over these sacred spots, and under the protection of the Roman eagles vast crowds visited the Holy Land at the end of the fourth century. The zeal with which these multitudes left the banks of the Rhine, the Rhone, and the Thames, to renew their baptism in the waters of the Jordan, and to gaze on the relics of the cross and to bow themselves before the tomb in Joseph's garden, shows how easily reverence may glide into superstition, and the material and the external be substituted for the spiritual and the inward.

A modern writer and traveller (Dean Stanley), speaking of a recent visit to Jerusalem, makes the following reflections, so apposite that I do not hesitate to quote them here. 'It is true' (he says) 'that the places bring before us vividly the scene, and in many instances they illustrate His words and works in detail. But the more we gaze at them the more do we feel that this interest and instruction are secondary, not primary; that their value is imaginative and historical, *not religious*. The desolation and degradation which have so often left on those who visit Jerusalem the impression of an accursed city, reads in this sense a true lesson: "He is not here, He is risen!"' And that this was intended to be the feeling is clear from the question of the angelic messengers, 'Why stand ye gazing up into heaven, ye men of Galilee?' and their added and significant declaration, 'This same Jesus, which is taken up from you into heaven, shall so come in like manner as ye have seen Him go into heaven' (Acts i. 11).

But when the presence of those who had gone in and out with the Saviour, and their immediate disciples, had been removed, no wonder if sentiment should take the place of Scriptural sobriety, and superstition supersede faith! And so men reversed the teaching of the Apostles; instead of looking not at 'the seen and the temporal,' they fixed all their thoughts on these, to the exclusion of ' the unseen and the eternal.'

And even the legitimate use of these sacred places was perverted into most unchristian practices, *e.g.*, they were made into sanctuaries, to which criminals might flee to escape the due reward of their crimes. A murderer returning from Jerusalem was revered as a saint! So Shakespeare makes Bolingbroke to say when he is apprised of the murder of Richard II. at Pontefract, and charged with instigating the crime:

> 'I'll make a voyage to the Holy Land,
> To wash this blood from off my guilty hand.'

Not only so, the Church of Rome in the eleventh century substituted pilgrimages for the penances of earlier days. And after a time these pilgrimages were enjoined not simply as meritorious, but even obligatory, and, as in our own days, those who could not go themselves might employ others to represent them. Hence hospitals and monasteries were built at Bethlehem and Mount Sinai, and rich merchants, such as those of Amalfi ('Les Moines d'Occident,' tome vii., p. 147), collected funds in the West even as far as Normandy for their maintenance.

A rage for relics also sprang up, and with these developments of superstition originated orders of professional pilgrims, called Palmers, also supported by the alms of the faithful, and held in high repute, as we read in 'Marmion,' where the abbess exclaims:

> 'O holy Palmer!
> For sure he must be sainted man
> Whose blessed feet have trod the ground
> Where the Redeemer's tomb is found.'

But when Syria was overrun by the Saracens, difficulties arose. Jerusalem fell into the hands of the Caliph Omar after a four months' siege, A.D. 636. A mosque was built on the site of Solomon's Temple. Tribute had to be paid by the Christians. Christian churches were profaned, and persecution arose. The cry went up:

> 'Therefore, friends,
> As far as to the sepulchre of Christ
> .   .   .   .
> Forthwith a power of English shall we levy
> .   .   .   .
> To chase these pagans in those holy fields,
> Over whose acres walked those blessed feet,
> Which fourteen hundred years ago were nailed
> For our advantage on the bitter cross.'
>
> *Henry IV.*, Part I., act i., scene 1.

Yes, then sprung up the crusades. Hildebrand saw how good an opportunity it would afford to consolidate the ecclesiastical empire he was building up; but he had work nearer home just then, and it was left to his successor, Urban II., to utilize the fanatical zeal of Peter of Amiens (or the Hermit, as he was called), who returned from the Holy Land furious at the Mussulman rule. Peter preached everywhere in churches and streets. He spoke of torrents of Christian blood being shed in Jerusalem. The people were deeply wrought upon by his fervid appeals, and promised to give themselves, their riches, and prayers for the deliverance of the holy places.

But the actual commencement of the crusades dates from the Council of Clermont, A.D. 1095. Pope Urban presided, and as he ascended a lofty platform in the market-place of that town, he skilfully set forth the dangerous prevalence of the Turkish rule over territories once Christian in Asia and Africa, 'and *exhorts* the present and *enjoins* the absent to unite in the expedition which is to drive back the advancing tide of Saracenic conquest, and rescue the tomb of Christ from the grasp of the infidel. The multitudes responded " Dieu le veut "— " It is the will of God. It is the will of God." They fell upon their knees, confessed their sins, received absolution. Bishops, barons, knights, all swore to avenge the cause of Jesus Christ. The Pope tells them to wear the cross on their garments. " A red cross," he said, " as an external mark on your breasts and shoulders, as a pledge of your sacred and irrevocable engagement. Let no love of relatives detain you, for man's chiefest love ought to be towards God. Let no attachment to your native soil be an impediment, because in different points of view all the world is exile to the Christian." Then he puts in an assurance which would meet the needs of modern times: " God will be gracious to those who undertake this expedition, that they may have a favourable year, both in abundance of produce and serenity of season. Those who may die will enter the mansions of heaven, while the living shall behold the sepulchre of the Lord." [1]

[1] One of the things which Pope Urban did to support the crusades was to exact the firstfruits (*i.e.*, the first year's income of benefices) and the tenth of every succeeding year as a tax in aid of these expeditions. When the crusades came to an end, not so this impost on the clergy, which went to swell the Papal exchequer. And when Henry VIII. rejected the Papal usurpation he coolly pocketed the tax laid on English benefices, and so it was received by the Crown until Queen Anne generously applied the money, amounting to some £16,000 or £17,000 per annum, to the augmentation of poor livings, under the name of Queen Anne's Bounty.

Great numbers of the clergy and laity at once impressed on their garments the sacred symbol, and begged the Pope to march at their head. This, however, he declined to do, and delegated that honour to Adhemar, the Bishop of Puy, who was the first to receive the cross from the Pope. As the council broke up, its members spread its spirit and resolve to all lands. An ancient chronicler quaintly remarks: 'The Welshman left his hunting, the Scot his fellowship with vermin, the Dane his drinking-party, and the Norwegian his raw fish!' Six millions of persons are said to have enrolled themselves as pilgrims of the Cross. In the month of March, 1096, the abortive movement, which cost Europe at least 250,000 people, took place under the leadership of Peter the Hermit and Walter the Penniless, *arcades ambo!* When they met the Turks at Nice in Bithynia in the month of May, only 3,000 were left! But as other portions of the crusading army came up under the leadership of Godfrey of Bouillon, the Turks were obliged to retire, A.D. 1097.

The next place captured was Antioch, by stratagem. It is said that a Yorkshire Templar, Stephen, Earl of Albemarle and Holderness, led the rear-guard in this battle with Robert, Duke of Normandy. Another Yorkshire crusader, Sir Miles Stapleton, son of Sir John Stapleton, Controller of the Household under King Stephen (of the Richmondshire family), and who on his return from the Holy Land married Penrodas, daughter of the King of Cyprus, was associated with this expedition (see 'The Stapletons of Richmondshire,' by H. E. Chetwynd-Stapylton, Yorks, *Archæological Journal*, p. 70).

The siege of Antioch left the crusaders with their numbers greatly reduced by sickness, desertion, famine, and intemperance, so that the hosts did not remove from Antioch until the month of May, 1099. After reaching Cæsarea, and gathering supplies from the Emirs of Tripoli, Tyre, Sidon, Acre, and Cæsarea, they advanced into the midland country of Palestine by Lydda, Ramleh, Emmaus, and Bethlehem (the very route now taken by the railway from Jaffa to Jerusalem), and descried the Holy City, the object of their toils and privations, on June 6. The horsemen dismounted from their steeds and walked barefoot. Some fell on their knees at the sight of the holy places, while others kissed the earth hallowed by the Saviour's footsteps. So the poet writes:

> 'Their naked feet trod on the dusty way,
> Following the example of their zealous guide ;
> Their scarf, their crests, their plumes, their feathers gay,
> They quickly doffed, and willing laid aside ;
> Their moulten hearts their wonted pride allay,
> Along their watery cheeks warm tears down slide.'

It was a full month, however, before they took the city, and planted the standard of the Cross where the Crescent had unfitly waved. Frightful was the carnage. At the mosque of Omar the Saracens' blood (it is said) reached to the bridle of their horses ; neither women nor children were spared by these misnamed soldiers of the Cross Godfrey of Bouillon was chosen King, but he refused to wear a crown of gold where his Saviour had worn one of thorns, and so preferred to style himself Defender and Baron of the Holy Sepulchre. He only reigned one year. and was buried on Mount Golgotha. His brother Baldwin succeeded him, and assigned apartments or lodgings to the crusaders in a building close to Solomon's temple, hence the name of Templars (*Militia Templi Solomonis ad Icrosoluma*).

The actual constitution of the order did not, however, take place before the year 1118, when Hugo de Paganis, Galfridu de St. Audemaro, and seven other French knights, joined themselves together professedly as the servants of Christ, adopting the so-called monastic vows of poverty, celibacy, and obedience, adding to these a fourth, viz., that of perpetual war against the infidel, so as to keep open the roads along which Christian pilgrims might travel in safety to the Holy Land. To these four rules were added others, drawn up by Bernard of Clairvaux (best known as the author of the hymn 'Jerusalem the Golden'), on the basis of the Cistercian statutes, and accepted at the Council of Troyes, 1128. The object of these rules was to combine monasticism with a military life. The Templars were also called the 'Poor Soldiers of Christ,' and their personal possessions were to be restricted to their horses and military equipments. They were expected to avoid superfluous articles of dress, to abstain from hawking and other sports, and to sleep under conditions which modern civilization would hardly permit to convicts. They were not allowed to write or receive letters or presents from parents or relatives without the consent of the Master. Other rules were enjoined which betray the belief that their vow of celibacy would be badly observed. In fact, great as was St. Bernard undoubtedly in purely monastic discipline, yet he showed his inexperience when he attempted to graft on to the rule of St. Benedict the habits of secular knighthood, and ere long symptoms of failure appeared.

But in the meantime the patronage of the famous Abbot of Clairvaux gave a fresh impulse to the crusading movement, and, by the vigour of his exhortations, a new expedition set forth from France and Germany, chiefly in 1147. The principal achievement of this crusade on the part of the Templars seems to have been the raising of the siege of Antioch, which, owing to the death of Raymond, its Christian prince, had fallen again into the power of the Saracens. But Baldwin, the King of Jerusalem, at the head of a body of Knight Templars, prevented the entrance of the foe into the city of Antioch, and followed up his successes so gloriously as to obtain possession of Ascalon, which had hitherto withstood all the efforts of the Christians.

But the Templars did not maintain their position in the East without many reverses, owing to the demoralization and disorder which seems to have overtaken them whenever they were disengaged from military operations. So, in 1187, Saladin recovered possession of the Holy City, in spite of the valour of a portion of its defenders, including now the two military orders of the Knight Templars and the Hospitallers. The treachery of Raymond, Count of Tripoli, had much to do with this disaster; but the fact of his unjust treatment by Lusignan, King of Jerusalem, shows at least the want of true Christian principle, which alone could maintain the dignity of such an enterprise.

The news of this calamity, however, raised Europe again to fresh efforts for beating back the victorious foe. This THIRD crusade is additionally interesting to us on account of the exploits of our own King, Richard the Lion-hearted. By his exertions, in which several Yorkshiremen, notably Sir Miles Stapleton, aided, the siege of St. Jean d'Acre was raised. Joppa and Ascalon fell as trophies to his prowess, and Jerusalem itself would probably have been added to his conquests had not the designs of Philip of France compelled Richard to enter on a three years' armistice with Saladin that he might return to England. Richard made over his conquest in Palestine to the Knights of St. John, who thus became a sovereign order, and established their headquarters at Acre, and in honour of their patron-saint called St. Jean d'Acre.

The appearance of this city at this time has been set forth in the following terms : 'Beautiful as it is even in our day' (modern travellers, such as Thomson, Bonar, Tristram, rather qualify this phrase), 'it was yet more beautiful when, seven centuries ago, it was the Christian capital of the East. Its snow-white palaces sparkled like jewels against the dark woods of Carmel, which rose towards the south. To the east there stretched away the glorious plain, over which the eye might wander till it lost itself in the blue outlines of hills on which no Christian eye could gaze unmoved, for they hid in their bosom the village of Nazareth and the waters of Tiberias, and had been trodden all about by the feet of One whose touch had made them holy ground. That rich and fertile plain, now marshy and deserted, but then a very labyrinth of fields and vineyards, circled Acre also to the north; but there the eye was met with a new boundary, the snowy summits of a lofty mountain range, whose bases were clothed with cedar; while all along the lovely coast broke the blue waves of that mighty sea whose shores are the confines of the world. And there Acre lay among her gardens; the long rows of her marble houses, with their flat roofs, forming terraces odorous with orange-trees and rich with flowers of a thousand hues. . . . You might walk from one end of the city to the other on these terraced roofs; and the streets themselves were wide and airy, and the shops brilliant with the choicest merchandise of the East, and thronged with the noblest chivalry of Europe. It was the gayest, gallantest city in existence; its gilded steeples stood out against the mountains, and above the horizon of those bright waters that tossed and sparkled in the flood of southern sunshine and in the fresh breeze that kissed them from the west. Every house was rich with painted glass, for this, though rare yet in Europe, was lavishly employed in Acre, and, perhaps, first brought from thence by the crusaders. Every nation had its street, inhabited by its own merchants and nobles, and crowned heads, including the Emperor of Germany, the Kings of England, France, Jerusalem, etc., had each their court and palace.' It is important to remember that this city is mentioned in the Old Testament as Accho, meaning sandy or sultry; and in the New, Acts xxi. 7, as Ptolemais; that it still has a place in history, and stands out conspicuously among those few cities which have a continuous existence of over three thousand years.

Three other crusades followed, but at length the Turks held undisputed sway over all the spots which had been so desecrated by unchristian strife, and polluted by unchristian vices, making the very name of Christianity an object of execration, instead of attraction, to those who might have been led to embrace its truths and exemplify its blessings under a course of procedure more consistent with its character. With the fall of St. Jean d'Acre, A.D. 1291, all hope of guarding the holy places of the East by the Templars and their allies passed away, and consequently the *raison d'être* of the organization was removed. It could not, then, be altogether surprising if some excuse were not pleaded sooner or later for appropriating the wealth of this richly endowed body by some of their numerous enemies.

We may, then, well pause and consider not only what possessions were attached to the Preceptory of Hirst in our own parish, as we have already done, but also consider the possessions of the Order in Yorkshire generally. Although Hirst was both in point of time and in other respects the chief of all the preceptories in the North of England, yet Ribstane enjoyed the distinction of being founded by Robert de Ros, owing to the friendly exhortations and a visit paid to England by Hugh Payen (or Hugo Paganus), the first of those knights who enrolled themselves in the Templar Order. During the two hundred years in which the Knight Templars flourished, they had numerous friends in Yorkshire. From a list by no means exhaustive, we find that the Templars held property, consisting of landed estates, houses, townships, advowsons of churches, tithes (as in this parish), water-mills, wind-mills, market-tolls, rights of free-warren, fisheries, and numberless other privileges, in some sixty places in Yorkshire. No wonder, then, that the failure of the Templars to protect the Holy Land from the intrusive power of the Arabs led some to question their right to retain the wealth lavished upon them as the sacred militia of the holy places. But before entering on this phase of Templar history, I think it right to refer to other parts of our parish than those so completely absorbed by the doings of this Order.

1333859

CHAPTER IV.

TOWNSHIP OF HADDLESEY—EARLIEST HISTORIC RECORDS.

WE turn now to those portions of the parish which not only give their name to the parochial entity, but are also in themselves of larger area, more numerous population, and of more enduring interest. The establishment of the Templar preceptory, in the twelfth century, in the eastern portion of the parish, absorbed for awhile attention to it as one of greatest publicity and prominence. But, nevertheless, we shall find, as we continue our story, material for interesting record in the west as well as in the east. The first mention of Haddlesey in any historic document is probably early in the thirteenth century.

From Yorkshire deeds in Public Record Office: 'B. 1022. Grant by Nicholas de Burstal to his daughter Agnes, of a portion of assart in the wood of Caiteford abutting upon Hadelsay Lane. Witnesses: Robert de Pauely, Hugh son of Hugh de Lascy, or rather, nephew of Ilbert de Lascy and others (named). Seal.' And Mr. E. H. Chetwynd-Stapylton, in his pedigree of Stapelton, kindly sent me privately, quotes a charter of 46 Hen. III., i.e. 1262, in which 'Miles Bassett is said to have free-warren East *Hamsy*, and Midel Hamsy, Ebor.'

But we may get, perhaps, the best idea of the sort of people inhabiting Haddlesey in the twelfth century by quoting some extracts from the first volume of the 'Coucher Book of Selby Abbey,' recently published under the auspices of the Yorkshire Archæological Association. And first, we may preface that the people of that day consisted of the lord and of his tenants. There were the sochemani, or sokemen: 'The works of the sokemen are these: Each one ought to plough once in winter before Christmas Day, according to the plough which he has. He who has no plough ought to find one for half a carucate of land. He ought also to plough once in spring in the same manner. The ploughman (*carucatores*) ought to have to eat wheaten-bread and flesh (*panem frum' et carnem*), and ale to drink in winter, while they have day (*dum diem habent*), in spring wheaten-bread and fish to eat, and ale to drink during their day's work. Every tenant of one bovate of land ought to find one harrow (*herciam*) in winter and another in spring, like one who holds two bovates, except six men who hold six bovates, of whom every one ought to find two harrows in winter and two others in spring. The harrowers ought to have to eat wheaten-bread and flesh or fish once a day. Every horse (*caballus*) shall have one sheaf (*garbam*) of oats in spring while the harrowers are eating, but in winter none. Also, every one ought to find a man to hoe for one day, with food like the harrowers. Every tenant of one bovate ought to find a man to reap in autumn for two days, like him who holds two bovates, except six men who hold twelve bovates, each of whom ought to find two men to reap two days, who are to eat once a day, and have wheaten-bread with flesh one day, and fish the other, with pottage (*potagio*). Every tenant of one bovate ought to give twopence for mowing meadow, like the tenant of two bovates, except six men holding twelve bovates, each of whom is to give fourpence. Also every one of them ought to find a man to toss the hay (*ad* [*fenum*] *levandum*) in meadows for one day, without food, except the six who are each to find two men. Every bovate ought to carry one cartload of hay and one cartload of corn, without food.

'It should be known that every ploughing is worth in winter without food 2d., and in spring 2d.; every harrowing without food, ½d.; hoeing one day without food, ½d.; mowing without food, ½d.; tossing hay in meadow, without food, ½d. Every cart carrying hay or corn is worth ½d.—Sum of the works in money, 27s. 6d.

'Work of one bovate without food, 5d.; and so one bovate yields with farms and services, 25d.

'The aforesaid sokemen hold one culture by itself containing forty acres, called Northmor, which yields half a marc.

'Every tenant of land owes suit of court, his relief, 16s., amercement, 5s. 4d.; and their merchete, 5s. 4d., etc.' (From a contributor to *Yorks. Weekly Post*.)

Secondly, the villani, or villains, though by no means necessarily villainous in our modern sense of the word, but persons very much in the position of the agricultural labourer as regards his work, but differing from him greatly in some other respects; *e.g.*, though they had a bovate or oxgang of land, and sometimes more, to cultivate, they could acquire no *private* property, neither land nor goods: their daughters could not be married without the lord's consent to what was considered an injury to his property. Still, the law forbade atrocious cruelty on the part of the lord to his villain. In course of time they acquired freedom, and they became copyholders of the manor to which they respectively belonged.

There were also the bordarii, or cotarii. Bordarii probably comes from *bord*, a cottage or wooden hut. They had no oxen, but cultivated some four or five acres of garden-ground. They performed inferior services of a miscellaneous character, such as grinding and thrashing corn, drawing water, and cutting wood. Both the villains and the bordarii had to do with crofts and tofts, as we shall see in many of the records we quote from in this history; so it may be well to explain now that 'tofts' were patches of land around the villains' houses; a 'croft,' an acre at the back of the same: 'feorm,' or 'farm,' was food and entertainment supplied by a villain to the lord of the manor when he visited his tenants.

There were also the serfs, or slaves; a class below the villains, though, like the nativi, or niefes, children of villains, bound to the soil, as much as their cattle or stock, though sometimes, as we shall see, set free, and so made liberi, or freemen.

CXXXIV. Charter of Peter, son of John Dodde of Selby: Gives to William, son of Gilbert of Hayelsay, *i.e.* Hathelsay ('y' being written for 'þ'), his heirs, assigns, etc., a 'certain messuage in the town of Selby, in Mikelgate, between the toft of Roger Marescall and the toft of Peter Hussald, one end whereof abuts on the highway, and the other over against the pond of the Lord Abbot of Selby,' to have and to hold, on payment annually to the Lord Abbot of twelvepence at Pentecost and Martinmas in two equal portions, for all services and claims, and 'to me and my heirs one grain of pepper on Christmas Day.' Witnesses: The Lord Walter the Chaplain, Henry Syward, and Roger Marescall.

CCCXXXVIII. Charter de Henry Vernoil: Alex, son of Thomas the Parson of Kellington, is mentioned.

CCCCLXI. Cartæ de Hath'say, *i.e.* Haddlesey. Charter of Robert of Stiveton, or Steeton (a township in the parish of Bolton Percy; contained $5\frac{1}{2}$ carucates of land, whereof Rd. de Stiveton held $4\frac{1}{2}$ carucates of Walter de Fauconberg, who held the same of the heirs of Brus, and they of the barons Mowbray, who held of the King *in capite*, by the annual rent of 7½d.): Deed of grant by the above to the sacristy of St. Germains, Selby, for service of the light at the altar of B. Mary, Hugh, son of Ailricus of Hausay, and his heirs, viz., of the tribute which was paid me for that land which he held of me freely and quietly and honourably, in the town of Hausay, viz., the toft where is a house and garden, which lies between the toft of Robert Sutor and the toft of John Dernel and the *new road*, and whatever belongs to me in Estker (*Carr*), and half an acre of meadow on the east. . . . xij^d for all secular exactions, etc.; vj^d at the feast of St. Martin, and vj^d at Pentecost.—Witness: DOMINUS JOHN DE BIRKIN, who also witnesses the deed of Alexander de Ruhale, CCCCLIX.

CCCCLXII. Charter of Ralph Miller of Haddlesay: The said Ralph binds himself and his heirs to pay to the Abbot and brotherhood of Selby xij^d annually, viz., half at Pentecost and half at St. Martin's, in return for a certain toft which he holds of them in the town of Hausay. Among the witnesses to this deed is THOMAS DE BELLA-AQUA.

CCCCLXIII. Charter of William de Euermu: The said William grants to Hugh, son of Walter, and his heirs, the tenement which Ralph the villain held in Hausay (*i.e.* Haddlesey) of Osbert of Bayeux, with all its appurtenances as Godfrey and Ralph held in same town—'to hold of me and my heirs, "in hereditary fee," on paying two pounds of pepper' annually at the feast of St. Peter ad Vincula. And for this concession and grant the aforesaid Hugh has given me vj^s. Witness: Robert de Euermu.

CCCCLXIV. Charter of Walter de Euermu: 'Gives to Hugh, the son of Walter, and his heirs, Ralph, the son of Ailsus (*nativus meus*), *i.e.*, the son of his serf of Hausay, with all his offspring, chattels, etc. And for this grant the aforesaid Hugh has given ' iiij solidos et unum talentum.' It is not easy to say what would be the equivalent of this sum in modern money, as the talent varied in value from £100 to £50, and even to £1. But this deed proves that the serf was a marketable commodity in England in the twelfth century; and that such transactions took place here in Haddlesey, Hugh, who was a small freeholder, buying Ralph, the son of Ailsus; the deed being witnessed by Robert de Euermowe, Sigerus de Archel, and others.

CCCCLXV. Charter of Alan, Prior of Drax and his convent: The Prior gives to Hugh, son of Walter, mentioned in the two previous deeds, his heirs, etc., one toft in *Middle Hausay* (for homage and service), on the west side of that town, and fifteen acres of land *in the wood of Hausay*, which lies in an *essart* (*i.e.* clearing) towards Gateford boundary (*i.e.* the site of the modern Paper House Farm), and six acres of meadow in the Mickelmarsh; to be held in fee and heirship honourably, with all easements and common rights of the *aforesaid town of Hausee*, 'by paying to us annually two pounds of pepper within the octave of St. Peter ad Vincula for all kinds of secular service'; and Hugh and his heirs are warranted the possession of the aforesaid land and *tenements* against all men. Witnesses: Paulinus the Deacon, and others.

CCCCLXVI. Hathelsay: Charter of Ralph, villain.—Grant of the aforesaid Ralph, villain to Hugh, the son of Walter, 'of all my land at Hausay' which I hold by gift of Osbert of Bayeux, and which Ralph, the son of Ailsus, held (see No. CCCCLXIII.), *i.e.*, one toft in Mediana Hayelsay (Middle Hathelsay) towards the west in the wood of Hausay in an *essart*, six acres of meadow in Mickelmarsh, to be held of me and my heirs, etc., in wood and clearing, and meadow and pasture, in roads and footpaths, in waters, and with all privileges and easements belonging to the town of Haddlesey, by paying to me, etc., annually, one pound of pepper at the feast of the apostles[1] Peter and Paul, for all secular service and demand. . . . For this grant the aforesaid Hugh has given me xx^s in acknowledgment. Witnesses: Osbert *Clericus de Schirburne*, Otho of Barkeston, Humphrey de Villi, and others.

CCCCLXVII. Charter of Hugh, son of Walter: Deed of grant of the above to God and the Church of St. Germain of Selby, and to the monks therein serving God, 'of all my lands in the town of Hathelsay, with its appurtenances; viz., below the town, two tofts and six acres of meadow, and in plough land, xx acres, to have and to hold in free alms, on payment of two pounds of pepper yearly at the feast of St. Peter ad Vincula (August 1); in the English Church (Lammas).' Witnesses: Henry Wales or Wallis, of Burgh Wallis, near Doncaster, Robert de Wykerlay, and others.

CCCCLXVIII. Charter of Roger, *son* of Goodrich de Hausay (Hathelsay): Greeting in the Lord. For the benefit of his own soul and that of his ancestors and descendants, and for the soul of Alicia his wife; he gives to God and the Church of St. Germain at Selby, and the Abbot and the monks therein serving God, two acres of land complete, and lying together in the eastern part below 'my essart, which lies between the assart of Lord Thomas Bella-aqua and the essart of Hugh de Lacy adjoining the wood of Gaiteford, to have and to hold, etc., in free alms; which two acres of meadow they may enclose with ditches without any hindrance or contradiction, at their own will and convenience, this I warrant and confirm with my seal.' Witnesses: Lord Thomas de Bella-aqua, Hugh de Mar.

CCCCLXIX. Charter of Robert de Willegby: Grant of one toft with buildings and appurtenances to the monks of St. Germain, Selby, in free alms for the soul of the said Robert de Willegby. The premises are described as

[1] June 29 and 30.

lying between the toft of Ralph, deacon of Kelington, and a toft of Ydannia de Polington. Witnesses: Thomas de Bella-aqua, Milo Basset, Ralph the Deacon.

Names of the Tenants of the Abbey of Selby at Hathelsay,
A.D. 1247.

William, son of Robert, holds of the Lord Abbot one messuage and twelve acres of land in Westhathelsay.

John Mallynson of Gaiteford, half of the toft which William, son of Nelson, had in Westhathelsay.

Thomas Gemme holds in Medilhathelsay one toft and half a bovate of land.

John, son of Adam of Medilhathelsay, holds one toft and one croft, one bovate containing 3 *acres of land* in Medilhathelsay.

William, son of Richard Balcok, *mercer*, holds one toft and one croft and a bovate of land in Medilhathelsay.

William, son of Miles, holds one acre of land in Westhathelsay, of the Lord Abbot, 'in the place called Est harr.'

CCCCLXX. Charter of David, Abbot of Selby (*i.e.* David de Cawood, A.D. 1262): To all whom it may concern, know that I, David, by the grace of God, give and demise to Eve, former wife of Adam de Barkston, and her daughters Isabella and Hawise, one messuage and bovate of land, with all appurtenances, in the town and territory of Hausey, which is a gift for the aforesaid women until we provide "maritagium"[1] for Isabella and Hawise, and for Eve a service by which she can get food and clothing, iij solidos being paid to us and our church half-yearly at the feast of St. Martin and Whitsuntide, so that the aforesaid Eve, Isabella, and Hawise can neither sell the land nor alienate it, nor marry without our permission.'

[1] That is, the duty which devolved on the owner of a serf to provide marriage for the daughters of his vassals.

If they do, the deed goes on to say, 'the property reverts to the monastery. In witness, etc., we have placed our hands: John de Selby.'

CCCCLXXI. Charter of Robert de Willeby, *son* and heir of Robert, Lord of Willeby: Know, all men, that I have appointed Ralph de Milford my attorney for placing the Abbot of Selby in full possession of a meadow in Westhausy, of which formerly there was a contention between us, saving the dowry of Lady Alicia, formerly my father's wife, concerning the same meadow, and all services to Lord Robert de Everingham, Hugh de Lascy of Gaiteford, and Henry of Burn, for tenements in the same town, due for a time to my father, and assigned to the Lady Alicia, formerly my father's wife. Given at Selby *die Lunæ proxima*.

CCCCLXXII. Hathelsay: Charter of Robert de Stiveton: Know all men, etc., that I, Robert of Stiveton, have quit-claimed for myself and heirs for ever, Ailsie de Hausay and Peter and Adam, and Hugh and Robert, his sons, with all their children, etc. In confirmation and witness of this I have placed my seal to this deed. Witness: Adam de Bella-aqua.

CCCCLXXIII. Charter of Cecilia, former wife of William de Nell de Hathelsay: Know all, that I, Cecilia, former wife of William Nell de Hathelsey, remit and give again to the quiet possession of the Abbot and monks of St. Germain, Selby, in the street called Mickelgate, all that I have or may have by way of dowry, etc. Witnesses: John le Chamberlain de Seleby, Henry Irnis, Walter de Linberght, John Etelaf, Thomas, son of Hugo, and many others.

After the preceding charters we come to Kirkby's Inquest of County of York, etc.

Kirkby's Inquest of County of York, taken in A.D. 1277 (Kirkby was consecrated Bishop of Ely, 1286, and died 1290 A.D.). The inquest was attested at Clifton, York,

March 5, 1281. We read 'Lord[1] Miles de Stapleton holds there with one carucate of land in Brayton which Walter Bassett held, with one carucate of land in Barneby, being a fourth part of a knight's fee, fifteen carucates going to the fee.'

Calendar of the Patent Rolls—Patent 9 Edw. I., No. 29, A.D. 1280. 'The King grants to Sir Nicholas Stapleton a house and 5 bovates of land (about 90 acres) at West Halsey. . . . Payment to be made to the King of 40s. per ann. for all service. December 1, by the King at Westminster.' This property was on the banks of the Aire, the site of Haddlesey House.

In 1293 the same Miles de Stapleton answers to a writ of Quo Warranto, 'That he has free warren in all his lands in Est Hausy and Middlehausy, by charter of the said King (Hen. III.) in 48th year of his reign, granted to Miles Bassett,[2] the grandfather (*avus*) of the said Miles de Stapleton, *whose heir he is*,' etc. He married Sibill, eldest daughter and co-heir of Sir John de Bella-aqua, or Bellew, Kt., and Baron, Lord of Carlton.

In the same inquisition we read, ' HATHELSAY. In the same town is half of a knight's fee, and it is held of the Earl of Lincoln, and the Earl holds it of the King, and pays for it ijs. vd.' Then at p. 344 of the same we read: 'Est and West Hathelsay, iij villis Nicholas de Stapleton.' And p. 439, Inquisition of articles touching movable goods liable to fine in the Wapentake of Barkston : 'They say that Lord Miles de Stapleton[3] holds two parts of the (villatæ) large town of West Haddlesey of the King in chief, and pays 40 shillings annually to the King ad sac-

[1] He was the first Baron.

[2] In Selby Coucher Book, p. 209, an essart of John de Mikelhurst, held of Agnes, wife of Miles Basset, is mentioned. At p. 211 of same book this Agnes is described as a widow, and her father's name given, J. de Lascels.

[3] A.D. 1304. Miles de Stapleton is mentioned as Constable of Knaresborough Castle.

cariam (the power of levying fines and exercising jurisdiction). Dated at Shireburn 4 of Edw. II. (1311).'

This same year Miles de Stapleton pays a fine to the King of twenty shillings for license to give certain tenements in West Hathelsey and East Hathelsey to a certain chaplain to perform Divine service every day in the chapel of St. John (the Baptist) about to *be rebuilt* by the said Miles in the aforesaid town of Est Hathelsay.

'8 of Edw. II. Milo de Stapleton is reputed to hold Esthathelsay Maner cum Westhathelsay 3 partes.'

'This Sir Miles granted to the Master and Brethren of the Knights of the Temple at Temple Hurst all his right and claim to a certain meadow called the Calf Enge; to a croft in which is a corn mill that the Master and Brethren held of his fee in Hathelsay, elsewhere described as "in Est Hathelsay, opposite to the gate of Hyrst." One toft and five acres which Ingelard, son of Roger of the Temple, holds in West Hathelsay. One toft and three acres which Robert de Camelford of the Temple has *in the same town*. One toft and four acres which Richard Ayr of the Temple holds in *the same place*. One toft and half a bovate that Hugh, the tailor of the Temple, holds in the same place. One toft that Adam, son of Hugh Balcok of the Temple, has in the same place, and one toft, one bovate, and seven acres that Alan Balcok of the Temple holds in Middel Hathelsay. Given at Ribstane the Friday nex after the feast of St. Matthew, Apostle, A.D. 1302.'—Cart. Harl. 84 A, 44 and 42.

This last quotation appropriately leads on to a resumption of our notice of the Templar preceptory in this parish. A preceptory was an establishment under the care of an officer called a Preceptor, appointed by the Master of the Order not only as a place of residence for a certain number of knights, but as a centre from which the estates of the Order in the neighbourhood could be supervised.

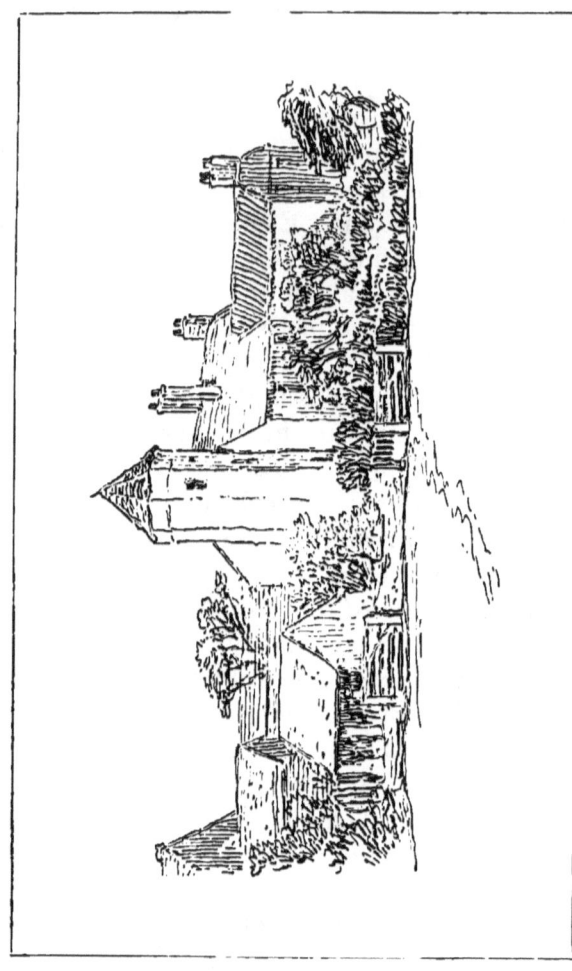

REMAINS OF TEMPLAR PRECEPTORY, TEMPLE HIRST.

CHAPTER V.

THE KNIGHT TEMPLARS: THEIR GROWTH AND THEIR DECAY.

WE closed our third chapter with some remarks on Templar history, suggested by the fall of St. Jean d'Acre, A.D. 1291. We now resume by remarking that from the time of the Templar settlement in England, viz., early in the twelfth century, they acquired immense possessions of lands and houses in nearly all parts of England. A very interesting record of the estates held by them in the year 1185 still exists in the Record Office in London. This book contains the results of an inquisition of the lands, churches, and mills bestowed upon the Templars, made, as stated at the commencement of the manuscript, by Geoffrey Fitz-Stephen, Master of the Order, when he was appointed to the Bailiwick in England. Here I may explain that the government of the Templars was vested in the Grand Master, who had his lieutenant immediately under him, also a Marshal Treasurer, etc. The different countries in which the

PILLAR HEAD OF SOUTH DOORWAY OF PRECEPTORY.

property of the Order was situated were called provinces, each province having its own Grand Prior, Grand Preceptor, or Master. Under the Provincial Master were the priors or bailiffs, and under the bailiffs were the preceptors, or heads of a local manor or establishment, such as Temple Hirst.

The book which contains this survey of the property of the Templars in England is in itself a great curiosity. Its covers are of stout oak covered with leather, on which are stamped various devices in the form of seals. The writing is good, and the capitals are coloured, but not illuminated.

To return to Temple Hirst. We have already remarked on the high place which this preceptory filled in the history of the Order, but we think also that it was chosen by Sir Walter Scott for perpetual fame when he wrote of Templestowe in his romance of 'Ivanhoe.' The readers of that volume will remember that the chief places which define the locality within whose limits the incidents of the story must be sought are Burton-on-Trent in the extreme South (see p. 271, Black's edition), and York or Copmanthorpe in the North—the chief transactions being near the Valley of the Don, and including the site of the present town of Rotherham and the castle of Coningsborough, the ruins of which yet remain. The only establishment of the Knight Templars sufficiently contiguous to the hermit's cell at Copmanhurst, the forest retreat of the outlaws, the castle of Athelstane and the hall of the Saxon Cedric, indicated by the name of Templestowe given by Scott, must be either Temple Hirst or Temple Newsam. Temple Hirst seems to be the more likely place, first because it lies more probably in the route which the work referred to seems to indicate as that which was taken by the leading characters in the romance, and furthermore the romance states that while the minstrel and Friar Tuck were con-

4

versing outside the walls of the preceptory of Templestowe, the heavy bell of the church of St. Michael, a venerable building situated in a hamlet at some distance from the preceptory, broke short their argument. Now, it is distinctly mentioned that the church at Kellington (Kelintoun) was a dependency of the manor of Temple Hirst, and is included in the returns made of the possessions of that manor; in addition to this, there are distinct proofs of its having been the church of the Templars, and its actual distance from the preceptory harmonizes with the statement that the tolling bell of that church might be heard from what we claim as the site of Templestowe, while I fail to find any similar arguments adduced on behalf of Temple Newsam as the competing site.[1]

Having dwelt on this point, let us proceed to consider the estates which were in possession of the Templars at the suppression of the Order so far as this county is concerned. By carefully comparing a large number of statements, published and unpublished, there seem to have been about seventy distinct properties in Yorkshire belonging to the Knight Templars at the time the Order was suppressed. The value of these lands, estimated by the standard of to-day, would be equal to a much larger sum than their nominal £2,500 per annum. No wonder that such an accumulation of wealth and influence as would accompany such large possessions made them an object of envy, so that their ruin was determined upon as mentioned in Chapter III. As early as 1307 a Bull had issued against them from the Papal Court, and in January

[1] Another consideration which greatly supports the previous contention arises from the fact that Mr. Morritt, of Rokeby (Scott's great friend), was the owner of Shirwood, the site of the ancient Potterlaw, once the property of the Templars. It is not too much to assume that this circumstance would be a matter of conversation between the author of 'Ivanhoe' and his friend. This property still belongs to a member of the same family, the Dowager Lady Barrington.

of the ensuing year orders were issued that the persons of the Templars should be seized and their possessions sequestrated throughout England. As regards Yorkshire, this order was executed by Sir John de Creppinge, High Sheriff of the county. Greenfield, Archbishop of York, summoned a provincial council to which Templars from all the northern counties were cited for the purpose of hearing the charge brought against them. Ivo de Elton, the last Preceptor at Temple Hirst, is not among those who were imprisoned at York, or examined by the council there (*Y. A. and T. Journal*, vol. x.). Some of the Templars, seeing that their position was a helpless one, pleaded guilty to the crimes and heresies of which they are accused, and threw themselves on the compassion of their enemies. By this they obtained absolution and small pensions, or corrodies, for their maintenance, or were drafted off into neighbouring monasteries, such as Selby and York. Whilst some of the Templars bowed their heads to the storm with cowardly pusillanimity, others courageously and indignantly repelled the odious and untrue charges made against them. Of these were an English Templar named Brother Humbert Blanke, Grand Preceptor of Auvergne. He appears to have been a knight of the highest character, and of stern, unbending pride. From first to last he had protested against the violent proceedings of the inquisitors, and fearlessly maintained, amid all trials, his own innocence and that of the Order. This illustrious Templar had fought under four successive Grand Masters in Palestine, had escaped the slaughter at St. Jean d'Acre, and after its fall led in person several daring expeditions against the infidels. He accompanied the Grand Master from Cyprus to France, from whence he crossed to England and was committed to the Tower of London. As he would not plead guilty to the charges brought against his Order, he was tortured and half starved for the space of five years, finally loaded with double chains, until at length death put an end to his sufferings.

James de Molay, the Grand Master of the Temple, was also confined in French prisons for five and a half years. He had yielded to the pressure brought to bear upon him so far as to make a confession, which 'he afterwards disowned and stigmatized as a forgery, swearing that if the cardinals who had subscribed to it had been of a different cloth he would have proclaimed them liars, and would have challenged them to mortal combat.'

On March 18, A.D. 1313, a striking scene was exhibited in Paris: a scaffold was erected before the Cathedral of Notre Dame, and the citizens were called together to hear the Order of the Knight Templars 'convicted by the mouths of its chief officers' of the crimes charged against it.

Four knights, loaded with chains and surrounded by guards, were then brought on to the scaffold, and the Bishop of Alba read aloud their pretended confessions. 'The Papal Legate then turned towards the Grand Master and his companions, and called upon them to renew the avowals previously made of the guilt of their Order.' 'Hugh de Peralt, Visitor-General of the Order, and the Grand Preceptor of the Temple of Aquitaine, assented; but the Grand Master, raising his arms bound with chains toward heaven, advancing towards the edge of the scaffold, declared with a loud voice that to say that which was not true was a crime both in the sight of God and man. "I do," said he, "confess my guilt, which consists in having suffered myself, through the pain of torture and fear of death, to give utterance to falsehoods, imputing scandalous sins and iniquities to an illustrious Order which hath nobly served the cause of Christianity. I disdain to seek a wretched and disgraceful existence by engrafting another lie on the original falsehood." He was here interrupted, and Guy, the Grand Preceptor (brother of the

Prince of Dauphiny), having protested his innocence in vigorous terms, they were both hurried back to prison. King Philip of France was no sooner informed of these proceedings than he commanded the instant execution of these brave men. At dusk of the same day they were led out of their dungeons and burned to death over a slow charcoal fire on the little island of the Seine, close to the spot where now stands the equestrian statue of Henri IV. au Pont Neuf.

It sounds like irony that the monarch who was guilty of these cruel and barbarous proceedings should bear the name of Philip the *Fair*. An old writer has quaintly remarked that this tyrant, 'thinking that the Templar hive was full of honey, determined to burn the bees.' This he did literally by wholesale barbarities all over his kingdom. In England the feeling was more favourable to the Templars, but as Philip was countenanced in all his plundering inhumanity by Pope Clement V. (a creature of his residing at Avignon instead of Rome), their persecution with a view to the overthrow of the Order extended to this country.

As early as the year 1307, April 3 (1 Edw. II.), a writ[1] (No. 9) was issued commanding the Sheriff of Yorkshire to

---

[1] Kenrick gives a list of these documents at p. 63. The bundle in the Public Record Office, London, is marked 'T. G. 41,156,' and contains several files and loose documents. First file:

No. 17 refers to Hyrst, Wednesday after Epiphany, 1 Edw. II.

No. 217 mentions an inquisition relative to a corrody claimed by William Constable of Ireland, out of the House of the Temple of Hyrst.

Roll endorsed, 'Ebor. Prime extente per Vic.':

No. 3: Inquisitions of lands in the wapentakes of Osgotcrosse and Barkeston *Potterlowe*, Sabbath, March 2, 1 Edw. II.

No. 9 (see above).

No. 10: Long inventory of goods at Temple Hirst, Potterlawe. And at Welington (Kelington), the last imperfect.

Separate roll marked 'H. C. H. 3.399,' indented, with writ annexed:

No. 1: Directing the Sheriff of Yorkshire to deliver to Adam Hoperton, whom the King had appointed steward, etc., of the Manors of deliver to Milo de Stapleton the Manor of Temple Hirst belonging to the Knight Templars, with all the lands and buildings belonging to the Order, both there and also at Birne, East Hirst, *West Hathelsay, and Middle Hathelsay* (sometimes called East Haddlesey, and, although erroneously, Chapel Haddlesey) together with the Manor of Kelyngton and the church there, and the Grange of Potterlawe and the lands there, as well as all the goods and chattels of the Templars to be found in these places, and the said Milo de Stapleton was to give account of the revenues arising from these places to the Barons of the King's Exchequer.

The number of these accounts and their excellent preservation in the Record Office, London, reads a lesson as to the change passing over earthly things, inasmuch as they show that a place which has nearly dropped out of all remembrance, now once occupied a large space in the eyes of the rulers of this country.

These compotuses take us back over five hundred years, and supply a vivid picture of the manner of life pursued by our forefathers at that period in the spots we now occupy. Instead of the sounds of military revelry and the presence of men who had fought beneath an Eastern sky with the renowned Saladin, we hear the piercing shriek of the railway whistle, and behold the rapid evolutions of machines which gather in crops in a few weeks instead of the months occupied by the agriculturists of the Middle Ages.

Temple Hurst, Neusom, and many other places (p. 66, Kenrick), with all goods and chattels, etc. (Langele, July 15, 3 Edw. II.).

P. 66, Kenrick, File No. 49, writs, etc., 5-7 Edw. II., marked 'H. C. H. 6,826':

No. 1 writ relates to allowances out of Hyrst Manor.

N.B.—Hyrst is mentioned in addition to Temple Hyrst in Roll 'H. C. H. 3,399.' Whether this is Hyrst Curtenay or Hyrst in the Isle of Axholme does not seem quite clear.

But to return to the accounts of Sir John de Crepping. We find him first of all giving credit for the sum of £4 7s. 9¼d. as rent and manor dues from the free tenants of Temple Hirst. He then accounts for £12 14s. 9d. realized by the sale of 14 quarters of wheat, 2.500 and 3 bushels of rye, 4 quarters of barley, 6 of peas, and 54 of oats. He also sold a horse and foal, 3 large pigs and 22 smaller ones, 9 capons, and 24 fowls for £4 12s. By the sale of hides of 25 animals, *which died from the murrain*, he makes 8s. 3d. He also sells the pigeon-cote for 10d., 3 oxen, 18 fat pigs, 8 sheep, 1 stone of soap and 5 of cheese for £2 16s. 2d., and for the hides of the cattle last mentioned he received 2s. 9d. more, making a grand total of £25 2s. 6¾d. His payments are first of all small claims to the *heirs of John de Courtency*, and to the Abbey of Selby, and to William Constable a *corrody*[1] of 2d. a day as keeper of the Manor of Potterlawe, then for repairs of carts and ploughs 10s. 3d. He has to purchase salt and other medicines for the shepherd's use for young cattle. He also paid wages at 2d. a day (equal to 2s. 6d. of our money), from January 10 to April 14, 15s. 8d. He, John de Crepping, further handed over to Milo de Stapleton 3 mares and 2 colts, the latter being down with the plague.

But we are favoured with a complete inventory of the stock and implements belonging to the preceptory at Temple Hirst, and as information of this kind is not very accessible to the majority of persons, and by no means uninteresting as a record of English life in this neighbourhood during a period from which we are daily receding, I do not like to withhold the details.

INVENTORY.

	s.	d.		s.	d.
29 Oxen valued at ...	12	0	9 Heifers	5	0
11 Cows and one Bull	9	0	4 Calves	1	6

[1] From *conrody*, eating together, referring to the custom of benefactors sending their old servants to feed in these institutions.

	s.	d.		s.	d.
1 Boar	3	0	1 Colt and 2 do., 2 years old	4	6
3 Sows	1	8	2 do. raised on the Farm	1	8
12 Hogs	1	3	288 (cciiij^{xx}viij) Wether Sheep	1	0
10 Pigs	0	8	226 Ewes	1	0
4 Mules for the carts	10	0	130 Lambs ... 0s. 8d.		
1 Mule and 3 Fillies, 3 years old	5	0			

In the Granary.

	s.	d.		s.	d.
46 quarters of mixed Wheat	3	4	132 quarters of large Oats	1	6
38 do. of Corn	4	0	58 do. small do.	1	0
57 acres of sown Corn	6	8	14 acres of Rye sown	1	0

Hay got in valued at £16. 12 oxen from Scotland, 6 ploughs with all their equipments valued at 12s.; 2 carts, 1 of which is broken, 13s.; 1 hand-cart with harness 3s., 2 waggons 5s; 3 dung forks, 2 spades, 4 flails, 4 forks for the corn, 18s. the lot.

In the forge—1 anvil, 1 pair of bellows, 2 pair of *tavellæ* (*i.e.*, instruments for branding cattle), and 1 curved anvil, all 10s.

In the hall—2 tables with tressels 2s., 2 sleeping tables or benches 2s. 8d.

In the cellar—1 alms-box value 6d., 3 chests 3s., 1 salt-cellar of pewter 2d., one tankard bound with iron, 2 do. not so bound, 6d., 1 large cask and 6 barrels 4s., hand-baskets 6d., and 2 tubs of salt meat.

In the kitchen—1 brass pot 1s., 3 smaller do. 12s., 1 small pitcher 1s., 2 brass pans 1s. 6d., 1 cooking-pot 2s. 6d., 1 mortar and pestle 2d., 2 tripods 8d., 3 knives 3d., iron chain 2d., an axe 4d., and 1 pair of mills (*molæ*) for mixing grits with salt 6d.

In the bakehouse—a leaden vessel 4s., 3 large measures 1s. 6d., 1 sleeping-table 8d., a cask for sifting flour 1s.

In the brewhouse—2 leaden vessels in the furnace 10s., 1 large vat 3s., 2 smaller do. 3s., 6 brewing vessels 3s., 3 measures (*algea*) 1s. 6d., 4 wine vessels (*lyma*) 1s. 8d., and a leaden vessel for steeping grain 13s. 4d.

In the dairy—1 leaden vessel 1s., 1 do. measure for liquids 3d.

In the chapel—1 chalice 13s. 4d., 1 missal 6s. 8d., 1 breviary in 2 volumes 6s., 1 Psalter 2s, 1 vestment for Sundays 8s., and for festivals with 2 *blessed* towels and a frontal 10s., 3 surplices and a *rochet* 2s. 6d.—the mention of this latter robe seems to imply that bishops occasionally officiated or visited at this Templar establishment; we shall probably refer to this point later on in our history. In addition to the preceding, the chapel contained a cross, 2 candlesticks, a pyx (*i.e.*, a box in which the Romish priests place the wafer after consecration), a thurible for incensing, and a boat for containing incense before placing it in the thurible or censer, also a chest. These last items were all valued at 4s.

In the dormitory also were 2 chests valued at 4s., and on the banks of the Aire, which flows close to the preceptory grounds, were 2 old boats and 3 old fishing-nets. There were also 4 corn measures and a winnowing-cloth valued at 8d., wherewith to conclude the list of goods and chattels.

But we have not done, for in the Grange at Potterlawe (a place we can now verify as Shirewood, in the township of Egborough) there were 35 quarters of small oats (by estimation, for the corn was still in sheaves) valued at 1s. per quarter, also 27 acres of sown rye priced at 5s. per acre. Also at Kelyngton, which we have before observed belonged to Temple Hirst, there were 5 cart-horses valued at 4s. each, 1 measure at 4d., 16 quarters of rye (in sheaves), only valued at 3s. 4d., and therefore seemingly not so good as that at Potterlawe and Temple Hirst ; 6 quarters of barley at 3s., 10 quarters of large oats at 1s. 6d., and 22 do. of small ones at 1s.

Then follows a statement that the inventory was sealed at Hirst on the first day of December, in the fifth year of Edward II., *i.e.* 1312.

And here I supplement this list of furniture, stock, implements, etc., from another inventory 'made on the Wednesday after the Epiphany 1 Ed. II. by Will. de Ros de Bolton " *miles* " and Laurence de Hethe' (? Heck) 'at the House of the Temple of Hyrst,' which appeared from the pen of Mr. E. H. Chetwynd-Stapylton, in the *Yorkshire Archæological Journal*, vol. x. :

Total of corn (*summa granarum*), £16 13s. 4d.

In the stable—a riding horse (*verrante*) valued at 30s., 1 colt at 20s., 8 pack-horses at 7s. each, 2 yearling colts 10s., and 10 foals at 2s. each. Also 36 cart-oxen at 10s., 1 bull at 7s., and 20 cows at 7s., 11 wether sheep and 246 ewes at 18d. Total £17 16s. 6d., with hay for the sheep and other animals. Also 43 pigs, including 3 boars and 6 sows at 18d., 12 hoggets at 9d., and 13 porkers at 3d. Also 9 capons, 9 cocks, 15 hens, worth together 3s. 1½d.

Implements—4 ploughs *with iron gear* at 8s., two old carts bound with iron at 13s. 4d. the two, 4 carts not bound at 7s., 4 waggons at 10s., 1 iron-bound wood-cart, 1 hand-cart at 3s., 10 dung-forks at 10d., and 7 hay-forks at 7d. ; forge tools and 15 pieces of iron worth altogether 9s. 10½d., and 2 books at 4d. At the fishery—2 boats, one worth 20s. and the other 7s. 8d., 1 large net and 1 cable 20s., 3 round nets and a seine 5s.

Chapel—1 silver chalice and one gilt do. 10s., 1 missal valued 6s. 8d., 1 breviary in 2 volumes 10s., 1 Psalter 2s., 2 graduals 10s., 1 ordinal 18d., 1 collect-book 18d., and another ordinal 8d., 1 vestment with 2 napkins 13s. 4d., 1 vestment *cum tuniclo de almaculo cum caponthoria.* These words are not a little puzzling; they may be intended for *cum tunic[u]lo dalma[ti]culo*, etc. Whether it be so or not, evidently these garments were intended for the vestment and stole of the sub-deacon at Mass. And here we may remark that the mention of silver and gilt chalices among the goods of the chapel shows that the Templars had their celebrations with the accompaniments of wealth. It was only richly-endowed churches or chapels which possessed such chalices; others had to be content with glass ones. It was at the Council held at Westminster A.D. 1175 that chalices of metal inferior to gold or silver were forbidden to be used. We resume the list of chapel furniture, and as it proceeds we see further proof of the fact that provision was made for a considerable number of clergy and a degree of pomp and dignity not customary in village churches, *e.g.*, 'one vestment for Sundays 8s., and one for festivals with two napkins 10s., three surplices and one rochet 2s. 6d.,' as in previous list.

In the hall (or treasury) there are thirty charters. How much we should like to have them to con over, but, alas! they have followed the way of the Order, *i.e.*, to destruction. But they were sealed up in one box, and two more charters in two other boxes, bearing the seal of Lord William Ros, before mentioned. Three trestle tables valued at 2s., and 2 dormant tables (*tabul. dor.*) attached to the wall 20s., a washing-basin 12d., 1 towel (*mappa*) and napkin (*manutergium*) 5s. 6d., 2 other towels and 2 napkins, 2 mazer cups, 1 iron-bound tankard 4d., 1 cask (*dolium*) 10d. (reminding one of the modern 'dolly-tub').

In the larder—8 barrels 4s. 4d., 2 troughs (*alvei*) for salting meat 12d., 3 carcases of beef (*carkōs boum*) at 4s. each, 18 pieces of bacon at 2s. each, 10 carcases of mutton 6d. each, and 1 piece and a half of goat's meat.

In the kitchen—1 brass pot (*olla*) 10s., and 4 more worth 13s., 2 wax tablets for writing on (*ceracula*) 2s. each, 1 brass vessel 2s., 2 salt-cellars (*patellæ*) 18d., 1 caldron (*cacabus*) 2s. 6d., 1 iron pot 8d., 2 pipkins (*cressett.*) 4d., 1 *imator* (? *imaginator*—embroiderer).

In the brewery and bakehouse—1 vat (*algea pro brasco fundrando in plumbato*) 10s., 1 copper (*plumbum*), 3 water-butts (*algeeaquæ*), two leaden boilers (*plumba in fornace*) 10s., 1 grater (*micatorium*) 3s., 3 tubs (*cuvæ*), 5 cheeses (*pan. casei*), etc.

Total value £124 8s. 7d.

Queen's Remembrancer's Office, T. G. 41,156, ¹⁷⁸⁄₂₃ Kt. Templars, Edw. II.

ADDITIONAL MSS. 6,165.

1307. An inquest was held at Potterlawe on March 2 (1 Edw. II.), by command of the King, to ascertain the value of all the lands and benefices held by the Templars in the wapentakes of Osgotcrosse and Barkston. The names of the valuers were :

Matthew Malling.	Hugo de Potterlawe.
Will. de Fal. de Kellington.	John Malyn de Egburgh.
Robert, son of Robert de Kellington.	Alex. Cocky de Rohall.
	Will. le Mareschall de Carleton.
John, son of German de Kellington.	
	John de Birne.
John Cocky de Kellington.	John Aleyn de Hathelesay.
Alexis, son of Sarre of Egburgh.	John, son of Will. de Thorp.
	Will. de Camelford de Hathelesay.
Ric. de Vendur of Kellington.	
Simeon de Monte of Kellington.	Ran. de Hirst.
	Peter de Bretton.
John, son of Ric. Vendur.	Peter ad Potam de Culeton.

The valuation of Temple Hirst includes the following items :

	£	s.	d.
A capital messuage (with a close containing a dovecote) value per annum	0	20	0
160 acres of arable land value per annum ...	4	0	0

KOAL HALL.

To face p. 60.

		£	s.	d.
5 acres of meadow value per annum	... ...	0	15	0
5 acres of pasture ,, ,,	... ...	0	10	0
40 acres of wood ,, ,,	... ...	0	6	8

And the said lands are in the hands of the King, and held of Henry de Lacy, Earl of Lincoln; but by what tenure the valuers are ignorant, and they also say that the said lands have been bestowed by the ancestors of the said Earl for a subsidy of land, of the site of which they are ignorant. There are also at Temple Hirst:

		£	s.	d.
3 acres of pasture value per annum	...	0	6	0
10 acres of meadow ,, ,,	... ...	0	30	0
1 windmill, which, with its site, is worth per annum	... ...	0	13	4

And these lands are in the hands of the King, and held by Milo de Stapleton, and the ancestors of the said Earl have bestowed them for a subsidy of land of the site of which the valuers are ignorant.

There are also in Birne 6 acres of arable land, the gift of John de Belowe (Bellew or Bella-aqua) for 2s. per annum for all rent and service.

There are also 30 acres of arable land in 'Est' Hirst value per annum 10s., which the Templars pay annually to John de Curtenay for all service.

They have also in Temple Hirst and East Hirst fixed free rents value 27s. 9d., and bond rents value 69s. 11d., both yearly.

Also in West Hathelsay and Middle Hathelsay fixed free rents value 8s. 9d. The yearly value of all these lands is £14 7s. 7½d.

At Kellington the premises are:

		£	s.	d.
1 capital messuage (with a close containing a dovecote) value per annum	... ...	0	6	8

	£	s.	d.
3 bovates of land value per annum	0	24	0
7 acres of land ,, ,,	0	2	4
1 acre of meadow ,, ,,	0	4	0
1 windmill	0	8	0
Also 8 bovates of land held in villeinage value per annum	0	64	0

The Templars also hold the church at Kelyngton for their own use, value per annum £33 6s. 8d.; except the vicarium, which is worth £40. Total value with the church, £40 13s. 2d.[1]

The lands and tenements of the said church are in the hands of the King, and are held by the heirs of Henry de Vernoil — in pure and perpetual charity and in aid (*in subsidio*) of the Holy Land of the grant of the said Henry de Vernoil.

In Potterlawe there is no house; there are 34 acres of arable land, value per annum 11s. 4d.; 15 acres of meadow land, value per annum 60s., held of the heirs of the said Henry de Vernoil as before.

Twelve acres of arable land, value per annum 4s., held of the heirs of Ralph de Roale on the same terms and for the same purpose as the preceding lands.

They have also at Potterlawe free fixed rents value per annum 2s., and rents of tenements held by the heirs of Henry de Vernoil as before. The total sum is £3 17s. 4d.

At Hethensale (Hensall) they have lands value per annum 3s. 2d.

At Smetheton (Kirk Smeaton) they have in free fixed rents 50s. held of the heirs of Richard Foliot by the presentation of the said Richard for a chaplain to celebrate divine service daily in the chapel at Temple Hirst.

---

[1] We should have expected this total to have been £73 6s. 8d. The explanation is that the revenues of the vicarium were leased away for twenty-eight years, so only a nominal sum was yearly left.

GATEWAY TO ROAL HALL.

Also Richard de Waleis pays a yearly rent of 15s. for a water-mill at Burghen-walleis, given by the ancestors of the said Richard in aid of the Holy Land (*i.e.*, Templar house there).

Total value £3 3s. 11d.

Total value in wapentakes of Osgotcrosse £50 7s. 7d. Sum of the preceding, £64 15s. 2½d.

The items given which should make up the total of £64 15s. 2½d. are:

	£	s.	d.
Temple Hirst...	14	7	7½
Kellington	40	13	2
Potterlawe	3	17	4
Hethensale	0	3	2
Smethall	3	3	11
	£62	5	2½

—but there is a deficit of £2 10s. 0d.

Under the heading Contrarient L-a-n-d-s—W. A. 3,352, 16 Edw. II. (*i.e.*, A.D. 1323), we find a roll of 2 membranes containing the extent of:

The Manor of Standale forfeited[1] by Roger Damoy. Query Downay, Daunay.

Also of Fanflet by John de Mowbray.

Also of Temple Newsom and Carleton (by the same).

Also of Temple Hirst by Robert de Holand.

Also of West Hathelsay and East H. by Nich. Stapleton.

A.D. 1323. Transcript of the manors of our lord the King in county York.

Under Temple Hirst we find the following:

It also appeared that Lord Robert of Holand (Sir Robert Holland, secretary to Thomas, Earl of Lancaster) had plough-land at Temple Hirst which contained a messuage with a garden which is worth vs. annually.

---

[1] Because of their part in Lancaster's rebellion. See forward. Chapter VIII.

And there is in the same place a dovecote which is worth xiid. annually, and used to be worth iijs. iiijd. There are also in the same place cc acres, whereof each x. acres is worth iiijd. annually. Total vjs. viijd., and each acre used to be worth vjd.

There are also xxv acres worth is. each acre annually. Total xxxs., and each acre used to be worth iiijs.

There is also pasture valued separately at xs. per acre, which used to be worth xxs. There is also pasture 'in water of the Ayre' (*i.e.*, the Ings) valued at vs., and not worth more.

There are four free tenants, viz., Alan 'de Melano,' who holds one messuage and xv acres, and three who hold 'for provision and service homage,' and pay iiijs., with suit of court twice a year (*duos advent. ad curiam*).

Also Richard Shippeman, who holds one messuage and pays xviijd. per annum, with suit of court twice a year.

Also John Hubbard, who holds one messuage and viij acres, and pays iis., etc. Also Alan Griffyn holds one messuage and 3 acres, and pays xviijd. per annum.

'There are also six villein tenants (*bondi*), who pay 15s. 10d. for 40 acres of land and meadow, and their houses, and 16 cottarii, who pay 27s. 6d.'[1] — the total being only £9 3s. 3d., as compared with £14 7s. 7½d. in 1308.

The following extracts from Yorkshire deeds in Public Record Office are worth quoting:

(51.)

'A 315. Grant by Matilda Bigot, Countess of Norfolk and Warenne, to Richard de Ottele, her chaplain, of the tenement with its appurtenances which she bought of Ranulf the Chaplain of Torn, in Torn and Fislac, to be held of her and her heirs, paying therefor yearly 3s. 8d.

---

[1] See *Yorks. A. and T. Journal*, vol. x., p. 442.

to the Knights Templars at Hurst. For this grant the said Richard has paid 15 marcs. Witnesses: Sir Adam de Neyreford, Sir John Lemveyse, Sir Roger de Lund[on], Master Richard de Freyssinfeld, Alexander de Stubbes, Thomas de Steynford, and Thomas de Mortemer, of Aitfeld.' *Fragment of seal.*

(52.)

'A 316. Grant by Ranulf the Chaplain of Torn, to Matilda Bigot, Countess of Norfolk and Warenne, of his tenement and appurtenances in Torn and Fislake, paying therefor yearly 3s. 8d. '*Fratribus Milicie Templi Salomonis,*' at Hurst. For this grant the aforesaid Matilda has paid 20 marcs. Witnesses: Sir Roger de Lund[on], Sir John Lenveyse, Richard de Castro, and others' (named).

These inventories are of great interest as giving us an insight into the domestic life of the period in general, as well as of that of the Templars in particular. The greater abundance of some articles in 1308 over those enumerated in the inventory of 1312 may suggest that in the interval the Templars had disposed of some of their goods, in view, it may be, of the impending troubles!

We note from a preceding page that it was as early as 1307 when a writ was issued to the Sheriff of Yorkshire to hand over to Miles Stapleton the manor of Temple Hirst, with lands and buildings, etc. From what we know of this nobleman, he would not act with harshness towards the Templars, but, on the contrary, may have been very willing to treat them with leniency, and so they may have reduced their movable goods and chattels before surrendering their premises.

Be this as it may, the buildings round the preceptory, and the preceptory itself, have suffered much less than the majority of such places, both from the ravages of time and the violence of the spoiler, or by the improvements (?) of modern iconoclasts, who think nothing perfect but that which their own unskilled hands have wrought. Remembering that the Templary preceptories were generally plain and substantial rather than ornamental buildings, we can trace the outlines of their erections without much misgiving as to their accuracy. In doing this I am greatly indebted to the kind help of Mr. E. H. Chetwynd-Stapylton, who explored the premises with me in 1882, and kindly allows me to use the ground-plan which he made for insertion here. I may add that the preceptory proper had evidently a moat

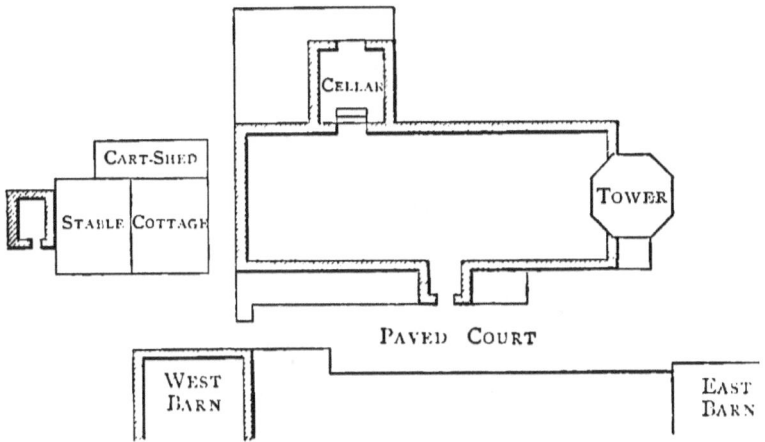

GROUND-PLAN OF PRECEPTORY.

around it at one time, of which there are remains on the north side, with the narrow gateway through which only one mounted horseman could pass at a time. This is another feature special to Templar establishments. What difference there is arises from the tower at the east end, now greatly reduced in height, and, as we write, being surmounted with over-sailing courses of brickwork on the top, which alters its appearance, especially as seen from the railway. There is a large room to the west of the tower, about forty feet by twenty feet, which would well serve as hall or refectory; then comes more westerly still an apartment which gives the idea of the chapel, and it has a projecting chamber or closet on the south side, with a raised daïs, which might have served for altar. The rough cast is now stripped from the walls, and barns and out-buildings remain much as they may have been 700 years ago. No doubt the use of the preceptory as a residence by the Darcys and others has greatly contributed to its preservation, but of this we need not speak now. The hour was approaching when those who had erected these buildings, as well as the Grange at Potterlawe, were to be scattered abroad, and other men were to occupy their premises and profit by the fruit of their labours in clearing the woods and cultivating the land.

> 'They perished, in one fate alike,
>   The vet'ran and the boy,
> Where'er the royal arm[1] could strike
>   To torture and destroy ;
> While darkly down the stream of time,
>   Devised by evil fame,
> Float murmurs of mysterious crime,
>   And tales of secret shame.'
>   Lord Houghton, ' Persecution of the Templars,'
>   *Yorkshire Archæological Journal*, vol. ix.

The Templars were conveyed to York from the northern counties, and confined in the castle during the autumn of 1309. A provincial council was summoned for May 20, 1310. Among the names of those who had been examined between April 27 and May 4 of that year occurs that of 'Ivo de Houghton,' which may mean Ivo de Etton, Preceptor of Hirst; if so, it does not appear

---

[1] If this refers to Philip, King of France, it is severely true ; but it must not be forgotten, in justice to the unfortunate King of England, Edward II., that he was coerced by the Pope and by Philip the Fair, whose daughter he unfortunately married, and whose shameful treatment of her husband was on a par with her father's conduct towards the Templars.

that he escaped imprisonment, and the supposition may only be due to the misnomer.

When we consider that occurrences which took place at this preceptory are the alleged cause of proceedings against the Templars north of the Humber (though not the exclusive cause, as we read of charges against them at Halton, Colton, and Newsam, for hunting contrary to the statutes of their Order), yet the prominence given to the evidence of 'Master John de Nassington, who declared that Milo de Stapleton and Adam de Evrington (? Everingham), knights, told him that they had once been invited to a great feast at the Preceptory of Templehirst, and were there informed that the Templars celebrated a solemn festival once a year, at which they worshipped a *calf !*'

Other most odious, disgusting, and self-contradictory charges were brought against the Templars, *e.g.*, that at their chapters they worshipped a cat, a man's head, a black idol, and then that their chaplains ended the proceedings by reading Psalm lxvii. The decree which declared the Order of Knight Templars to be forever abolished in England was promulgated by Archbishop Greenfield from Cawood on August 14, 1312. In 1323 the King appointed Humphrey de Waleden and Richard de Ikene seneschals of the castles and towns of Tykhill and Scarborough, and keepers of the Park of Heyura (? Healaugh), and the manors of Faxflete, Carlton, *Hachelsey*, *Temple Hirst*, Barley (*i.e.*, Barlow, modern name), Sandall (? *Sandhall* upon the Ouse), and Temple Newsam, with their respective appurtenances in the county of York. Next year some of these places fell to the Hospitallers.

Here we may pause to note what happened to those who were the chief actors in the destruction of the Templar Order. Thirteen months after the execution of the last Grand Master of the Temple, James de Molay, in Paris, the Pope was attacked by dysentery and speedily died. His dead body was placed in the church at Carpentras, and, taking fire, was unintentionally cremated! His relatives quarrelled over the immense wealth he left behind him, and a large sum deposited in a church at Lucca for safety was abstracted by a band of robbers.

Before the close of the same year, Philip, the King of France, probably the most criminal of all the enemies of the Templars, had his last days embittered by misfortune; the nobility and clergy combined to resist his exactions, his family were disgraced by their infamies, and he himself died of an incurable disease.

The malefactor whose evidence was used as a pretence for the arrest of the Templars was himself hanged for additional crimes. Whilst our own King Edward II., the least culpable of all the sovereigns responsible for the ruin of the Templars, had from the time of their downfall misfortune following misfortune, until his miserable life was ended by a horrible crime in Berkeley Castle.

Having thus dwelt briefly on the miserable results to the leading actors in this great tragedy, we may well devote a few lines to a review of the effects of the Templar movement on the social, moral, and intellectual character of the age during which the Order existed. To begin, we learn that, however great the enthusiasm of those who undertake an enterprise, yet if there be zeal without knowledge the design must fail. The idea of combining the profession of a monk with that of a soldier only needed the cold breath of adversity to dispel the vapouring sentiment of mistaken piety from which the design was evolved. The complete failure of the crusades well illustrates the value of the homely proverb that 'the cobbler should stick to his last.' When Bernard of Clairvaux foretold the success of the crusades, he showed that though he could pen sweet melodies, and soar aloft in holy meditation; that though he was mighty in the synod and in the monastery; yet that in the organization of military expeditions he failed painfully and hopelessly. Still, dark and disastrous as were the doings of the Templars for the most part on the sacred soil of Syria, it would not be right to say that the mighty conception of the monk of Clairvaux yielded no fruit. The very gathering of the multitudes for the ostensible purpose of promoting religion and morality, humanity and brotherhood of man as *men*; the defence of women from outrage, and the suffering from oppression, breathed a new thought into the stagnant body of brutality and violence which more or less prevailed among the nations in the eleventh and twelfth centuries. The crusades gave a new idea to chivalry, which had heretofore been limited to the possession of wealth and the bearing of arms. According to the notions of the eleventh and twelfth centuries, a landless being could not be a gentleman, as arms could only be carried by way of vassalage and for hire. When, therefore, men went forth at their own charges, as during the crusades, not simply in obedience to a lord or sovereign as the token of their subjection, but willingly impelled by an unselfish and not a servile motive, it lifted the profession of arms on to a higher platform, and made it possible to a wider circle of society.

Again, we may assert that the crusaders extended knowledge both geographically and historically. They created historians as well as furnished material for their pens. Navigation and commerce also participated in the stimulus furnished by the crusades. These expeditions also introduced to the West the literature and languages of the East, also many useful herbs and fruit-trees. The roughness of military life in Europe was also softened to some extent, probably, by the romance which glowed in the breasts of these new soldiers of the Cross. Whilst theologically the crusades doubtless gave an impulse to what we may call Mariolatry, yet the ostensible profession of a Templar Knight carried with it the recognition of the claims of womanhood from a more Scriptural aspect than was current generally before. In spite of such bad specimens as Bois de Gilbert, we may hope that there were many of the Brotherhood who regarded themselves as the pledged protectors of the defenceless and the fair. I think we may assume that the three great virtues of loyalty, courtesy, and munificence were more or less exhibited by the Knight Templars. It is true they have been charged with overbearing pride and insolence, among others by one who knew them well, viz., Richard Cœur de Lion, yet he himself as a Templar showed great magnanimity in dealing with the perfidy of his brother and the treachery of a colleague in the wars.

As to courtesy, the very name of a knight carried this obligation on its shield as its patent of nobility, and its presence is an essential element of bravery, otherwise courage might degenerate into brutality and bring down the lordly knight to the level of the uncultivated boor.

But high above all other knightly graces shone out that of munificence. In the flood-tide of their enthusiasm the Templars literally accepted the counsels of Urban II.; though, looking back, their lot was indeed a hard one, to go forth under the benedictions of one Pope, and then some two hundred years later to be crushed beneath the curse of another. However, under the intoxicating fumes of Papal benediction and popular applause the Templars, obedient to the counsels of Urban II., affixed the red cross to their garments, sold their estates at any price, quitted their castles and their family endearments, and went south with their lives in their hands. Whilst those absolutely unable to leave country and kindred gave their lands *in subsidio Terræ Sanctæ*.

In this act we see at least a fundamental principle of Christian discipleship, viz., that all should share either in person or by deputy in the high call and claims of that service which seeks to win an alienated world to the love and service of its Sovereign Lord and King, Christ Jesus.

Everywhere at home and abroad, in the thinly populated rural district as well as in the crowded streets of the city, in the unreclaimed masses and unsanctified classes of our English civilization as well as the millions of the untaught heathen in far-off lands, the cry for good soldiers of Jesus Christ sounds aloud. These knights need to wear no outward sign upon their cloaks, but within to feel the power of that which urged the noblest missionary of Europe and Asia 'to labours more abundant than they all,' viz., the love of Christ, for he wrote: 'We thus judge, that if one died for all, then were all dead; and that He died for all, that they which live should not henceforth live unto themselves, but unto Him who died for them and rose again.' Glorious sentiment — the Gospel in miniature! and not unworthily epitomized in the motto on the white-crossed flag of the Swiss Confederation:

'Un pour tous, et tous pour un.'

TEMPLARS' SEAL.

CHAPTER VI.

THE KINGDOM OF GOD AND HOUSE OF PRAYER IN OUR PARISH.

WHATEVER other interests there may be in any community, to the Christian mind one is paramount beyond all others, viz., that which concerns the worship of God and the salvation of souls. It is time for us, therefore, in our review of the past history of Haddlesey, to address ourselves to the question of what was done in this connection. We have seen that the Knight Templars not only had their own chapel at the preceptory at Hirst, but that also they had their own special church at Kellington. But this provision was for their own members. There was also the small church at Birkin, which in early days was doubtless regarded[1] as the parish church of the five townships of Birkin, West Hathelsay, Est Hathelsay, and East and West Hyrst. But this arrangement was soon found unsatisfactory; so we learn that

[1] I say regarded because it is so spoken of from time to time, and certainly *after* the confusion of the Civil Wars claimed and exercised the rights of a mother church even to the extent of levying a church-rate on the inhabitants of the four townships, who, nevertheless, had to maintain their own separate church and churchyard. But the greater difficulty in regarding Birkin as the mother church of all these townships in the usual sense of the word is the existence of separate manors from a very early date, it being notorious that the boundaries of ancient parishes were coterminous with the manors of their founders.

Archbishop Walter Gray consecrated a parochial chapel at Haddlesey, A.D. 1237. Here it is well to explain the difference between a parochial chapel and a chapel-of-ease, as there is much confusion of ideas on this subject. During the first six or seven centuries of the Christian era, the parish was the district of the Bishop, what was afterwards called the diocese. In this district the Bishop and his clergy lived together at the cathedral church, and the tithes and offerings of the faithful made one common fund for the support of the Bishop and his clergy and the erection and maintenance of places of worship, and the carrying on of what was to a large extent a diocesan mission. This sort of collegiate life of the Bishop and his clergy was characteristic of the British and Anglo-Saxon Churches.

In process of time, however, it was found necessary to build additional sanctuaries in such places as invited the itinerant preachers to settle down to pastoral work in their midst. The most frequent cause of this was the offer of some large landowner to build a church and maintain a resident clergyman, for the benefit of himself, his family, and tenants, within a given area. On doing this, the founder of the church became its patron, and the bounds of a parish extended over his manor. In almost every case the church, in its initiation, was a chapel of the thane for parochial uses. *Most* of these parochial chapels were made into parish churches in the modern sense of the word, at a period beginning at the end of the ninth century and ceasing about the end of the twelfth. What gives Birkin its real priority and rank as a quasi mother church to Haddlesey is the very interesting fact that it probably had a resident priest at the end of the eleventh century. So we read in Mountain's 'History of Selby' that 'John, son and heir of Hugh de Lacy' (Abbot of Selby, 1097-1123), 'of Gateforth, gave Alfwyn de Byrkhouse, the vassal of his brother

Robert, with the land that he bought of *Osbert, the priest of Byrkin*, to Selby Abbey.'

However, this process was only gradual, and so from time to time we read still of chapels built upon the manors and ancient demesnes of the Crown, like Haddlesey; their incumbents or chaplains were instituted by the Bishop and inducted by the Archdeacon. These parochial chapels differed from chapels-of-ease in that they had the right of christening and burying, and that the minister was presented by a patron to the Bishop for institution, and that he was irremovable by the rector of the mother-church. By the law of King Edgar (about A.D. 970), it was ordained that a thane might give one-third part of his tithes to a parochial chapel. How these different points bear on the history of the church at Haddlesey we shall note as we continue. According to Torre MSS., the first church at Haddlesey was consecrated by one of the greatest prelates which ever filled the archiepiscopal See of York, Walter Gray. He was a zealous reorganizer of parishes and great reformer of past negligences in his diocese. It is difficult to be quite sure of the date of the consecration, but it has been supposed to be about 1237. Archbishop Gray's episcopate extended from 1215 to 1255.

The existence of this building is abundantly plain from the language of Sir Miles Stapleton : 'Seriously considering (says Dodsworth) that his tenants at Hathelsay, and other inhabitants of the towns of Est Hurst and Temple Hurst, being oftentimes in the year prevented from attending the mother church at Birkin, " for the inondacion," *had built at their proper charges a certain decent chapel for celebration of Divine worship.*' A.D. 1310-11 he paid a fine of 20s.—about £20 of our present money—to the King for license to give certain lands in East and West Haddlesey for *rebuilding* the Chapel of St. John the Baptist ('de novo construendo'), and on August 29, 1313, *he further granted a messuage and lands next the chapel*, and other lands at East and West Haddlesey, to the 'lord Wm. de Calthorn, chaplain, and his successors for ever.'[1]

It is important to note the gift 'of a *messuage* and *lands* next *the chapel*,' because no such messuage or lands *now* belong to what was then the chapel. When and by whom this messuage and lands were alienated is not an improper question in these days, when claims on Church property are being multiplied and the incomes of the clergy greatly reduced. I have my own opinion as to the time and method of this alienation, but as at present I cannot support it with documentary proof, I refrain from mentioning the grounds.

The particulars of the gift are : ' Unum messagium in Est Hathelsay infra precinctas ejusdem capellæ scituatum ; et unam bovatam et sex acras terræ in West Hathelsay, cum tofto ad p'dam bovat. terræ spectando, quæ quidem toft. et bovat Robertus de Camelfford ad voluntatem meam aliquando de me tenuit ; et quatuor acras prati in Est Hathelsay, simul jacentes in quodam prato voc. le Vestyenge, ex parte occident. ; et duas acras bosci in Est Hathelsay, jacent. in bosco meo qui vocatur le Westwode ; et viginti solid. annui reddit. percipiend. de H'bagh cujusd. pastur. in Est Hathelsay, que locatur Kidcholm. Hend et tenend eisd. Capellanis, &c. Dat. 29 Augt., 1313, cum sig.—Cart. Harl., 84 A 45, extracted by Mr. E. H. Chetwynd-Stapylton, which may be translated as follows : One messuage in East Hathelsay, situated

---

[1] *Yorkshire Deeds.*—This gift is further certified by a license of Henry de Lacy, Earl of Lincoln, Constable of Chester, to Miles de Stapleton, to grant land in *Esthathelsay*, held of him in frank almoign, to the *chaplain of the chapel to be built by him in Esthathelsay,* in accordance with a license in mortmain of the present King to him to grant 1 oxgang, 6 acres of land, 4 acres of meadow, 2 acres of wood, and 3 acres of pasture in Westhathelsay and Esthathelsay for the above purpose. London, Sunday after SS. Simon and Jude, 4 Edw. II. (A 106). — (*Yorkshire A. and T. Journal*, vol. xii.), A.D. 1311, October 24.

below the precincts of the same chapel; and a bovate and six acres of land in West Hathelsay, with a toft looking out upon the aforesaid bovate of land, which toft and bovate Robert de Camelfford for some time held of me at my pleasure; and four acres of meadow in Est Hathelsay, lying together in a certain meadow called 'le Vestyenge,' on the west; and two acres of wood in Est Hathelsay, lying in my wood which is called 'le Westwode'; and twenty solidi of yearly rent to be received from the herbage (?) of a certain pasture in Est Hathelsay, which is called Rideholm. To have and to hold to the said chaplains, etc.

As regards the name given to this pasture, it is interesting to note that in the terrier of lands belonging to this benefice there is still land going by the name of Royds, supposing we are right in conjecturing that 'ride' may be a corruption of 'riod' or 'royd,' meaning land cleared of wood for pasture or cultivation. As regards Holme, that name is also preserved as Keed Holm, but this land is in West Haddlesey. Westwode would be the tract lying between Westfield, where the rectory house now stands, and the land abutting on the Paperhouse farm. The next addition to the revenues of the church at Haddlesey appears to have been made in the year 1331, and reads as follows: ' To all the faithful of Christ that shall see or hear this triptite (? probably tripartite) charter. John de Hathelsay, citizen of York, greeting. Know ye that I, for the health of my soul, and of the souls of Robert de Hathelsay my father, and of Agnes my wife, and Emma my wife, and of Sir Nicolas Stapleton, Kt., William Camelford, and of Bettrice his wife, have confirmed to Sir Richard Warthill, chaplain, and his successors that shall celebrate divine service in the chapel of St. John the Baptist in Est Hathelsey . . . . . 2 messuages, 38 acres of land, 3 acres of meadow, 2s. of yearly rent, and pasture for 15 beasts, with its appurtenances in West Hathelsey.' This document was witnessed by Sir Nicholas Stapleton, Sir John Travers, and others, and is dated at West Hathelsey, July 15, 5 Edw. III.

As regards this John Hathelsey, it appears from the Register of Archbishop Melton (kindly lent me by Canon Raine) that he was chamberlain of the city of York, 1318; bailiff, 1319-20, having been admitted freeman 1301. From Canon Raine's 'History of York' we further learn that the city of York had three bailiffs up to the year 1397. In this year the three bailiffs were changed into two sheriffs. It is satisfactory to know that one bearing the name of Haddlesey was so distinguished a citizen of what is to-day no mean city, but which was in the fourteenth century still more important as regards its connection with the affairs of the nation. Many Parliaments were assembled within its walls, and kings and queens were frequent sojourners in their journeys backwards and forwards to Scotland.

Royal marriages, too, were celebrated in the grand minster of the Northern capital, while the castle of the Archbishops of York at Cawood, and that of the princely house of Percy at Wressil, to say nothing of Pontefract Castle,[1] another royal residence, the key of the county of York, put Haddlesey at this time within constant touch of all the moving activities of the period. This we shall see more fully as we revert to the main stream of our history in connection with the Stapleton family.

Now, it must suffice to remember that our first church was erected at the cost of the inhabitants of the four townships which hereafter were to constitute the ecclesiastical parish of Haddlesey. And it is a noteworthy fact that this church, in its first instance, owed its origin, not to the gift of a landowner, however munificent, but to

---

[1] 'Quod castrum de Pontefracto quod est quasi clavis in comitatu Eborum,' etc. Letter of R. de Grevill to King Henry III. in 1263, quoted by Mr. Wheater, *Yorkshire Weekly Post*, March 28, 1891.

the people who craved its services. Our parish church *as a building* is inferior to many, but I think, in point of spiritual parentage and historic record, it is also superior to some. The poorest building, raised by pious hearts and used by those who are seeking after God, is infinitely more illustrious than the grandest pile ever constructed, lacking these essential conditions. But, again, we have another advantage, that when the heart of Lord Miles Stapleton was moved by the zeal of his tenants to *rebuild* the structure which they had put up, we have in this work the co-operation of an illustrious name; for Lord Miles Stapleton, as we have previously seen, was no mere owner of vast estates and numerous tenants. He was a statesman in the widest sense of the word, a friend and counsellor of one of England's greatest monarchs, Edward I., and also a friend, and would have been a counsellor, of his weak successor, Edward II. There is a glory, then, greater than that of marble and masonry, of carving and sculpture, of 'long-ribbed' aisle and painted window, of lofty tower and arched roof, in the thought that our house of prayer was in its earlier history the gift and conception of a man who played so conspicuous a part in the history, not only of his parish and county, but of his nation and that of Europe in the wars of Edward I.—a man who, having served his country well in many other spheres, at last yielded up his patriotic life on the inglorious field of Bannockburn in the vain attempt to neutralize the follies of his sovereign and to retrieve misfortune caused by the disasters of his times.

Of this centurion it might be said, as of one long before his time: 'He loveth our nation, and he hath built us a synagogue.' And so from that time, through many vicissitudes, as we shall have to trace, there has been for over 500 years a house of God on this same site. Other houses and their owners have passed away beyond all means of recognition, but this one building, humble and modest as it was, has lived on. Our only regret is that when it became too small, and probably dilapidated, in 1834, it was pulled to the ground, instead of having the new incorporated with the old, and so keeping up the continuity in the material structure of the building, so symbolizing one of the glories of the spiritual Church of our nation, which, tracing its foundations back to Apostolic times, surviving the violence of Northern heathen tribes and the parasitic growth of mediæval Romanism; lifting up its voice in the darkest night of superstition from time to time in witness to the truths of primitive Christianity, and then, after many struggles, going forth like a mighty giant under the stimulating breath of the Holy Ghost, and reasserting at the glorious Reformation the doctrines of God's Word as the only ground of hope and guide of conscience. The few scattered fragments which tell us of the presence and progress of the kingdom of God in our parish seem to say that at least some of those who ministered here had the reputation of faithful shepherds. Having said thus much with regard to the commencement of ecclesiastical organization in our parish, it may be well to insert some more detailed information from Torre's MSS. of the archdeaconry of York [1]:

'EAST HADDLESEY.

'A town in the p'h of Birkin, belonged anciently to the Bella-aquas, and from them descended to the Stapletons

[1] James Torre, the celebrated antiquary, was the son of Gregory de Turre, of Haxey, Lincolnshire. One of his ancestors — Roger de Turre — was Vicar of Owston in 1469 and Haxey in 1473. He was twice married, and settled in York probably for the purpose of devoting himself to the study of ecclesiastical antiquities. It appears from a note appended to his works that he began to arrange his MS. for this work on March 15, 1691, and completed it in June, 1692. It contains 1255 columns folio and a complete index. He died in 1699, aged forty-nine, and was buried in Normanton Church. See further particulars in *Yorkshire Weekly Post*, April 25, 1891.

of Carlton, and at last came to the Wethams, K. S. R. C. $\frac{227}{233}$.¹

'In 58 of Hy., Nicholas Stapilton obtained a charter and freewarren Feb. 9th, 1312.

'Sir Miles Stapelton, Kt., etc., sufficiently endowed for the support of one chaplain. And Wm., Archbishop of York, having called before him Sir Hugh Sampson, Rector of ye p'h of Birkin (1289 A.D.); Sir Adame de Everingham, patron thereof, both voluntarily submitting to the ordination. The Archbishop ordained that every chaplain who shall celebrate in sd church shall be deputed by Sir Miles Stapelton and his heirs to be presented, and being *instituted* shall have, by the grant of the said Hugh, Rector, and Sir Adam de Everingham, Patron (who presented their charter sealed thereupon), the tithe hay of a certain place which the sd Sir Myles in Squalleyker, now enclosed, and which same place is vulgarly called Toun mannersyth.² *The tythes whereof this chaplain* shall have and hold for himself and his successors. Moreover, the founder of this chappel, his heirs and tenants, are and shall be bound to repair and reedify this building. No burials allowed in the chapel yard.'

CATALOGUE OF CHAPLAINS.

Temp. Institut.	Capellani.	Patroni.	Vacat.
1302.	Wm. de Hathelsay.		
1304.	F. John de Stokes.		

¹ In Compoti of the Yorkshire estates of Henry de Lacy, Earl of Lincoln, Pontefract Castle, the morrow of St. Michael anno regni regis Edwardi, xxiiij—*i.e.*, 1295 — occur the following payments: De xij*d.* de firma (farm) of Hugo, son of H. of Westhathelessaye, vj*d.* of farm of Gilbert of Hathelessey, Michaelmas term.

² This word 'Toun mannersyth,' sounding to modern ears unintelligible, is very significant, as indicating the place where the manor court was held, the word being literally in modern phrase the town manor seeing. This spot was given by Sir M. Stapelton to the chaplain, and is described by its original name of Squallyacre.

Temp. Institut.	Capellani.	Patroni.	Vacat.
1312.	D'ns Wm. de Calthorn.	Sir Miles Stapleton.	Mort.
1331.	Sir Rd. Warthill.	Sir Nicholas Stapleton.	,,
1342.	John Bonvalet.	Sir Miles Stapleton.	
March 23rd, 1346.	Ds. John de Basine, pr'b'r.	Robert de Camelford.	
1349.	John Byron Wetwang.	Sir Miles Stapleton.	Resigned.
1351.	John de Curteys.	Archbishop by lapse.	
1364.	Ds. John de Clone.	,,	
1376.	Wm. de Calthorn.	Sir Miles Stapleton, who calls him *the parson of Hathelsey* in a deed giving him and the parson of Sprotborough one messuage and 5 bovates of land in West Hathelsay.	
Jan. 1st, 1385-6.	*Rd. Seringe.[1] Wm. de Birkin. *Wm. de Sprotburg.	Doubtful. Sir Wm. Fitzwilliam, Esthathelsay, has a license to assign 17 marks annual rent issuing from his manor of Est, Midel, and Westhathelsay, held of John, King of Castile, Duke of Lancaster, as of the honour of Pontefract, to two chaplains to celebrate divine service daily for the soul of Thos. Stapleton, formerly L. of ye manor aforesaid, dated 10 Nov., 9 Rd. II.; cf. two grants appointing chaplains as above.—Patent Rolls. ii. 269*b*.	Mort.

---

[1] It is possible that those marked with a star were only chantry priests, and not 'chaplains or parsons,' whilst more frequently the chantry priest and chaplain were the same person, as in the case of Richard Warthill and others, as above.

SIR WM. FITZWILLIAM AND LADY, WHO DIED AT HADDLESEY, A.D. 1474.
(From the brass in Sprotborough Church, kindly supplied by
Dr. Fairbanks.)

| Temp. Institut. | Capellani. | Patroni. | Vacat. |

May 23rd, 1394. } Ds. Thos. Toveton, or (?) Towton.

May, 1399. Ds. Thos. de Chaworth. Sir John de Fitzwilliam.

Sir John de Fitzwilliam of Sprotboro died at Rouen, 1421. His son, Sir William Fitzwilliam, married Elizabeth, daughter of Sir Thos. Chaworth. Therefore it is probable that her brother had been appointed by her father-in-law to the church at Haddlesey in 1399. Her own father died in 1459, and her husband in 1474. The date of her own decease is not given, but that it was after her husband is shown by the blank space in the brass let into the stone covering her husband's grave in the chancel of Sprotborough Church, *which was erected the same year as Haddlesey was rebuilt.*

The inscription above referred to is as follows : ' Hic jacent Wills. Fitzwilliam do'nus de Sprotboug armiger et Elizabeth uxor ejus filia Thome Chaworth militis qui quidem Will'ms obiit apud *Hathilsay* primodie mensis decembr a'd'ni 1474;' and afterward aforesaid Elizabeth, day, month, year, A.D. 14 . . .

The Sir William Fitzwilliam just mentioned was the eighth in descent from Albreda, the heiress of the De Lacys, a knight of the Holy Sepulchre, and had the manor of Darrington about the year 1400, which manor seems to have remained in the family about a hundred years longer, for in 1514 it belonged to William Fitzwilliam of Sprotborough, also (by that evasion of the Act forbidding bequests of land which was so customary in the early part of the reign of Hen. VIII.) made William Lord Conyers, and others his feoffees, by a deed of February 27, 7 Hen. VIII.: ' They were to suffer Thos. Southill and others his executors yearly to take the issues of the manors of Elmley, *Haddlesey*, and Darrington to the use of Thos. Southill and Margery his wife, then to the use of Elizth., their daughter, and then to revert to his right heirs.' This Fitzwilliam, as shown above, who was a De Lacy in the female line, was the last of the elder branch, and Thomas Southill[1] was his uncle by marriage ; whose only daughter Elizabeth (the next to her parents in succession to the manor, according to the will of William Fitzwilliam, dated March 4, 1516-17 ; proved April 29, 1518) married, first, Sir Henry Saville, of Thornhill, and secondly, *Richard Gascoigne*, of Lasing-croft. She died July, 1571. Richard Gascoigne married again, but died in 1592 without leaving any children. Hunter, in his ' History of Doncaster,' says that William Fitzwilliam was buried at Haddlesey 1542. See pedigree to follow.

Temp. Institut.	Capellani.	Patroni.	Vacat.
Apl. 12th, 1412.	Hugh de Shirley.	Lady Matilda Fitzwilliam.	

(February 12, 1426. Robert Lacy, of Gaytford, bequeathed two acres of priestland[2] between John Strensall, Vicar of Brayton, and Hugh Sherley, priest of Haddlesey.)

May 25th, 1424.	D'ns. Thos. Mansell.	Sir Thos. Clarell.[3]	

---

[1] This may be a convenient place to note that, according to deed 703, No. 144, Public Record Office, transcribed into *Yorkshire Weekly Post*, November 7, 1891, a grant was made by Thomas Sotehyll to his kinsmen Thomas Gryce ; William Gryce, clerk ; and Oswald Gryce, of the next *advowson or presentation* to his chantries in St. Philip's Chapel in Haddilsay, co. York.— Sotehyll Hall, February 18, 13 Hen. VIII. (Soothill seems to be a township in Dewsbury parish.) Then, as regards Oswald Grice, mentioned above, he makes a grant at the instance of Lord Darcy to Edmond Seynter, of the offices of surveyor and bailiff of lands, etc., in Middle, East, and West Haddelsey, belonging to Thomas Sotchill, as the said were granted to him by the said Thomas for twenty-four years, from January 23, 13 Hen. VIII. Dated December 20, 18 Hen. VIII. Lord Darcy was head steward under the Honour of Pontefract, and Thomas Gryce was clerk.

[2] According to Canon Isaac Taylor, the tenth of the ploughland was reserved for the priest, and in process of time these lands were permanently set apart, and so were called priestlands. As regards Shirley, he seems to have been a chantry priest, not a chaplain.

[3] Sir Thomas Clarell, of Aldwarke, born about 1394 ; married, 1407, Elizabeth, daughter of Sir John Scroope, and co-heiress with her sister, wife of Sir Richard Hastings, who died *s.p.*

Temp. Institut.	Capellani.	Patroni.	Vacat.
Feb. 3rd, 1433.	Wm. Arrowsmith, pbr.	Lady Fitzwilliam,[1] widow of Sir John de Fitzwilliam.	Mort.
March 2nd, 1434. 1439.	John Rose, or Box, pbr. Ds. Wm. Cowper.	Sir John Clarell.[2] Doubtful.	Resigned.
Jany. 22nd, 1440.	Ds. Rd. Beane.	Sir Wm. Fitzwilliam.	Mort.
July 1st, 1444.	Ds. John Pykering.	,,	,,
Feb. 25, 1453.	John Aleyn, pbr.	Sir Wm. Gascoigne (by right of his wife, the Lady Fitzwilliam, of p. 84, who was then the widow of Sir Robt. Waterton). He was High Sheriff of co. of York in 1422, and died about 1465.	,,
1455.	Ds. Thos. Riplay.	Doubtful.	
Jany. 28th, 1475.	Ds. Henry Whetelay.	Sir Wm. Fitzwilliam.	Resigned.
Aug. 25th, 1482.	Ds. Thos. Ryedale, or Ryhall.	,, ,,	
Jany. 9th, 1484.	Ds. Ed. Seyntor, i.e., Santerre (Holy Land) probably a descendant from a Kt. Templar.	,, ,,	Mort.
Apl. 25th, 1491.	Thos. Boothroyd.	,, ,,	,,
July 2nd, 1497.	Christr. Conyers.	Lady Fitzwilliam.	,,
Jany. 23rd, 1506.	John Richardson.	,, ,,	,,
Augt. 21st, 1506.	Adam Hugh.	,, ,, (widow)	,,

[1] This lady was the daughter of Sir Thomas Clarell, and married Sir William Gascoigne clandestinely either in 1425 or 1426.

[2] Sir John Clarell, of Marshburg Hall, married Elizabeth, widow of Thomas Metham, 1422.

Temp. Institut.	Capellani.	Patroni.	Vacat.
Augt. 6, 1507.	Christr. Rooke.	Lady Fitzwilliam.	Mort.
Jany. 13th, 1508.	John Richardson.		
Nov. 10, 1545.	D'ns Ralph Levet.	Henry Saville, Kt., by right of his wife Elizth., dgr. and co-heiress of Thos. Soothill, by Margaret, dgr. and co-heiress of William Fitzwilliam, of Sprotboro. She married secondly to Rd. Gascoigne of Barnbow, co. York, 1596.	
Dec. 6, 1545.	John Good.		

This Sir Henry Saville, K.B., was a man of considerable importance, he took part in the coronation of Queen Anne Boleyn, May 30, 1534; was Steward the same year of the Honour of Pontefract and of the Manor of Wakefield; and High Sheriff of the county in 1538 and 1542. He died April 5, 1558, seized of thirty manors in Yorkshire, including Sothill, Saxton, Haddlesey, Darrington, etc.

As the name of Ralph Levet is the last in Torre's MSS., I think I can well make a break here to resume the *general* history of the parish, as the succession of the clergy will naturally come on again. Many of the above names, however, are not found in Torre's list, and are due to independent research.

CHAPTER VII.

THE STAPLETON DYNASTY, WHICH EXTENDED FROM 1262 TO THE DEATH OF THOMAS STAPLETON, ABOUT 1380.

AT our last reference, we left Baron Miles Stapleton engaged in plans for rebuilding and endowing the chapel at Hathelsay, A.D. 1312. This year was an exciting one for this part of England. The barons, under the leadership of the Earl of Lancaster, were in open conflict with the young King, Edward II., because of his unworthy favouritism towards Gaveston, whom the King having left in Scarborough Castle for safety, the barons pursued and made prisoner there. As soon as this quarrel was patched up, the young King arranges for a new campaign against the Scots. He summons Miles Stapleton to Roxburgh in terms which remind us of former intimacies; c.g., when Edward came to the throne in 1307, being only twenty-three years of age, Stapleton was made Lord Steward. Then in 1308 he was in attendance on the King at Boulogne, where his marriage was celebrated with great magnificence on January 25. Sir Miles took his countryman, we might say fellow-Yorkshireman, John de Maulever, with him. Stapleton should have presided at the King's coronation by virtue of his office, but, to the great disgust of the barons, Gaveston thrust himself forward and carried the crown before all the magnates of the realm. So Stapleton withdraws from Court, although the King treats him with substantial proofs of his goodwill, and in this summons to Roxburgh he says: 'We affectionately request you to hasten to the parts of Scotland with all the men and arms you can collect.' This muster appears to have fallen through, and while Edward was celebrating his Christmas at York Gaveston reappeared. In June, 1312, there was a much more peremptory summons for Stapleton and his neighbours, Adam de Byrkin and William Roos of Inmangthorpe, 'to join the King at Battle Bridge with all the horse and arms they could muster.' This hasty summons was only obeyed by few, and the next year, 1313, we find him summoned to Parliament at Westminster three times, viz., on January 8, when the Parliament sat from March 18 to April 7; secondly, on May 23; and thirdly, on July 26, when the Parliament sat from September 23 to November 18. The urgent business on this occasion was the war in Scotland. It seems as if Baron Stapleton was summoned to the House of Lords by writ. Mr. Hallam says the only baronies known for two centuries after the Norman Conquest were incidental to the tenure of land immediately from the Crown, and under the Great Charter of John all tenants-in-chief were entitled to a summons by *particular* writ (see further Hallam's 'Middle Ages').

Sir Miles Stapleton did not, however, long enjoy his dignity as baron. The Scottish King, Robert Bruce, laid siege to Stirling, where Philip de Mowbray was shut up, and Edward called out the whole military force of his kingdom to meet at Berwick June 11, 1314. This must have been a stirring time in Hathelsay, when its great chieftain went forth at the head of his retainers, supported by Adam de Byrkin and William Roos of Inmangthorpe, to repel the rising forces of King Robert of Scotland. No doubt they prefaced their expedition by a service in the little church of the village, newly rebuilt, little thinking perhaps that many of those would never worship again in their own sanctuary. It may help us to realize a little more vividly how war was carried on in these days if I give a copy of a writ issued by the same King from York on November 6, 1319. This writ 'requires that every man of 20 years old up to 60, having 40 shillings in land, or chattels to the value of 60 shillings, shall be provided with an aketon (*i.e.*, a coarse linen or leathern doublet stuffed with cotton wool), a bacinett (*i.e.*, an iron skull-cap shaped like a basin, hence its name), and a gauntlet.' This was held to be sufficient equipment for a hobeler, *i.e.*, a kind of light horseman employed in skirmishing and securing forage, and reconnoitring the movements of the enemy. The same writ required that every man above sixty years of age should provide himself with a horse and man-at-arms, *i.e.*, a man much better mounted and clad with stronger armour than the hobelers (Poulton's 'History of Holderness').

Well, when the Hathelsay contingent met the King at Berwick, they found the total force consisted of some 30,000 horsemen; to these must be added the troops already in Scotland and foot-soldiers, as the slain in the ensuing battle are reported to be 146 lords and knights, 700 gentlemen, and 10,000 common soldiers. It seems that Robert Bruce posted his troops in four divisions on the banks of the little river Bannock, about three miles south of Stirling. Sir Walter Scott gives a spirited representation of the scene in his 'Lord of the Isles,' canto vi. :

> 'Of all the Scottish conquests made
> By the first Edward's ruthless blade,
> His own retained no more.

Northward of Tweed, but Stirling's towers,
Beleaguered by King Robert's powers ;
  And they took term of truce,
If England's king should not relieve
The siege ere *John the Baptist's Eve*,
  To yield them to the Bruce.
England was roused on every side,
Courier and post and herald hied
  To summon prince and peer,
At Berwick bounds to meet their Liege,
Prepared to raise fair Stirling's siege,
  With buckler, brand, and spear.
The term was nigh ; they mustered fast,
By beacon and by bugle blast.
  Forth marshalled for the field.
There rode each knight of noble name.
There England's hardy archers came.
The land they trode seemed all on flame
  With banner, blade, and shield !
And not famed England's powers alone,
Renowned in arms, the summons own ;
  For Neustria's knights obeyed ;
Gascoyne hath lent her horsemen good,
And Cambria, but of late subdued,
Sent forth her mountain multitude,
And Connaught poured from waste and wood
Her hundred tribes whose sceptre rude
  Dark Eth O'Connor swayed.'

Bruce had posted his troops to great advantage ; between himself and the English was a deep morass. But the Scots were not content with the natural disadvantages of the spot ; they dug trenches three feet deep and three feet broad, over which they placed hurdles, and beneath which they planted sharp stakes, so that when the English made their charge with cavalry a scene of terrible confusion resulted, and by this destruction and flight of the cavalry the rout of the whole of Edward's army was effected. Quoting again from Scott describing the night before the battle (June 23, 1314), he says:

> 'It was a night of lovely June;
> High rode in cloudless blue the moon.
>
> . . . .
>
> Old Stirling's towers arose in light,
> And, turned in links of silver bright,
> Her winding river lay.'

Then at sunrise the next day, he continues:

> 'Now onward, and in open view,
> The countless ranks of England drew,
> Dark rolling like the ocean tide,
> When the rough west hath chafed his pride,
> And his deep roar sends challenge wide
>   To all that bars his way!
> In front the gallant archers trode,
> The men-at-arms behind them rode,
> And midmost of the phalanx broad
>   The monarch held his sway.'

After describing the opening charge, he comes to the surprise of Edward at the flight of his men and the crisis of the day in these words:

> 'The King with scorn beheld their flight.
> "Are these," said he, "our yeomen wight?
> Each braggart churl could boast before,
> Twelve Scottish lives his baldric bore!
>
> . . . .
>
> "Forward, each gentleman and knight!
> Let gentle blood show generous might,
> And chivalry redeem the fight!"
> To rightward of the wild affray,
> The field showed fair and level way;
>   But in mid space the Bruce's care
> Had bored the ground with many a pit,
> With turf and brushwood hidden yet,
>   That formed a ghastly snare.
> Rushing, ten thousand horsemen came,
> With spears in rest, and hearts on flame,
>   That panted for the shock!

With blazing crests and banners spread,
And trumpet clang and clamour dread,
The wide plain thundered to their tread
   As far as Stirling rock.
Down ! down ! in headlong overthrow,
Horseman and horse the foremost go,
   Wild floundering on the field !
The first are in destruction's gorge,
Their followers wildly o'er them urge ;—
   The knightly helm and shield,
The mail, the aketon, and the spear,
Strong hand, high heart are useless here.

     .   .   .   .

Too strong in courage and in might
Was England yet to yield the fight.
   Her noblest all are here ;
Names that to fear were never known,
Bold Norfolk's Earl de Brotherton,
   And Oxford's famed De Vere.
There Gloster plied the bloody sword,
And Berkeley, Grey, and Hereford,
   (Stapleton) and Sanzavere.
Ross, Montague, and Manley came,
And Courtenay's pride, and Percy's fame—
Names too well known in Scottish war,
At Falkirk, Methven, and Dunbar,
Blazed broader yet in after-years
At Cressy red and fell Poitiers.
Pembroke with these and Argentine
Brought up the rearward battle line.
With caution o'er the ground they tread,
Slippery with blood and piled with dead,
Till hand to hand in battle set,
The bills with spears and axes met.

     .   .   .   .

Unflinching foot 'gainst foot was set,
Unceasing blow by blow was met ;
   The groans of those who fell
Were drowned amid the shriller clang
That from the blades and harness rang,
   And in the battle yell.'

It is scarcely needful to add anything to this thrilling and pictorial narrative, but it may be well to remark that the victory of Bannockburn was decisive for Scottish independence ; that the Earl of Gloucester died fighting bravely at the head of his tenants; that whilst the King himself escaped to Dunbar with about 500 knights, Miles Stapleton was amongst the slain. In the records of the cathedral at Durham is a memorandum that on December 23, 1314, the Lord Bishop granted eleven days' indulgence for the souls of Miles de Stapleton and Cecilia (Sibilla), formerly his wife. He seems to have died intestate. A note in the registry of Archbishop Greenfield at York, September 18, 1314, shows that the archbishop had taken possession of his goods, but afterwards delivered them to the heirs.

Sir Miles de Stapleton was succeeded by his eldest son, Nicholas, who was twenty-five years of age at his father's death. He seems to have inherited the Bruce estates and part of Stapleton as soon as he came of age, A.D. 1310, and did homage to the King December 27, 1311. He was affianced in marriage in 1304 to Isabella, daughter and one of the heirs of John de Brittayne, Earl of Richmond, and grand-daughter of the Duke of Brittany, by Beatrix, daughter of King Henry III. The Lady Isabella brought him increased estate in Fletham and Kirkby ; out of regard to his father's death at Bannockburn, Edward released Sir Nicholas from payment of arrears of scutage due on account of the same, November 1, 1314. His descent from the Bruces is set out in the Marshall's roll (Rot. Maresc., 8 Edw. II., m. 5 dors, Palgrave Writs).

After the flight from Bannockburn the King took up his residence in York and the neighbourhood, including a considerable space of time at Haddlesey, so that I will close this chapter by remarking that a Parliament was held in York February, 1315, 'that Sir Nicholas had letters of credence March 5 concerning the defence of the Scottish borders,' that the same year the three brothers, Dominus Nicholas, Gilbert, and John de Stapleton were summoned by Archbishop Greenfield to Doncaster among the knights of Yorkshire to discuss the same business.

7

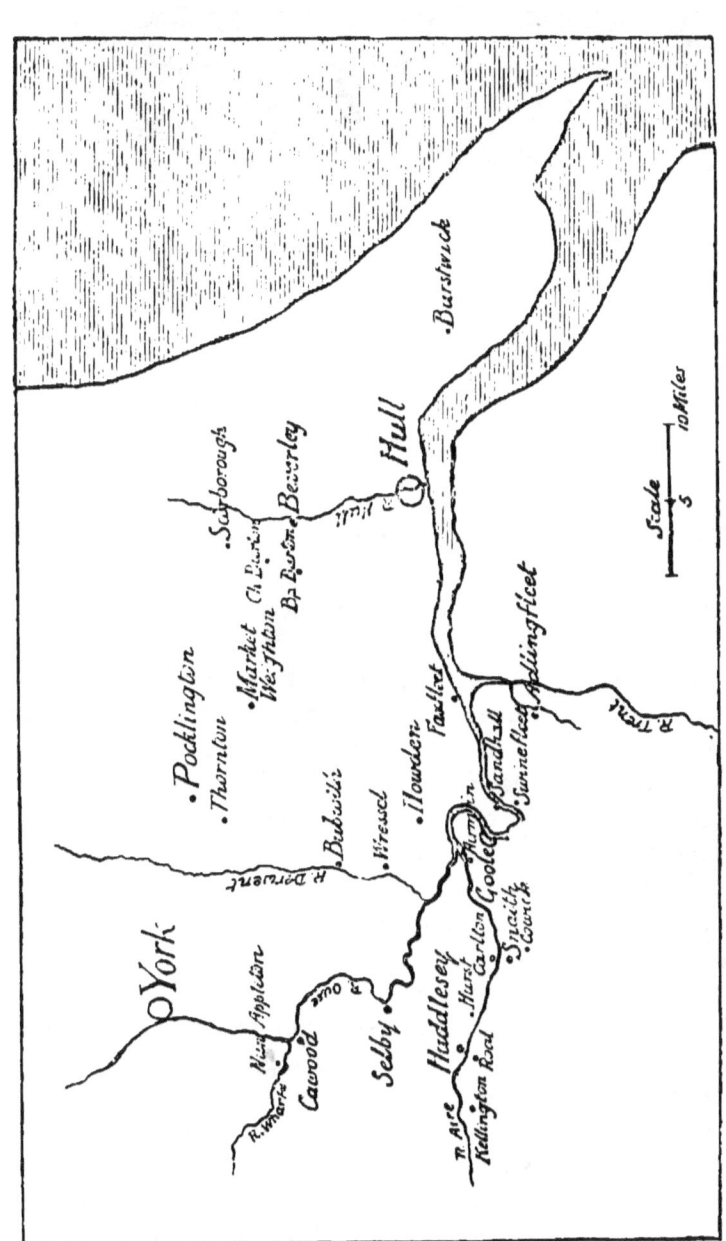

MAP TO ILLUSTRATE THE ITINERARY OF EDWARD II. AT HADDLESEY AND GENERAL TOPOGRAPHICAL REFERENCES IN THIS WORK.

CHAPTER VIII.

EDWARD II. AT HADDLESEY.

THE King's stay at Hathelsay was so prolonged in 1322, that, as owing to the kindness of Miss Holt I am able to give such interesting details of his manner of life and the events of the period, I feel I must devote a separate chapter to the record; for though weak and unfortunate as Edward of Carnarvon undoubtedly was, yet it does not happen to every country parish to have its reigning Sovereign resident in its borders for over three weeks. However, the first visit of Edward II. to Hathelsay seems to have been in 1313, during the lifetime of his old tutor and steward, the first Baron Stapleton, for in the Wardrobe Account, 16 Edw. II., 23/17, we read:

1313. Monday before St. John Baptist, *i.e.*, June 20, 2d. is given to a page who takes wine from Hathelseye to Athelingflete to our lord (the King). Friday, Nativ. S. John B. (24th), 2d. again to a lad from the Friars of Swynflete to my Lord *at Hathelseye*. On the way to Hathelseye, 4 bushels of oats 2s. 6d.

1322, June 8. Mandates of the King were dated from Hathelsay (Rot. Liberate, 15 Edw. II.), and December 17. (Rot. Fin., 16 *ib*.)

Wardrobe Roll, 16 Edw. II., 23, 17.

Thursday (June 16). Bread 7d., beer 6½d., flesh of beef and mutton 9d., 'potag' (probably soup) 1d., fuel 1d., 'erba pro equis' (probably hay for the horses) 7d., 2 bushels of oats 16d., one bushel 'senfur' 2d., mending a saddle 2d. wine 5d., parchment 1d.

Friday (17th). Bread 7d., 2 bushels of oats 16d., beer 6d., 'erba pro equis' 7d., 2 bushels 'fursur' 4d., passage of Ouse Water . . . . times 3d., fish 3d.

Saturday (18th). Passage of 'Bugwith water' (probably the Derwent at *Bubwith*) 2d., 'In falcacione libere' (possibly a day's mowing, or for mowing freely) ½d., expenses of grooms and horses at 'Dossele' (? Wressil) 4½d., dinner at Fexflete, *i.e.*, Faxfleet of to-day, 7d.

Sunday (19th). At Faxflete, shoeing horses 1d., passage of waters and carriage from York to *Brustwyk* £6. Burstwick was one of the manors granted to Miles Stapleton in 1308. It was in Holderness, near Hedon, and fell to the Crown by escheat.

Monday before St. John Bapt. (20th). Passage of the waters at Apelton and Ayremynne 3d., bread and 'herba' for the horses at Selby 6d., horses at Cowik 4¾d. Passage of the water at Karleton 2d. At Athelingflete, bread 12d., beer 14½d., given to pages bringing wine from *Hathelseye to Athelingflete* to my Lord (King) 2d., 6 chickens bought 8d., one hen 2d., 6½ bushels of oats 4¾d. (either of inferior quality to others at 4d. per bushel, or else the markets were falling), 3 lb. of almonds and ½ lb. of 'seminum' (? seminellum), 1 lb. 'dainz officii' and of sugar in plate (no prices).

Tuesday (21st). At Berton (? Burton), bread for grooms and horses 16d., cheese 2½d., 4 baskets 'in cordis' 9d., boy and 2 horses to Athingflete for two days 18d.

Wednesday (22nd). At Thornton.

Thursday (23rd). At Borton (*i.e.*, Burton), butter 1d., salt fish 5d., salmon 6d., eggs 1d. To Swynflete.

Friday, St. John Baptist's Day. To the groom of the friars of Swinflete *coming to my Lord (the King) to Hathelsaye* 2d., 'In prebenda usque Hathelsaye' 4 bushels of oats 2s. 6d.

Saturday (25th). At Selby to York, salt 1½d., litter 1s., carrying coffee from Selby to York by water, 12d., 'Cupis' 2d. (probably cipum, grease).

Sunday (26th). 3½ lagena vini 17½d. (the lagena was a large vessel, mostly of earthenware, with a neck and handle, containing generally one gallon), 3 birds ancis (geese) 16d., 4 chickens 6d., milk 2½d., flour 2d., 6 pigeons 4½d., apples 1d.

Monday (27th). Honey for the horses 1d.

Tuesday (28th). Herrings 6d., turbot 6d., one pickerell 18d., playces 6d., Pastry 'pascellas' and flannes (cheesecakes) 6d.

'Thursday (29th).'[1] Grease 2d., boat from Thorp (? Bishopsthorp) to York for 'erba,' 6 days, 12d.

Friday (30th). 2 lbs. almonds, 4d.

Saturday (July 1st). Eels, 6d.

Sunday (July 2nd). Goose, 5d.

Monday (3rd July). Drink 1d., ginger 'cinap' and vinegar for 9 days 8d., candles 2d. Scouynstedbrigge, Poklyngton, Wyghton (Weighton), and York.

Tuesday (4 July). At Beverley.

Monday (10th). Do. at York. Salt ½d.

Tuesday (11th). At Howden. Mutton 13d., saffron ½d. At Faxflete, supper for the grooms, 4d.

King Ed. II. dates mandates from *Hathelsaye*, once going thence to York in one day, A.D. 1322, May 20th; also June 8, 10, 16, 18, 20, and Dec. 17th; A.D. 1323, June 16, 18, 22. Close Rolls.

Dec. 13th, 1325, Ed. II. sends letters to the *Bailiff of Hathelsaye*. (Wardrobe Roll, 19 Edw. II., 25/1.—Q.R.)

[1] There is a puzzle here about the day of the week, which the author is unable to explain.

The preceding details of royal expenditure are interesting, as showing us the kind of food placed on the King's table five and a half centuries ago. Although some persons have accused Edward II. of indolence and pleasure-loving pursuits, he does not from these records appear to have given way to excessive eating or drinking. Another question may suggest itself, Why should the King have tarried in these parts for so long a time, as is above recorded? We have observed in previous chapters that after the Battle of Bannockburn Edward took up his residence in York and *neighbourhood*. The Scots, encouraged by their military successes, ravaged the Northern counties with pitiless barbarity. And Sir Nicholas Stapleton of Haddlesey received summonses from the King in 1316, and again thrice in 1317. In 1318 a Parliament was assembled at York, and every city and township in the kingdom was ordered to contribute men for the war, under penalty of forfeiture of life and limb (*sub foris factura vitæ et membrorum*). Sir Nicholas Stapleton was made Commissioner of Array, with Adam de Everingham of Birkin for the Wapentake of Barkston Ash. Nearly 5,000 foot-soldiers were soon under arms in York; but as the summons was only for forty days, they dispersed without accomplishing any result. The King spent his Christmas at Beverley, and again the army was called out. In the spring of 1319 Stapleton was ordered to join his father-in-law, the Earl of Richmond, 'with horse and arms.' In June of the same year Stapleton is again Commissioner of Array for the West Riding of York, with seven others, 'to raise and train 4,000 foot-soldiers for service ag'st the Scots.' These men joined the King at Berwick to invest this town. To hinder the success of the English in reducing the place, Bruce made a sudden diversion by breaking into Yorkshire with the fury of a whirlwind, causing terror and devastation everywhere. Had it not been for a fortunate providence, the

Queen of Edward II. would have fallen into their hands. She was staying at Cawood Castle, and a body of 10,000 Scots under Douglas marched with great secrecy near to the village. One of his soldiers, however, fell into the hands of the Archbishop of York and the King's Councillor, who, after being threatened with torture, promised, if they would spare him, to show the great danger that Queen Isabella and her children were in. They pretended to scorn his information, but were induced, on the man's staking his life on the truth of his statements, to send out spies in the direction he mentioned as to the nearness of the Scots. Alarmed by the results they collected, all their retinue and the men at arms that York could supply brought the Queen to York, afterwards sending her to Nottingham for greater safety.[1]

In addition to other troubles, famine and pestilence added their horrors to the situation. The famine was so terrible that it is said that thieves in prison devoured each other. One wise thing the Parliament of London did in 1316—viz., forbid the use of corn for brewing purposes.

But we return to the siege of Berwick, which place had been surrendered by the treachery of Peter Spalding, the Governor. It seems that the King, notwithstanding the formidable preparations he had made with movable towers filled with men, catapults, grappling-hooks, and piles of faggots, was so alarmed by the news of Bruce's ravages in Yorkshire that he hastened back, only to find the army of ecclesiastics led by Archbishop Melton of York utterly routed at Myton Bridge.

After this a temporary truce was arranged between the two Kings of England and Scotland. But the favouritism of Edward for the two Despensers—father and son, the eldest being created Earl of Winchester, and the son Lord Chamberlain—brought on fresh troubles. William

[1] Wheater's 'Cawood.'

de Braose, Lord of Gower, had settled his estate in Wales on his son-in-law, John, Lord Mowbray, with remainder to De Bohun, Earl of Hereford. Mowbray accordingly claimed it at Gower's death, but was immediately deprived of it by the King, to confer it on young Despenser. Thomas, Earl of Lancaster, who was greatly incensed against the Despensers, called together all who shared in his dislike of the favourites, and took up arms to procure their expulsion from the kingdom. Indeed, it is said he deserted the King at the siege of Berwick, and induced others to withdraw their troops when the castle was being surrendered, merely on hearing an authorized report that Lord Hugh Despenser was to be made its Governor. Among those whom Lancaster called out were his liege-men in Yorkshire, to meet him at Sherburn. It seems as if Stapleton yielded to this call because of the claims of Lancaster for his Haddlesey manors and to Mowbray for Rydale, and so we understand how he came under the King's displeasure. Lancaster's revolt was most disastrous for himself. He first of all seized Burton-on-Trent (perhaps, more correctly, Tutbury Castle), but his forces fled even before they were attacked. The Duke goes to Pontefract, thence towards Scotland by Castleford and Wetherby, looking for help from Bruce, with whom he had formed a treasonable alliance; but he met with a complete and ruinous repulse at Boroughbridge, March 16, 1321, chiefly by means of Sir Andrew Harcla, Governor of Carlisle, and Sir Simon Ward, Governor of York. The Earl of Hereford, Bohun, whose claim had to do with the quarrel, was killed by a Welshman, who thrust a spear through a crevice in the planks of a narrow foot-bridge over which he was crossing, having dismounted. Lancaster himself was taken prisoner, and conveyed to Pontefract, where he was tried by his peers in the presence of the King himself, March 20, and beheaded with five or six other barons, who were hanged and

quartered at Pontefract. Lords Clifford, Mowbray and
Dayville were hanged in chains at York. Many others
fell into the King's power, and were put to death. Eighty-
six were imprisoned; *only five* were liberated. On July 11,
138 persons submitted to a fine to save their lands and
lives. Sir Nichol de Stapelton,[1] Bacheler (*i.e.*, bas-
chevalier), was fined 2,000 marks, and ordered to send
two casks of wine every year to the King's exchequer,
John de Stapelton, his brother, John de *Crumbwell*,
George Salvayn, and Robert de Colvill, all of Yorkshire,
John D'Arcy, nephew of his father's friend, the Earl of
Lincoln, and John de Camton, of Northumberland, being
sureties for his future good behaviour. His manors of
Kirkely, Helham, Stapelton, Dighton, Crethorn, and
Wath were committed to the custody of Walter de Kil-
vington as security for the payment of the fine.'[2] In
these transactions we understand partly why Edward
spent so much of his time at Haddlesey and the neighbourhood in the summer of 1322, and we shall now understand more fully the following records:

'West Hathelsay.—Extent of this manor on the same
roll (as that containing the manor of Sterndale, FOR-
FEITED by Roger Dawnay; see Chapter V., p. 63);
FORFEITED by Sir Nicholas de Stapleton. *There was a
ferry across the Ayre here*, which, with the cottage attached
to it, was worth 8s. per ann. A right of fishing in the
same river also belonged to this manor, and was worth
3s. per annum.'

A.D. 1322. The Ayre is recorded to have overflowed
in the autumn of this year, so that the meadow-land

---

[1] Lincoln's Inn MSS., p. 35, has the following note: 'Inquisition respecting the breaking of the "purgation" of Nicholas de Stapliton at West Haddlesey in Yorkshire.'

[2] Speed and Stapletons of Richmondshire (*Yorkshire A. and T. Journal*, vol. viii.).

could not be cut. Thus we learn that inundations are unpleasantly characteristic of this stream.

1322. East Hathelsay was also held by Sir Nicholas de Stapleton of the Manor of Pontefract, value £12 3s. 11½d.

Temple Hirst, which belonged to Robert de Holland, was sublet to Robert de Lathun for £20 per annum. *But on September 29 of this year the King for certain reasons took the manor into his own hands, together with the wheat and the hay in the Grange.* Was it arranging these various matters that Edward found it desirable to make the prolonged visit to Haddlesey of which we have been writing? The relative value and importance of townships in our parish as compared with neighbouring localities at this time may be inferred from the accounts of Richard de Moseley, parson of the church of Friston, who was the King's receiver of the revenues of the Honour of Pomfret, and the lands which lately belonged to Thomas, Duke of Lancaster, and to the other rebels who took up arms to compel the King to dismiss the Spensers from his undue affection. The list includes the following with other places, viz.: Birkin, £3 9s. 3d.; Byrom, £1 7s. 8d.; Est Hathelsey, £2 2s. 1¾d.; West Hathelsey, £6 0s. 2d.; Temple Hirst, £10[1]; Knottingley, £13 15s. 6½d.; so that the territory included in the present parish of Haddlesey represented a higher valuation than that of the neighbouring districts. It is of interest also to note that during the many visits paid by Edward II. to Yorkshire, we have records of many visits paid to Haddlesey, and Cowick and Sandhall, but only one to Selby.

We think we cannot better conclude this portion of our narrative than by quoting a very interesting contribution of Mr. Wheater's to the *Weekly Yorkshire Post* respecting Sandhall and its connection with Edward II.:

[1] It is worthy of note, however, that Temple Hirst was valued at £14 7s. 7½d. ten years before. See p. 61.

'SANDHALL—A FORGOTTEN MANSION.

'On the banks of the Ouse and opposite Goole stands the ancient residence Sandhall, now forgotten and in obscurity. And yet the place is historic. In 1316 the King granted to Roger de Damory[1] in fee the manor of Sandhall by the service due. Roger, one of the disgraceful parasites of that age, married Elizabeth, third sister and heir of Gilbert de Clare, late Earl of Gloucester; Hugh le Dispenser, jun., having married Alianor, the eldest sister, and Hugh de Audeley, jun., Margaret, the second. Damory took possession, and two years later, in 1318, the King granted to Roger and Elizabeth " Nepti Regis " in general tail the manor of Sandhall, co. Ebor, Halghton, co. Oxon, and Faukeshall, co. Surr., by the service due. The hall had previously belonged to the ancient family of Salvayne of Duffield, of whom Sir Gerald had been a prominent soldier in Scotland. The history of the reign explains the termination of the Damory holding, and in a few years Sandhall is in the possession of the Lady Agnes de Vesci. When Edward Baliol was fetched from France in 1332 to stir up revolt in Scotland, he was brought to Sandhall as the guest of Lady Agnes, and there was planned the expedition which resulted in the overthrow of Scotland at Dupplin and Baliol's temporary restoration to the throne. The adventure was one of the romances of history. With the assistance of Lords Wake, Talbot, Vesci, and Beaumont, Sir Gilbert Umfraville claiming the earldom of Angus, Lord Percy claiming that of Galloway, David Strathbolgi that of Athol, Sir Geoffrey Mowbray, and others, "he gathered together 25,000 well-appointed men," and sailed from the now lost port of Ravenser, and landed at King-

---

[1] See this name among those punished for their share in Lancaster's rebellion, Chapter V., p. 63, but afterwards pardoned by the King, so that he died a natural death.

horn in Fife. A series of four actions were quickly fought, in which the Scots were so disastrously defeated that in a few weeks Baliol was crowned. In a few months he was again a fugitive, receiving a pension from the English Government, and resident at Hatfield Hall, near Doncaster, where he ended his life, and with it the historic line of the Baliols. Sandhall had shortly afterwards become a royal manor, and a residence which the King used with some dignity. In 1339 the King's butler is ordered to deliver " at the manor of Sandhalle " two tuns of wine " for the private use of our lord the King." Other places in the neighbourhood were similarly supplied, as " the manoirs of Hathelseye and Cowyk," the supply to one or other extending over some years. And so we have a pleasant glimpse of Edward's doings on the banks of the Ouse and in the region of Snaith Marsh. It is little to be suspected now, when the steamer hurries the impatient traveller past the bowery surroundings of the old house, that the kings and princes of England were wont to resort thither for their sports and rural ease.

'" On Thorne's brown moor, on marshland wild, by banks of reedy Don,
When Longshanks warred on Scottish ground, where Crecy's field was won,
The royal bugle called the spot, the royal hunter strove
By marshy mere, on pasture green, or in the sylvan Grove.
From Falkirk's rout, from Poictiers, and Agincourt's red plain
The princely hunters hither came, their royal sport to gain ;
Good Margaret fared at Brotherton, Philippa Hatfield sought,
And there, to swell our roll of fame, their matron's burden brought,
When joyful hearts, with loyal glee, from Cowick raised the call
That spread from Hathelsea's bright stream to echo from Sandhall."'

And inasmuch as the Despensers and their connections are so closely associated with the fortunes of Edward and of others mentioned in these pages, I add their pedigree, as kindly supplied by Miss Holt, who compiled it for use in her own valuable work, 'In all Time of our Tribulation' (Shaw and Co.).

II. THE DESPENSERS.

Hugh le Despenser, *the Elder*, son of Hugh le Despenser, Justiciary of England, and Alina Basset, and so related to the Stapletons : *born* Mar. 1-8, 1261 (*Inq. Post Mort. Alinæ La Dispensere*, 9 Edw. I., 9); sponsor of Edward III., 1312; created Earl of Winchester, 1322; *beheaded* at Bristol, Oct. 27 (Harl. MS. 6124), 1326. [This is not improbably the true date ; that of Froissart, Oct. 8, is certainly a mistake, as the Queen had only reached Wallingford, on her way to Bristol, by the 15th.] As his body was cast to the dogs, he had *no burial*. *Married*

    Isabel, dr. of William de Beauchamp, Earl of Warwick, and Maud Fitz John ; *widow* of Patrick de Chaworth (see Fitzwilliam pedigree), by whom she was mother of Maud, wife of Henry, Duke of Lancaster : *married* 1281-2 (fine 2,000 marks); *died* before July 22, 1306.

Issue :—1. Hugh, *the Younger*, *born* probably about 1283 ; created Earl of Gloucester in right of wife; *hanged* and afterwards beheaded (but after death) at Hereford, Nov. 24, 1326; quarters of body sent to Dover, Bristol, York and Newcastle, and head set on London Bridge ; finally *buried* in Tewkesbury Abbey. The Abbot and Chapter had granted to Hugh and Alianora, Mar. 24, 1325, in consideration of benefits received, that four masses per annum should be said for them during life, at the four chief feasts, and 300 per annum for either or both after death for ever ; on the anniversary of Hugh, the Abbot bound himself to feed the poor with bread, beer, pottage, and one mess from the kitchen, for ever (*Rot. Pat.*, 20 Edw. II.). Hugh the Younger *married*

    Alianora, eldest daughter of Gilbert de Clare, The Red, Earl of Gloucester, and the Princess Joan of

Acre (daughter of Edward I.), *born* at Caerphilly Castle, Nov., 1292; *married* May 20, 1306, with a dowry of £2,000 from the Crown, in part payment of which the custody of Philip Paynel, or Paganel, the founder of Drax Abbey, was granted to Hugh the Elder, June 3, 1304 (*Rot. Claus.*, 1 Edw. II.). Her youngest child was born at Northampton, in December, 1326, and she sent William de Culpho with the news to the King, who gave him a silver-gilt cup in reward (Wardrobe Accounts, 25/1 and 31/19). On the 19th of April, 1326, and for 49 days afterwards, she was in charge of Prince John of Eltham, who was ill at Kenilworth in April. She left that place on May 22, arriving at Shene in four days, and in June she was at Rochester and Ledes Castle, Kent, the seat of Lord Bradlesmere. Three interesting Wardrobe Accounts are extant, showing her expenses at this time (31,17 to 31/19); but the last is almost illegible. 'Divers decoctions and recipes' made up at Northampton for the young Prince came to 6s. 9d. 'Litter for my Lady's bed' (to put under the feather bed in the box-like bedstead) cost 6d. Either her ladyship or her royal charge must have entertained a strong predilection for 'shrimpis,' judging from the frequency with which that entry occurs. Four quarters of wheat, we are told, made 1,200 loaves. There is evidence of a good deal of company, the principal guests beside Priors and Canons being the Lady of Montzone, the Lady of Hastings (Julian, mother of Lawrence, Earl of Pembroke), Eneas de Bohun (son of Princess Elizabeth), Sir John Neville (one of the captors of Mortimer), and John de Bentley (probably the ex-gaoler of Elizabeth, Queen of Scotland. Sundry young people seem to have been also in Lady La

Despenser's care, as companions to the Prince:—
Earl Lawrence of Pembroke; Margery de Verdon,
step-daughter of Alianora's sister Elizabeth; and
Joan Jeremy, or Jermyn, sister of Alice, wife of
Prince Thomas de Brotherton, i.e. Thomas, Duke
of Lancaster, hanged at Pomfret. The provision
for April 30, the vigil of St. Philip, and therefore a
fast-day, is as follows (a few words are illegible):
Pantry :—60 loaves of the King's bread, at 5 and 4
to the penny, 13½d. *Butlery :*—One pitcher of wine
from the King's stores at Kenilworth; 22 gallons
of beer, at 1½d. per gallon, 2s. 6d. *Wardrobe :*—
... lights, a farthing; a halfpennyworth of candles
of cotton ... *Kitchen :*—50 herrings, 2½d.; 3 cod-
fish, 9¾d.; 4 stockfish ... salmon, 12d.; 3 tench,
9d.; 1 pickerel, 12 roach and perch, ½ gallon of
loaches, 13½d.; one large eel ... 1½ qrs. pimpernel,
7½d.; one piece of sturgeon, 6d. *Poultry :*—100
eggs, 5d.; cheese and butter, 3¾d.; ... milk, 1¼d.;
drink, 1d. *Saltry :*—½ qr. mustard, a halfpenny;
½ qr. vinegar, ¾d.; ... parsley, a farthing. For
May 1st, St. Philip's and a feast-day: *Pantry :*—
100 loaves, 22½d. *Butlery :*—one sextarius, 3½
pitchers of wine from the King's stores at Kenilworth; 27 gallons of beer, 2s. 8½d., being 17 at 1d.,
and 12 at 1½d. One quarter of hanaps, 12d.
Wardrobe :—3 lbs. wax, 15d.; lights, ½d.; ½ lb.
candles of Paris, 1d. *Kitchen :*—12 messes of
powdered beef, 18d.; 3 messes of fresh beef, 9d.;
one piece of bacon, 12d.; half a mutton, powdered,
9d.; one quarter of fresh mutton, 3d.; one pestle
of pork, 3½d.; half a veal, 14d. *Poultry :*—One
purcel, 4½d.; 2 hens, 15d.; one bird (*oisoux*), 12d.;
15 ponce, 7½d.; 8 pigeons, 9½d.; 100 eggs, 5d.; 3
gallons milk, 3½d. ... *Saltry :*—¼ quarter of mustard, ½d.; ... ½ qr. verjuice, 1½d.; garlic, a farthing;

parsley, ½d. Wages of Richard Attegrove (keeper of the horses) and the laundress, 4d.; of 18 grooms and two pages, 2s. 5d. (Ward. Acct., 19 Edw. II., 31/17). When King Edward left London for the West, on Oct. 2nd, he committed to Lady La Despenser the custody of his son and of the Tower. On the 16th the citizens captured the Tower, brought out the Prince and the Chatelaine, and conveyed them to the Wardrobe. On Nov. 17th she was brought a prisoner to the Tower, with her children and her damsel Joan (Issue Roll, *Michs.*, 20 Edw. II.; Close Roll, 20 Edw. II.), their expenses being calculated at the rate of 10s., per day. Alianora and her children were delivered from the Tower, with all her goods and chattels, on Feb. 25, 1328, and on the 26th of November following her 'rights and rents, according to her right and heritage,' were ordered to be restored to her (*Rot. Claus.*, 2 Edw. III.). She was not, however, granted full liberty, or else she forfeited it again very quickly; for on Feb. 5, 1329, William Lord Zouche of Haringworth was summoned to Court, and commanded to 'bring with him quickly our cousin Alianora, who is in his company,' with a hint that unpleasant consequences would follow neglect of the order (*Rot. Pat.*, 3 Edw. III., Part 1). A further entry on Dec. 30 tells us that Alianora, wife of William La Zouche of Mortimer (so that her marriage with her gaoler's cousin had occurred in the interim), had been impeached by the Crown concerning certain jewels, florins, and other goods of the King, to a large amount, which had been '*esloignez*' from the Tower of London: doubtless by the citizens when they seized the fortress, and the impeachment was, of course, like many other things, an outcome of Queen Isabelle's private spite. 'The said William and Alianora, for pardon of all hindrances, actions, quarrels, and demands, until the present date, have granted, of their will and without coercion, for themselves and the heirs of the said Alianora, all castles, manors, towns, honours, and other lands and tenements, being of her heritage, in the county of Glamorgan and Morgannon, in Wales, the manor of Hanley, the town of Worcester, and the manor of Tewkesbury for ever to the King.' The King, on his part, undertook to restore the lands in the hour that the original owners should pay him £10,000 in one day. The real nature of this non-coercive and voluntary agreement was shown in November, 1330, when (one month after the arrest of Mortimer), at the petition of Parliament itself, one-half of this £10,000 was remitted. Alianora *died* June 30, 1337, and was *buried* in Tewkesbury Abbey.

2. Philip, *died* before Apr. 22, 1214. *Married* Margaret, daughter of Ralph de Goushill; *born* July 25, 1296; *married* before 1313; *died* July 29, 1349. (She *married*, secondly, John de Ros.)

3. Isabel, *married* (1) John Lord Hastings, (2) about 1319, Ralph de Monthermer; *died* Dec. 4 or 5, 1335. Left issue by first marriage. The daughters of Edward II. were brought up in her care.

4. Aveline, *married* before 1329, Edward Lord Burnel: *died* in May or June, 1363. No issue.

5. Elizabeth, *married* before 1321 Ralph Lord Camoys: living 1370. Left issue.

6. Joan, *married* Almaric Lord St. Amand. [Doubtful if of this family.]

7. Joan, *nun* at Sempringham before 1337; *dead* Feb. 15, 1351.

8. Alianora, *nun* at Sempringham before 1337: living 1351.

Issue of Hugh the younger and Alianora: 1. Hugh, *born* 1308. He held Caerphilly Castle (which belonged to his mother) against Queen Isabelle: on Jan. 4 of that year life was granted to all in the castle except himself, probably as a bribe for surrender, which was extended to himself on Mar. 20; but Hugh held out till Easter (Apr. 12), when the castle was taken. He remained a prisoner in the custody of his father's great enemy, Roger Earl of March, till Dec. 5, 1328, when March was ordered to deliver him to Thomas de Gournay, one of the murderers of King Edward, and Constable of Bristol Castle, where he was to be kept till further order (*Rot. Claus.,* 1 and 2 Edw. III.; *Rot. Pat.,* 1 Edw. III.). On July 5, 1331, he was ordered to be set at liberty within 15 days after Michaelmas, Ebulo L'Estrange, Ralph Basset,[1] John le Ros, Richard Talbot, and others being sureties for him (*Rot. Claus.,* 5 Edw. III.). In 1338 he was dwelling in Scotland in the King's service (*Ib.,* 12 Edw. III.), and in 1342 in Gascony, with a suite of one banneret, 14 knights, 44 scutifers, 60 archers, and 60 men-at-arms (*Ib.,* 16 *ib.*). He *died* s.p. Feb. 8, 1349; *buried* at Tewkesbury. *Married*
>Elizabeth, dr. of William de Montacute, first Earl of Salisbury, and Katherine de Grandison (*widow* of Giles Lord Badlesmere, who was put to death at Canterbury in 1321 as an adherent of Lancaster, *remarried* Guy de Bryan); *married* 1338-44; *died* at Astley, June 20, 1359; *buried* at Tewkesbury.

2. Edward, *died* 1341. *Married* (and left issue)
>Anne, dr. of Henry Lord Ferrers of Groby, and Margaret Segrave (*remarried* Thomas Ferrers); living Oct. 14, 1366.

3. Gilbert, *died* Apr. 22, 1382. *Married*, and left issue: but his wife's name and family are unknown.

---

[1] This Ralph Basset was the last peer of his race. He died in 1390, unmarried.

4. Joan, *nun* at Shaftesbury, in or before 1343; *died* Apr. 26, 1384.

5. Elizabeth, *married* 1338 Maurice Lord Berkeley; *died* Aug. 14, 1389; left issue. [Doubtful if of this family.]

6. Isabel, *married* at Havering, Feb. 9, 1321, Richard Earl of Arundel; *divorced* 1345; *buried* in Westminster Abbey. No issue.

7. Alianora, contracted July 27, 1325, to Lawrence de Hastings, Earl of Pembroke; contract broken by Queen Isabelle, who on Jan. 1st, 1327, sent a mandate to the Prioress of Sempringham, commanding her to receive the child and 'veil her immediately, that she may dwell there perpetually as a regular nun' (*Rot. Claus.*, 1 Edw. III.). Since it was not usual for a nun to receive the black veil before her sixteenth year, this was a complete irregularity. Nothing further is known of her.

8. Margaret, consigned by Edward II. to the care of Thomas de Houk, with her nurse and a large household; she remained in his charge 'for three years and more,' according to his petition presented to the King, May 1st, 1327 (*Rot. Claus.*, 1 Edw. III.). On the previous 1st of January the Queen had sent to the Prioress of Watton a similar mandate to that mentioned above, requiring that Margaret should at once be professed a regular nun. No further record remains of her.

CHAPTER IX.

TEMPLE HIRST UNDER THE DARCYS.

NOTWITHSTANDING that Henry VIII. reproached the Darcys as 'but mean, scarce well-born gentlemen, and yet of no great lands till they were promoted by us,' they seem to have been among the followers of William the Norman, and from his time to have taken a more or less prominent part in public affairs. The one with whom our story begins, as the possessor of the manors of Temple Hirst and Temple Newsam by grant from Edward III. in 1338, is Sir John Darcy, nephew of the great Earl of Lincoln, and an old friend of Sir Nicholas Stapleton. The following extract from Yorkshire deeds in the Record Office will come in here appropriately: 'C. 805. Grant by John de Arcy, knight, lord of Notton, to Peter del Hill, of Notton, of lands, etc., which the grantor had by the feoffment of Richard, son of John de la Wodehall, of Cotheworth, within the boundaries of the same place, for life; with remainders to his son Ralph and the heirs of his body, and others.' [Thirteenth century.]

This Lord Darcy held high office in the household of Edward III., first as Lord Steward, and afterwards as Chamberlain. It was probably in this capacity he was

1. Rosamond, d. of Sir Peter Fretchvile.=John, Lord Darcy and Meinel, *obt.* July, 1635.=2. Isabel, d. of Sir Chr. Wray, Lord Chief Justice; wid. 1st of Godfrey Foljambe, Esq., of Walton, and afterwards of Sir Wm. Bowes. She was called 'The good Lady Darcy.'=3. Mary, d. of Thos., Lord Falconberg.=4. Eliz., d. of Wm. West, Esq.

Anne=Hen. Savile, Esq.

Marg., not mar.

John. Rosamond. Eliz. All died young.

Conyers, Lord Darcy and Conyers, created Earl of Holderness 1682; *obt.* 1688.=Grace, d. and h. of Thomas Rokeby of Skiers, Esq.

Sir William.

Henry. Thomas. Marm. James.

Barbara=Matt. Hutton, Esq.
Ursula=Jo. Stillington, Esq.
Marg.=Sir Thos. Harrison.
Doro.=John Dalton, Esq.

Ann=Thos. Metcalf, Esq.
Grace=1. George Best, Esq.
2. Fran. Molineux, Esq
Mary=Acton Burnet, Esq.

1. Cath., d. of Francis, Earl of Westmorland, *s.p.*=Conyers, Lord Darcy, Earl of Holderness; *obt.* 1692.=2. Frances, d. of Thos., Earl of Berkshire.=3. Frances, d. of William, Duke of Somerset, wid. of Thomas, Earl of Southampton, Lord Treasurer.

Ursula=Sir Christ. Wyvil, Bart.

Eliza.=Sir Henry Stapleton, Bart.=Grace=Sir John Legard.

Marg.=Hen. s. and h. to Sir George Marwood, Bart.

Anne.

John, Lord Darcy, s. and h., died before his father.=Bridget, d. of Robert, Lord Lexington.

Philip.

Charles.

Robert, Earl of Holderness, *obt.* 1722.= . . . .

Conyers, Guidon of the Guards.

Eliz., mar. in May, 1708.=Sir Ralph Milbank, Bart.

Charlotte.

Robert, Earl of Holderness, *obt.* 1778.= . . . .

1. Sir Cavendish Butler Wentworth, Bart.=Bridget, *s.p.*=2. Mr. Murray.

1. Robt., Duke of Leeds, father of the present Duke.=Lady Amelia Darcy, sole heiress.=2. John Byron, Esq., father of the present Lord Byron.

The continuation is found in Burke's 'Extinct Peerage.'

[*To face Chap. IX.*

CHAPTER IX.

TEMPLE HIRST UNDER THE DARCYS.

NOTWITHSTANDING that Henry VIII. reproached the Darcys as 'but mean, scarce well-born gentlemen, and yet of no great lands till they were promoted by us,' they seem to have been among the followers of William the Norman, and from his time to have taken a more or less prominent part in public affairs. The one with whom our story begins, as the possessor of the manors of Temple Hirst and Temple Newsam by grant from Edward III. in 1338, is Sir John Darcy, nephew of the great Earl of Lincoln, and an old friend of Sir Nicholas Stapleton. The following extract from Yorkshire deeds in the Record Office will come in here appropriately: 'C. 805. Grant by John de Arcy, knight, lord of Notton, to Peter del Hill, of Notton, of lands, etc., which the grantor had by the feoffment of Richard, son of John de la Wodehall, of Cotheworth, within the boundaries of the same place, for life; with remainders to his son Ralph and the heirs of his body, and others.' [Thirteenth century.]

This Lord Darcy held high office in the household of Edward III., first as Lord Steward, and afterwards as Chamberlain. It was probably in this capacity he was

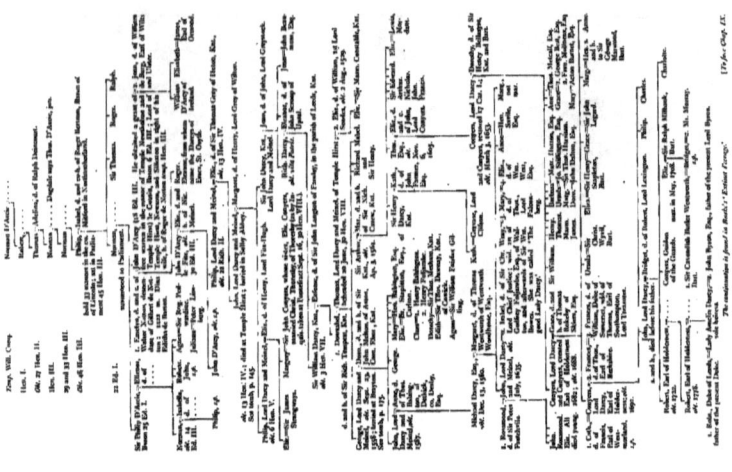

appointed to superintend the funeral of the King's ill-treated father. The received narrative of the burial of Edward II. by the Abbot and monks of Gloucester does not harmonize with the Wardrobe Accounts. From them it appears the young King sent the Bishop of Llandaff, three knights, and a priest, with four lesser officials, ' to dwell at Gloucester with the corpse of the said King, his father,' which was taken from Berkeley Castle to Gloucester Abbey on October 21st. Among many other items of expenditure indicating considerable funereal pomp stands an entry : ' Wages of *John Darcy*, appointed to superintend the funeral, from Nov. 22 to Dec. 21 (1327), £19 6s. 8d.' (Ward. Acct., 1 Edw. III., 33/2). Lord John Darcy was ordered in 1333 by Edward III. to attack the Scotch at Hallidon Hill in flank with a body of light armed foot from Ireland. In 1335 the Lord Justice Darcy brought a body of forces from Ireland in thirty-six vessels, with which he ravaged the isles of Bute and Arran. (*Lord Beaumont* also took part in these expeditions—Smollett's Hist., vol. iii., p. 340.) He was in Flanders raising a loan for the King's wants, 1339, and the next year at the siege of Tournay. In 1342 he was sent into Brittany with the Earl of Northampton to aid the brave Countess of Montfort in her defence of Hennebon,[1] while her husband was a prisoner in the Louvre. By the help of Edward III. and of the brave wife, Jane of Flanders, the expedition was successful, and John of Montfort became fourth Duke of Brittany.

Darcy was again in France in 1345, and Miles (Stapleton) and his cousin were in his service. After taking several towns from the French, and defeating them near

---

[1] Hennebon is a small port near the Blavet's mouth, up which the English fleet sailed to support the Countess of Montfort when she was besieged in her castle. A few small vessels still trade from it, and near are mineral springs. It has a Gothic church of the fourteenth century, with ruins of an abbey.

Morlaix, a considerable port on the English Channel, they returned to England, but only for Darcy to join Northampton in the great expedition, which landed at La Hogue in the spring of 1346, and overran Barfleur, Valognes, St. Lo, Caen, Lisieux, Honfleur. Wherever they went, remarks P. P. N. Thomas, they pillaged and plundered, and at length reached Picardy, winning what he calls 'la funeste battaille de Crecy.' 'Shiploads of clothes, jewels, and gold and silver plate' were sent to England.

Englishmen naturally take a different view, and admire the courage and skill of their young King Edward III., who divided his forces into two divisions. The one under Arundel and Northampton included Darcy and his friends. From Crecy the victors laid siege to Calais. In this siege Darcy had in his retinue 12 knights, 68 squires, and 80 archers, Sir Miles Stapleton contributing 8 squires and 8 archers. Darcy was sent by the King soon after the commencement of the siege to meet the Parliament, September, A.D. 1347, with a message from him, and, as Constable of the Tower, went down to the North to take charge of David King of Scotland and other prisoners captured at the battle of Neville's Cross (October 17). He died soon after (May 30, 21 of Edward III., 1348), leaving John Lord Darcy his son and heir, then thirty years of age. His mother was Emmeline, daughter and heir of Walter Notton, or Nocton. This nobleman does not appear in connection with Temple Hirst; indeed, his life was short, and he died at Notton, or Nocton, Saturday next after the feast of St. Chad (March 2, 30 of Edward III., 1357). He married Elizabeth, daughter and heir of Nicholas Meinill, from whom it is said the Darcys of Essex descend. This Lord Darcy left a son, John, aged five, at his father's death, and died six years afterwards seised of Notton, or Nocton, Woolley, Silkstone, etc., as given in our pedigree.

Some records of work done at Temple Hirst about this time—*i.e.*, 1327—deserve a space here—viz., that carpenters received 2d. a day for work, and slaters 4d. Later on, also—A.D. 1522—there appear some curious entries relative to payments for labour at Temple Hirst—*e.g.*, 'iij heggers that made the hedge about the pounde at Hirst ij of them for iij daies, the iij man iiij daies at iiij part of the day iijs. ivd.

'For mending the slayht house wall, and the oxen stall iiijd. . . . For hegging the cow pastures and oxcloses 4d. a day. "Old Stokkall of Hirst" was paid 4d. a day for leading thorns to the cow pastures for hedging. Three loads of hay for the fat oxen cost 10s., and another load bought of Robert Pulley 4s. For stubbing of thorns the payment was 4d. a day. A man was also paid 1s. 4d. for carrying thorns *by boat* to Poterlay, being employed for four days in this work. For mowing the payment was 6d. per day, and sometimes 8d. Stokkall also received 8d. per day for leading thorns and wood out of the holmes that was stubbed. Haymakers received 2d. per day. The total quantity of hay made in 1522 was 141 loads from Temple Hirst; viz., from the corn close and Hollins 60 loads, and from the *Park* 81, to which must be added 8 loads from Poterlay.'

There is also an account of fish taken from March 2, 1517, to the feast of St. Martin in the same year by Will Wail, keeper of Lord Darcy's—viz., of the greatest sorte xxxiij pikes, middle do. 1, best do. lxvij.

CHAPTER X.

SECOND BARON MILES STAPLETON.

WE must now leave Temple Hirst and the Darcys for a space to resume our narrative as regards other parts of the parish, and to inquire after Sir Miles, who returned from France to England in 1347[1] to claim his estates at Hathelsay, Carlton, Stapleton, Kirkby, Fletham, etc., assigned to him in 1343 when aged twenty-four. He married Isabel, daughter of Sir Henry Vavasour, of Hazlewood, A.D. 1348, and two children were born in 1349 and 1350. His cousin, Miles Stapleton of Bedale, was one of the founders (*primus fundator* he is called on his Garter plate in St. George's Chapel, Windsor) of the most distinguished order of chivalry ever known, not only in England, but in Europe, instituted by Edward I. after his series of military successes in France, stimulated, it may be, by the enormous wealth which enriched England at this time, and the consequent passion for pageantry and pleasure which showed itself throughout the land. The exact date for the founding of the order seems open to dispute. M. H. Gourdon de Genouillac, in his 'Dictionnaire Historique

---

[1] In this year John de Hathelsay, of Selby, is dismissed from an essart called Senesfield, in Thorp Bylghby, at Martinmas (Selby Coucher Book, vol. ii.).

des Ordres de Chevalière,' mentions January 19, 1350, as the period, and assigns as its occasion Edward's victory at Crecy, rather than the more usual and romantic story of the incident at Lady Salisbury's ball. It seems, however, that magnificent jousts were held at Bury St. Edmunds, Eltham, and Windsor. In the King's accounts for 1347 orders for twelve garters of blue embroidered with gold and silk, and the motto 'Honi soit qui mal y pense,' are found to be used at the great tournament at Eltham. Nine of the knights who took part in these are numbered later on with the founders of the order—viz., the Prince of Wales, the Earl of Lancaster, Earl of Warwick, Sir John L'Isle, Sir John Gray, Hugh Courtenay, Sir MILES STAPLETON, Sir John Beauchamp, and Sir John Chandos. On April 9, 1348, materials are again ordered for dresses for the jousts at Lichfield—viz., for the King, and other lords, ladies, and demoiselles, and for eleven knights of the King's Chamber, *Sir Miles* being one of them. The same month he received a present of a war-horse from the Black Prince. These tournaments seem to have been both a military exercise and a social function. As a rule, the knights were divided into two sides, twelve on 'the King's side' and twelve on 'the Prince's side,' and had their stalls assigned in St. George's Chapel, Windsor. Milo de Stapulton occupied the ninth stall on the King's side, being seventeenth on the list. He bore for his arms 'a lion rampant surcharged on the breast, with a mullet gu., denoting the third House.'

All these particulars show how great a personage was this nobleman, whose history is so closely connected with the leading family in our parish, and whose fame ought to stir the hearts of Haddlesians to-day to raise the reputation of a place which once numbered among its residents the friends and companions of one of England's greatest monarchs; for there is no question that Edward III. was the foremost prince of his time, and laid the foundation for the after-progress of our land in all the elements of national greatness, social amelioration, and commercial development. One proof alike of his patriotism and his sagacity was the choice of John Wycliffe, the famous Oxford reformer, as his chaplain and representative at Bruges at the conference evoked by the national resistance to Papal encroachments and extortions.

But we must return to Sir Miles. The outbreak of the plague in 1351 put a stop to a contemplated new expedition to France. We have no means of telling how the pestilence affected this parish, but it is said that Yorkshire suffered severely, as well as Norfolk and London, where people died at the rate of 200 daily. In these calamitous times Baron Stapleton exchanged military for civil pursuits. He became Sheriff of Yorkshire in 1353,[1] and perhaps again in 1355. I say perhaps, because it is said that in this last year Milo de Stapleton, 'dn's de Hathelsay,' and his cousin Milo, 'dn's de Bedale and

---

[1] The following is from the Selby Coucher Book, vol. i., Record Series, Yorkshire A. and T. Society, and shows not only the confidential employment of Sir Miles Stapleton, but also the relative importance of Haddlesey in the fourteenth century :

'Inquisitio capta apud Selby coram MILONE DE STAPLETON DE HATHELSAY, escaetore domini Regis in Com. Ebor. die Lunæ prox. post festum Omnium Sanctorum, anno Regis Edwardi tertii post conquestum Angliæ vicesimo septimo (A.D. 1353) secundum tenorem brevis domini Regis huic inquisitioni attachiati, per sacramentum Johannis de Fenton (of Est Heathelsay), Roberti Ryhill, Johannis de Okelesthorp, Roberti de Berley (*i.e.*, Barlow), Gilberti de Schirburne, Henrie de Stockbrig, Johannis Lovet de Fenton, Ricardi le Clerk de Bretton (? Brayton), Thomas *atte Wode de Birne*, Roberti filii Margeriæ de Kithire, Petri de Preston, et Johannis de Berley (Barlow) juratorum qui dicunt super sacramentum suum quod Thos. de Acastre,' etc. (P. 81, Inquisition taken Nov. 4 at Selby, f. 30.)

Then follow awards of lands in Acaster Selby to the Abbot of Selby, who produces two charters dated January 25, 1315, and October 1, same year. These awards were confirmed by letters patent from the King at Westminster, December 1, 1353.

Ingham,' were sent out with the Black Prince and Henry Earl of Derby (afterwards Duke of Lancaster) and other Commissioners to meet the French Ambassadors at Avignon. In 1356 Sir Miles received, for taking David Bruys (Bruce), King of Scotland, from Newcastle-on-Tyne to London, 200 marks, paid for the expenses of the King—a large sum; this, multiplied by fifteen, as equivalent to modern money, brings it up to £1,800. In 1358, while still Sheriff, Sir Miles was summoned as a baron to Parliament. This seems to have been his last attendance at Westminster. He seems to have lived, for a time at least, at Kentmere, at Kirkby, Fletham, and Stapleton-on-Tees, and to have accumulated wealth by lending large sums on mortgage to his cousin of Ingham. This appears from a suit (*finalis concordia*) concluded at the Westmoreland Assizes, February 3, 1364, whereby 'Milo de Stapleton, of Bedale, chivaler, grants to MILO DE STAPLETON, of Hathelsay, chivaler, Brianis de Stapleton, chivaler (afterwards of Wighill), Richard de Richmund, John de Kirkeby, and others the manors of Ingham and Waxtonesham, co. Norfolk, Bedale and Cotherstone, co. York, and North Morton, Berks, for Hathelsay's life.' In return for which Hathelsay, on the part of the feoffees, undertakes to pay Sir Miles of Bedale 500 marks a year—nearly £5,000 of our money—during the life of the latter. And if Hathelsay should survive his cousin, he is to have still the estates for life at a nominal rent of one rose a year, but at his death the whole of the estates revert to the heirs of Bedale and Ingham. And for this grant Sir Miles of Hathelsay agrees to pay his cousin down £1,000—equal to £15,000 of our money.

In 1359 Sir Miles seems to have had disputes with some of his tenants at Carlton about some waste lands there, including William de Ayremin, who made complaint to the King that they went in fear of bodily injury and the loss of their goods. So the King orders his bailiffs to protect them for one year (Rot. Pat., 33 Edw. III. m. 28). After this he has a dispute with Queen Philippa, in which he claims half the river Aire within his demesne at Carlton, of which she on the Snaith side tried to deprive him. The King appointed a commission of inquiry by letters patent, dated at Westminster, January 27, 1365, but we do not know the result. However, he outlived these controversies, and made his will at Hathelsay, on the Sunday next before the Feast of St. Bartholomew, August 24, 1372, as follows : ' In the name of God, amen. I, Milo de Stapilton, chivaler, make my testament after this manner. First, I commit my soul to God and the Blessed Virgin Mary and All Saints, and my body to be buried in the Church of St. Nicholas of Drax. And I appoint Dn's Brian de Stapelton, and Dn's Johannes Legett, parson of Melshamby, my executors, to whom I bequeath all my goods, personalty and realty. And to this I have affixed my seal.' This will was proved on January 5, Sir Miles having died about the year 1373, leaving behind him his son and heir Thomas ; his daughter Elizabeth, wife of Sir Thomas Metham, who carried a great part of his estates to that family. An elder daughter, Sibill, seems to have died before her father, the Sibill Stapelton mentioned in the above will being the wife of Thomas. She was the eldest daughter of Sir John Fitzwilliam, of Sprotborough, chivaler. In the Stapelton pedigree (Foster's) she is called Sibill, but in the Fitzwilliam pedigree of the same compiler she is called Joan ; also in proceedings in Chancery (see forward). In like manner her second husband is called John Felton, Esq., in one document, and *Enoch* Felton in another. Thomas Stapelton had livery of his father's estates in 1373, but was never summoned to Parliament, having died on August 10 of the same year, at the early age of twenty-three. On his death his sister Elizabeth, wife of Sir Thomas de Metham, was declared next heir to all her father's estates;

but a few months later, February, 1374, another suit is commenced by the King against the widow and her father, Sir Thomas Metham and his wife, and the chaplains of Hathelsay and Sprotburgh. On this arises protracted litigation, and although I have found Mr. Chetwynd's painstaking papers in the *Yorkshire Archæological Journal*, as well as others he has kindly furnished me with privately, most valuable help, yet in the puzzled labyrinth arising after the death of Sir Thomas de Stapelton in 1373, I am glad to avail myself of extracts kindly furnished by Mr. Paley Baildon, as they came to hand in preparing his own book ' History of Baildon.'

'PLEAS BEFORE THE KING IN HIS CHANCERY AT WESTMINSTER ON THE OCTAVE OF S. MARTIN, A.R. 47, A.D. 1374.

'It was found by an inquest made by William de Ergum, the Escheator for Yorkshire, at the King's command, that Thomas de Stapelton, deceased, held on the day that he died, in fee tail, the manor of Haddlesey (except a certain place called *Sqwalley*[1] (or Sqwerker) and £6 rent assigned to a certain chantry), to himself and Joan his wife, and the heirs of their bodies lawfully issuing, so that if they died without such heir of their bodies, then the manor would remain to the right heirs of Thomas for ever. And also that Thomas held in his demesne as of fee a messuage and 5 bovates of land in West Haddlesey of the King in chief by his charter, rendering therefore at the Exchequer, by the hands of the Sheriff of Yorkshire for the time being, 40s. And also that Thomas held in his demesne, as of fee, divers lands and tenements in Baildon, which are burdened to John Vavasour in 100s. a year for life, and which are held of Sir Simon Warde by the service of the fourth part of a

[1] See this name in charter of February 9, 1312, Chapter VI. of this work.

knight's fee. And that Elizabeth, wife of Sir Thomas de Metham, is sister and next heir of said Thomas de Stapelton, and is aged 24 years and more.

'And thereupon Hugh Rene, clerk (parson of Sprotboro'), William de Calthorn (parson of Hathelsay), and William Spynk, of Sprotburgh, appeared personally and denied that Thomas de Stapelton was seised of the manor of Haddlesey and the lands in West Haddlesey the day that he died, because they say that, long before he died, the said Thomas de Stapelton by his charter, which was produced in Court, and which was dated at Sprotburgh, 10 July, 47 Edw. III., enfeoffed the said Rene, Calthorn, and Spynk of the said manor and of all the lands that he had in East Haddlesey, Middle H. and West H., to hold to them and their heirs for ever, and they were seised and possessed of the same until the Escheator put them out. And all this they are prepared to prove.

'And the said Joan, widow of Thomas, appeared by Thomas de Thwayt, her guardian, and Thomas de Metham and Elizabeth his wife appeared by their attorney, and said that Stapelton held the property exactly as the inquest said, and they prayed that it might be inquired into.

'And John Fitz-William and William de Calthorn also appeared and denied that Stapelton was seised of the lands, etc., in Baildon the day that he died, because they say that, long before his death, he, by his charter, produced in Court and dated 1 July, 47 Edw. III., enfeoffed Fitz-William and Calthorn in the same, by the name of his manor of Baildon, with the appurtenances, to hold to them and their heirs for ever, and they were seised and possessed of the same until the Escheator put them out.

'And Thomas de Metham and Elizabeth his wife appeared and said that Stapelton held exactly as the inquest said, and they prayed that it might be inquired into.

'And thereupon Michael Skyllyng, who sued for the King, prayed that all the property might remain in the King's hands until the truth be known.

'A day is given on the octave of St. Hilary, and the Sheriff of Yorkshire is commanded to cause to come 24, as well knights as other proved and lawful men of the view of Haddlesey, West Haddlesey, and Baildon, by whom the truth of the matter can be made known.

'After various adjournments, the case was heard at York on the Monday after the Assumption of the Blessed Mary (August 15), before William de Finchden, Chief Justice of the Common Bench, Thomas de Ingleby, and Brian de Stapelton. John Fitz-William produced a letter, under the King's Privy Seal, to the Justices, directing them to proceed in the matter. And when the jury were sworn, John Fitz-William produced also, and put in evidence, a certain writing, in the hand of Thomas de Stapelton, as he asserted, and sealed with Stapelton's two seals, that is, with his great seal and with his signet, which was said to be his last will; and Fitz-William also produced a purse containing the said two seals, and prayed the Justices that they would cause the writing to be read. This was done, and in the writing it was stated that the last will of Thomas de Stapelton was that Joan, his wife, should have the manor and tenements contained in the record for life, and that after her decease they should go to John Fitz-William and his heirs, on condition that he should found two perpetual chantries in the chapel of Haddlesey for the souls of Thomas de Stapelton and his ancestors; and if Fitz-William would not do this, the property was to go to Brian de Stapelton and his heirs on the same condition; and if he would not do it, then to Miles, son of Miles de Stapelton, of Bedale; and if he would not do it, then to Isabella de Neuland; and if she would not found the chantries, then to his own right heirs. This writing Thomas de Stapelton had left in the keeping of Fitz-William when he last went abroad, and it was not to be opened during his life.

'The jury found that as to the Manor of Haddlesey and one messuage and 5 bovates in West Haddlesey, the said Thomas de Stapelton, long before his death, being of sound mind and of full age, made a certain charter of feoffment in fee simple, which was put in evidence, to Rene, Calthorn, and Spynk, by the name of his Manor of Haddlesey and all that he had in East H., Middle H., and West H., to hold to them and their heirs for ever; and he gave letters of attorney to John de Shirwode, John de Cateby, and John Tilleson, of Esholt, to deliver seisin of the premises to the feoffees, which was done accordingly a month before Stapelton's death. By virtue whereof Rene, Calthorn, and Spynk were seised of the premises in Stapelton's lifetime, and held their court at Haddlesey, and all the tenants of the manor attorned to them, except one John Lascy, who held of the manor by the service of 2d. a year. And they say that Rene, Calthorn, and Spynk held possession all the life of Stapelton, and continued in possession after his death until the Escheator removed them; and that Stapelton at the time of his death had nothing in the manor and lands, except the service of John Lascy, who had not attorned. And they say, being asked, that there was no condition imposed.

'And as to the lands in Baildon, the jury say that those lands and tenements form the Manor of Baildon, and that Thomas de Stapelton, long before his death, being of sound mind and full age, made a charter of feoffment in fee simple, produced here in court, to John Fitz-William and William de Calthorn, of his Manor of Baildon, to hold to them and their heirs for ever; and he also gave a letter of attorney to Shirwood and the others to deliver seisin thereof, which was done accordingly long before the death of Stapelton, whereby Fitz-William and Calthorn were seised, and all the tenants of the manor attorned in the lifetime of Stapelton, and they remained in possession during his life and after his death, until they were removed by the Escheator. And they say that Stapelton had no estate in the premises at the time of his death, and that the said gift was unconditional.

'Thereupon Rene, Calthorn, and Spynk produce letters patent from the King, pardoning the trespass which they had committed in acquiring the land held of him in West Haddlesey without license.

'They also produce a writ close from the King, witnessing that the manor of Haddlesey is held of the Castle and Honor of Pontefract in socage at a rent of 2s. for all services, and that it is charged with a yearly rent of 10 marks to Sibilla de Stapelton for life, and with 33s. 4d. to William de Brune for life. Dated at Westminster, 18 Nov., A.R. 48.

'Whereupon Rene and the others pray that the manor and tenements and the mean issues may be delivered to them; and the court so awards, excepting the said place called Sqwalley, and the £6 rent belonging to the chantry, and the services of John Lascy.

'And the court also awards that the land and tenements in Baildon and the mean issues thereof be delivered to John Fitz-William and William de Calthorn.

'Saving always the rights of the King, if any.'—Coram Rege Roll, Hil. 48 Edw. III., No. 184, m. 4.

Before discussing the points raised by the documents just quoted, I give a translation of Cart. Harl. 83, C. 15, kindly supplied by Mr. Chetwynd-Stapylton:

'48 Hathelsay and Baildon put in trust pending trial, 1375. Edward, King, etc. Know all men that it was decreed before us concerning our Manor of Hathelsay with its appurtenances, and concerning a messuage and five bovates of land (from 40 to 60 acres) with appurtenances in West Hathelsay, and other lands and tenements in Bayldon, co. Ebor, which belonged to Thos. de Stapelton, deceased, who held under us in chief, and which, by the death of the said Thomas, were taken into our own hands by *Wm. Brymer,* lately our escheator. Between us and Joan, late wife of Thos. de Stapelton, and Thos. de Metham and Elizabeth his wife, sister and heir of the aforesaid Thos. de Stapelton and John Fitzwilliam (chevalier), Wm. de Calthorn, Hugh Rene (clerk), and William Spink, of Sprotborough,—We commit the safe keeping of the aforesaid manors, etc., in Westhathelsay and Baildon, to our beloved Ralph Bracebridge while the aforesaid remains undecided.'

Referring to the documents which I presume have escaped Mr. Chetwynd - Stapylton's vigilant search, it seems that the act of the King just quoted, and which Mr. Stapylton refers to in *Archæological Journal* (vol. viii., p. 116), was issued between the commencement of proceedings in the Court of Chancery at Westminster, the end of November, 1374, and the trial at York before Chief Justice William de Finchden, towards the end of August, 1375, so that the binding over the manors, etc., to the care of Ralph Bracebridge was an interim proceeding early in the year 1375, and before the trial at York.

Litigation, however, did not cease, for there is another trial at York in 1384. This fact, and the names occurring below, seem to upset the statement that Thomas de Stapleton, brother of the last Sir Miles, succeeded to the Hathelsay estates in 1382, as both Mr. Chetwynd-Stapylton and Foster, in his pedigree of Yorkshire families, assert. Let us note the following:

'PLEAS AT YORK. MONDAY, IN THE FEAST OF S. PETER AD VINCULA, 8 RIC. II., 1384.

'Thomas de Metham, chivaler, and Elizabeth his wife, against William de Calthorn and John de Felton, chivaler, and Joan his wife, in a plea of novel disseisin of the manor of Haddlesey and land, etc., in West Haddlesey. Felton did not come; Joan his wife was dead. Calthorn came and said that *Thomas de Stapleton, son and heir of Miles, brother of Elizabeth, the plaintiff*, she being his heir, was formerly seised of the manor and premises, and gave them to Hugh Rene, clerk, William Spynk of Sprotburgh, and the said William de Calthorn, to hold the said manor and appurtenances, and whatsoever he had in the vills of West, Middle, and East Haddlesey, to said Hugh, Wm., and Wm., their heirs and assigns for ever, and Calthorn produces the charter, dated 10 July, 1373, and says that Rene and Spynk are dead, and he is now seised.' [The result does not appear.]—Assize Roll, Yorkshire, N 2, 29—3, m. 21.

In the above no reference in made to Thomas Stapleton, uncle of the Thomas who died in 1373. Moreover, Elizabeth Metham, the sister of the late lord of Hathelsay, is alive. John de Felton was the husband of the late Sir Thomas de Stapelton's widow Joan, daughter of Sir John Fitzwilliam. The latter seems to have been in possession of the Baildon property in 1378, for in that year he sues John Nant, of Baildon, for breaking his close there, and taking his goods and chattels to the value of 100s. In the same year also John Fitzwilliam and William de Calthorn bring an action for waste at Baildon. This John Fitzwilliam having been killed about 1384, he was succeeded at Baildon and at Hathelsey by his son William. This William, in 1387, sues for cutting trees at Baildon, and in 1389 for waste. In 1394 he calls himself 'Dominus de Baildon.' He settles Baildon on his third son, Ralph, who afterwards succeeded to Hathelsay in 1398, so that there is good reason for thinking that John Fitzwilliam succeeded to the Haddlesey estate by virtue of the charter produced by Rene, Calthorn, and Spink, who were trustees for the said John Fitzwilliam.

CHAPTER XI.

EST HATHELSAY.

HERE we leave the reigning families awhile to get an idea of the inhabitants of the parish generally, furnished by the Poll-tax returns in the second year of the reign of Richard II. We begin with Est Hathelsay, and find at the head of the roll John Felton, chevalier, who figured in the preceding lawsuits, and was also one of the jurors in the Selby Abbey inquisition A.D. 1352. He and his wife are put down for xxs. We may speculate as to the exact spot where this gentleman, connected by marriage with the Stapletons and Fitzwilliams, resided in East Haddlesey. There are three possible sites. We read that the first Baron Stapleton 'gave a croft and windmill opposite the door or gate of Temple Hirst in East Hathelsey.' This may have been either the site of the old house so long held by the Bromleys, the land of which reaches up near to the Hirst boundary, or, less likely, the farmhouse, etc., in Eastfield, now the property of the governors of the Wakefield Charities, or site No. 2, the spot called by the Ordnance surveyors 'Hall Garth.' This site measures about 120 yards square, and is surrounded by a broad, deep moat, in some parts double, and joined to the river Aire on its north bank. Here there are indications of buildings in the past, and it is pretty certain that the Fitzwilliams had a residence here later on, but whether quite so soon as John Felton's date is not clear. If, however, we give up the two previous sites, we have only another left. That is Haddlesey Hall, the property of the Duke of Ancaster in the seventeenth and eighteenth centuries. In reference to this we have remains of buildings which must have belonged to a large house; measuring from east to west about 100 yards, with lofty and spacious interior rooms, walled gardens, a park stretching out to the north and east by the banks of the Aire. This house was only destroyed at a comparatively recent date, viz., the time of Mr. John Sawyer, and is in many ways the most likely spot for the residence of a 'chevalier,' or nobleman.

That East Haddlesey filled a relatively important position in the early part of the fourteenth century appears from the Poll-tax returns of Richard II., 'Est Hathelsay' heading the returns for 'Barkston Wapentagium,' and John Felton,[1] chivaler, pays xxs., while Gaytford only has an attorney at 6s. 8d.; Birkyn a franklin (Thos. de Midilton), 6s. 8d.; Brayton an Esq. at 6s 8d., and Selby an Esquier in service, 3s. 4d.; equalling Eggboro, with a cattle merchant. And Snayth figures with an attorney at 6s. 8d., which, though in the adjoining wapentake of Osgoldcross, was and is closely associated with Hathelsay in many ways. In this connection we must bring in the Poll-tax returns for Kellington. Fifty-nine persons were assessed at a total of 20s. 4d. Among these names we find John *Presteson* and Johanna *Prestdaghter*. As it is interesting to know the names of the inhabitants of our parish over 500 years ago (the date of this tax being 1379), I give the names of those in addition to Chevalier Felton

[1] This gentleman was probably the son of William Felton *temp.* Edward III., who was the first cousin of Robert de Felton, who was a baron of Parliament in the reigns of Edward I. and Edward II.

who paid a tax of 4d. each in Est Hathelsay, viz., John Watson and Alfreda his wife, John Swayne, Matilda Swayne, Gilbert Vower and wife, John de Pole and wife, John Hudson and wife, Rd. Swayne and wife, Wm. de Hewensall and wife, Rd. Wryght and wife, Wm. Ibotson and wife, Thos. Walkoc and wife, Wm. Walcok and wife, Rd. Scotte and wife, Robert Fox and wife, Wm. Lambe and wife, Robt. Balcoc and wife, John Chaumberlayn and wife, Robt. *Abbot* and wife, John Fox, John Gardiner, Cecilia Warde, Robert Prestman, John son of Richard, Alice daughter of William, Christina *Lamberd*, Alicia de Selby: making a total of 18 married couples, 4 single men, and 4 single women—in all 44 tax-payers, the amount of money from this township being 28s. 4d., *i.e.*, about £22 of our money.

WEST HATHELSAY.

The names are: Wm. Clerk and wife, carpenter, 6d.; John Jouet, tailor, and wife, 6d.; all the others 4d. each., viz., Adam Spenser and wife, John Brown and wife, Robt. Rowlay and wife, John Cooper and wife, Hugh Nelson and wife, Thos. Smyth and wife, John Nanson and wife, Henry Baret and wife, Wm. Brown and wife, Thos. Rygge and wife, Thos. Leper and wife, Rd. Franks and wife, Wm. Wodcok and wife, John Baret and wife, Hugh Leuthe and wife, John Dawson and wife, John Vower and wife, Thos. Prestman and wife, John Souter and wife, John son of Adam, Amicia daughter of Adam, Agnes daughter of John, Emma daughter of John, Wm. son of Robert (from these names come the Adamsons, Johnsons, Robertsons, Williamsons of later date), Juliana Knyth, Agnes daughter of William, Wm. son of John, Agnes widow of Thomas. Total, 21 married couples, 3 single men, 5 single women, and one widow—in all 29 taxpayers, with a total of 10s. 4d., about £8 of our money. In the two Hyrstes we find :

Adam Baron and wife,	Robt. Lascy and wife,
John Palmer and wife,	Ingram and wife,
Henry de Chaumbir and wife,	John son of Adam and wife,
	Thos. Alcok and wife,
Robert Byrkin and wife,	John fflynt and wife,
Gemasius and wife,	John at ye Wode and wife,
Henry Fysser and wife,	Richard Turnour and wife,
Nicholas Gryffin and wife,	Matilda Griffyn,
Wm. Skinner and wife,	John Griffyn,
John Theker and wife,	Robert, servant of Matilda,
Thos. Skinner and wife,	John Bull,
Wm. Turnour and wife,	John Bakester (*i.e.*, Baxter modern),
Robert Griffyn and wife,	
Wm. Huekyn and wife,	Elizabeth de Chester,
Henry Leeget and wife,	Joan Palmer,
John Turner and wife,	John Schypman,
John Basselaw and wife,	John Smyth,
John de Lane and wife,	Joan Smyth,
Thos. Smyth and wife,	Alicia Smyth,
Thos. Randolf and wife,	Wm. Alcok,
Edmund Adkynson and wife,	Henry fflynt,
Rd. Gemme and wife,	Agnes, servant of Hugh,
Wm. fflynt and wife,	Elizabeth, servant of Henry.

Total, 29 married couples, 7 single men, and 8 single women—in all 71 taxpayers, with a total of 13s. 8d., *i.e.*, about £11 of our money, showing a grand total for the whole of our existing parish of about £40. It is a very remarkable thing that not one individual of the name of Hathelsay occurs in these lists, although in the Gateforth list we find not only Amicia de Hirst, but also JULIANA DE HATHELSAY, and in Selby WM. DE HATHELSAY and wife (Lyster), and as such pays a xiid. tax. In the same list there is also a *John Hathelsay* and wife (no 'de') and only iiij*d*. tax. It seems, then, that the Hathelsays were so bound up in the fortunes of the early Baron Stapletons that they either migrated with them or were killed off in the wars. One considerable migration we have full information about, viz., that to South Duffield, in 1310, when William de Hathelsaye goes there as steward of the first baron Miles de Stapelton. But before going over to South Duffield under the pleasant guidance of Mr. Thomas Burton's 'History of Hemingborough,' edited by Canon Raine, let us recall what our own history tells us of the Hathelsay family. We have then Roger de Beghal (or Beghby) in Hausy, and Richard the son of Alan de Hausey, as witnesses to a charter of Adam, Lord Newmarket, about the year 1230. Again, in 1207, John Aleyn de Hathelsay and William Camelford de Hathelsay are among the names of those appointed to value the farming stock and furniture of the Templars at their preceptory at Hirst. Peter de Hathilsey is also mentioned in an inquisition of 8 Edw. I., 1280, so we can see that those people were a recognised factor in the place in the thirteenth century. In the fourteenth century, A.D. 1349, February 14, John de Hathelsay and John de Spalding are the sureties of Lord William de Aton in an indenture between him and the Abbot of Selby. So in a memorandum dated January 24, 1350, the Act permitting Henry de Salley to leave Selby Abbey, in order to join a mendicant order, is signed in the presence of John de Hemingboro', *John de Hathelsay*, and others who are described as *fide dignorum*. And at the settling down of Miles de Stapelton at West Hathelsay he evidently found them a class of people to assist him in the management of his outlying estates, so he despatches William de Hathelsay to South Duffield as his local agent early in the fourteenth century. I say early, because Miles de Stapleton was killed at Bannockburn in 1314, and William de Hathelsay appears as farming the tithes of Hemingborough under Cardinal Joscelin d'Ossat, the absentee[1] rector of that important parish in 1317. We can start, then, on firm ground as regards the migration of the leading portion of the Hathelsays to South Duffield, where for some 600 years they seem to have maintained a leading position, as there was a house called Haddlesey Hall, and the south end of the cross aisle, or south transept of the church, was reserved as a place of interment for the occupants of that house and Topham Hall. As the first of the South Duffield Haddleseys was William, so that name seems to have survived through many generations. A marble tablet reads, 'Sacred to the memory of Wm. Haddlesey, Esq., of South Duffield, who departed this life Apl. 14, 1824, aged 74 years.' Another William Haddlesey dies on August 13, 1857; and another September 16, 1872. One or two entries in the parish registers give us a view of the character borne by the Haddleseys in South Duffield; *e.g.*, in 1675 the vicar writes: ' Oct. 26, Henry Saltmarsh, of Hemingborough, gent.; and Madam Frances Hadlesay, of South Duffield, both my very choice friends, w^r married at Howden per me, Thos. Revell, vic. Hemb. 1676, May 29.—Mem^m. that Markham Haddelsay, of South Duffield, gent., my dear friend, died May 28th, and was buried May ye 29th.' At the present time the South Duffield Haddleseys seem to have sold their estates, but there is still a family of which a William Haddlesey is the head, as our pedigree will show.

---

[1] This Cardinal Rector of Hemingborough is a striking specimen of the evils inflicted by the Court of Rome on the Church of England in the Middle Ages. Joscelin, it appears, while holding the rectory of Hemingborough, lived at Rome, never visiting England, much less residing on his benefice. Beyond this, when the Prior of Durham sent officials to visit the church, the servants of Joscelin closed the church doors against them and drove them away on two occasions.

THE HADDLESEY PEDIGREE.

William de Hathelsay, steward of first Baron Miles de Stapelton of West Hathelsay, 1317.

Robert and William de Hathelsaye are mentioned in 1342 and 1345.

Thomas de Hathelsaye was appointed Rector of St. Edward's Church in Walmgate, York, June 10; 1342, and Cantarist to Naylor's Chantry in Church of St. Crux, February 9, 1349.

Richard de Hethelsay was appointed Vicar of Drax, December 21, 1343.

William de Hathelsaye, son of William of South Duffield and Alicia, his wife, occurs 1379. Robert, son of Thomas de Hathelsaye, in Subsidy Roll of same year. William de Hathelsaye occurs in rental of 1426, John Hathelsaye in Prior's rental same year, and John Hathelsaye, jun., in Bishop's rental in 1440. William Hathelsaye occurs 1467 and 1478.

William Haddlesay occurs from 1515 to 1532. He died November 5, 1540; married Margaret ———; died January 13 following. From these were born:

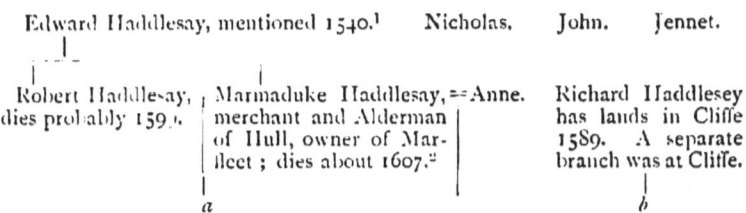

Edward Haddlesay, mentioned 1540.[1]   Nicholas.   John.   Jennet.

Robert Haddlesay, dies probably 159_.	Marmaduke Haddlesay, merchant and Alderman of Hull, owner of Marflect; dies about 1607.[2]	=Anne.	Richard Haddlesey has lands in Cliffe 1589. A separate branch was at Cliffe.
a			*b*

---

[1] 'Thos. Blake of Catton Park bequeaths by will Aug. 31st, 1566, to *Edward, son* of Thos. Haddlesey, xli. and all my land in Reapon. To Thos. Haddlesey the farmhold of Cathwet [we note later on how the Haddleseys were associated with *Catwick*], willing him to give to children of Maude Lodge every year xls., and then if it chance the said Thos. to die then his son Edward shall have the rest of my years. Francis Blake, whose will was proved 1553, bequeaths £40 to his son-in-law, Thos. Haddlesey.'—*Yorkshire Archæological Journal*, vol. x.

[2] Marmaduke Haddlesay, son of William Haddlesay, is baptized at St. Mary's, Hull, September 19, 1619.

Haddlesey.

The Name of Haddlesay as a family name, was first taken from a place in the West riding of Yorkshire, not far from Selby.

This family Arms is given in the following way, viz. Argent, a chevron embattled at the top edge, Sable, between three Eagles, Gules, on the chevron a crescent for a younger line.

Crest, an Arm in plate Armour, lying fesseways, holding in the hand, a broken spear, erect, all proper — Motto - Cui Debeo Fidus. Translation — Faithful to whom I owe faith.

This Bearing is ascribed to Joseph Haddlesey, Esqr of Essex and Herts. dated, 1648. which family appears to have been concerned in the Political events of the Commonwealth.

Correctly drawn by J.^{no} Thorold. 27- Posterngate, Hull. 1860.

Between pp. 138-139.

The Haddlesey Pedigree.

a
William,[1] Thomas. Kay. Abigail.
Samuel. Robert. Hamp- Esther.
Michael. ton. Anne.

b
George Haddlesey of Cliffe, bur. Jan. 19, 1626-7.

Wm. Haddlesey, of South Duffield; will proved Nov. 13, 1641.

Anne, d. Aug. 1, 1609.

Anne Haddlesey, of South Duffield, bur. Jan. 4, 1642.

Edward Haddlesey, of Brackenholme; bur. Oct. 13, 1620.

Dorothy Fawkes.

Wm. H. — Eliz. Hache 1637, and Mabel Kirlew, Nov. 29, 1640.

Wm. Haddlesey, of South Duffield, bur. May 7, 1663.

Mary, dau. of Markham.

Catherine.[2] Dorothy. Robert, bur. at Selby Jan. 18, 1603-4.

Marmaduke. Philip. Robert.

Michael. Thomas.

Joan. Mary.

George Haddlesey, bap. 1632-3. Philip, bap. 1641.

Markham Haddlesey of South Duffield, bap. Nov. 15, 1635; d. May 28, 1676.

Frances.

Susanna, bap. Oct. 30, 1634. Anne, bap. July 10, 1637. Elizth., bap. July 25, 1638. Mary, bap. Sept. 21, 1643.

Wm. Haddlesey, bap. May 31, 1664.

Pelham Haddlesey = Henrietta Maria, of South Duffield, dau. of Marmabap. Nov. 6, 1666; duke Norcliff, bur. Aug. 14, 1702. Aug. 1, 1691.

Anne, bur. Dec. 27, 1660. Mary, bap. Feb 5, 1662. Frances, bap. July 8, 1673; bur. Jan. 26, 1679-80.

Markham Haddlesey of South Duffield, bur. May 15, 1729.

Anne Blythe, ..., m. at York Minster Oct. 16, 1712; bur. Nov. 14, 1744.
Markham = Anne.

William. Pelham. Nathaniel.

Henrietta = John Smith of Maria South Duffield, Oct. 31, 1725.
Alice, bap. May 21, 1700.

Wm. Haddlesey, bap. Jan. 14, 1713; bur. Dec. 31, 1715.

Thomas, bap. July 30, 1722.

John Haddlesey, of South Duffield, bap. June 20, 1724; bur. Apl. 14, 1765.

Mary, dau. of — Hobson, of Copmanthorpe; bur. Oct. 11, 1788, aged 59.

a

---

[1] A William Haddlesey, of Holy Trinity, Hull, married Joan Barnard same place 1608.

[2] A Cathron Hadelsie was married to Joseph Curtis at St. Mary's Church, Hull, November 27, 1651.

Wm. Haddle-=Jane, dau. 1. Mary,=John Haddle- Anne, Mary=Thos.
sey of South   of — Snow- daughter sey, gent., bap. dau. Hornby of
Duffield, bap. ball of Mal- of — Feb. 21, 1758; of — Snaith.
Jan. 30, 1749; ton, who re- Wood. d. at Thorne Philip- Anne=Thos.
d. April 14, married — 1820, and bur. son. Jewitt.
1824, aged 74. Tomlinson. there. Frances=Robt.
Markham, bap. Clark, Holy
Feb. 29, 1764; Trinity, Hull.
bur. May 31, Elizth., bap.
1787. Jan. 9, 1760.
Joshua, posthumous, Maria, bap.
bap. Jan. 2, 1766; Mar., 1762;
d. unmarried 1846. bur. Apl. 17,
  1765.

Wm. Haddlesey Charlotte, d. Ashforth in Mary= — Stephenson;
of South Duffield, d. Aug. 1816; d. June 13, 1865, d. 1865.
13, 1857, aged 61. aged 72.

William, born Wm. Haddlesey Hannah, dau. of Jane, bap. 1819.
1817; d. an of South Duf- Thos. Cawkill Anne, bap. 1821; d. May
infant. field, bap. 1827; of Cliffe, m. 14, 1855, aged 34.
John, bap. died Sept. 16, July, 1850; d. Mary, bap. 1823.
1825. 1872, aged 45. Sept. 27, 1872, Charlotte, bap. 1830; d.
Joseph, bap. aged 43. infant.
1828. Elizabeth, bap. 1833.
  Charlotte Anderson, bap.
  1834; d. July 24, 1862,
  aged 27.
  Susanna, bap. 1837.

Charlotte Ashforth, John Wm. Mary Moun- Wm. Thos. Haddlesey,
born Dec. 3, 1853. Haddlesey, tain Shaw of born Sept. 22, 1857.
Frances Annie, born born April Selby, 1878. Arthur Ed. Haddlesey,
March 11, 1862. 8, 1856. born Oct. 27, 1859.
Susanna, born May Markham Chas. Had-
14, 1870. dlesey, born Sept. 28,
  1863.

Wm. Henry, b. Oct. 14, 1878.
Ernest John, b. June 3, 1883.
Beatrice Hannah, b. Jan. 17, 1886.
Chas. Pearsey, b. March 11, 1889.
Thos. Cawkill, b. Jan. 3, 1892.

The Marmaduke Haddlesey, merchant and Alderman of Hull, who died in 1607, mentioned above, is supposed to be the father of Thomas Haddlesey, Vicar of Kirkby

The Haddlesey Pedigree.

Grindal 1618, and Rector of Thorpe Bassett 1625-26. Also probably the father of:

Robert Haddlesey, = Eliz. Hampton, Oct. 24, 1604. Rector of Catwick in Holderness, 1602-3.

Ann, bap. Nov. 13, 1605. Elizth., bap. July 12, 1607. Dorothy, bap. Jan., 1612-13.

Margaret, bap. May 5, 1614. Susanna, bap. June 29, 1615. Abigail, bap. July 30; bur. Aug. 8, 1617.

Marmaduke, bap. Sept. 21, 1618. Michael, bap. Nov. 5, 1620.

The residence of the Haddleseys is said to have been panelled with oak and of considerable age. Near the entrance is a rudely sculptured stone representing a lion on the back of a tortoise, symbolizing the old motto, 'Festina lente,' which seems appropriate to the career of the Haddleseys. On the death of Mr. William Haddlesey in 1872 the estate of 125 acres, with a corn mill, was sold, other property having been previously disposed of.

There seems, however, to have been a branch of this family settled in Lincolnshire in the fifteenth century, who intermarried with the Fitzwilliams of Mablethorp. This branch is supposed to be descended from Robert Haddlesey, Rector of Catwick in 1602. Samuel Fitzwilliam Haddlesey, solicitor of Caistor, now represents this branch.

HADDLESEY — COATES. — August 19, at St. Nicholas' Church, Searby, Lincolnshire, by the Rev. J. F. Kirk, assisted by the Rev. J. R. Hill, George Haddlesey, third son of G. R. F. Haddlesey, Esq., Caistor, to Ethel Margaret, eldest daughter of W. H. Coates, Esq., J.P., of Searby Manor, Caistor, Lincolnshire.

One meets with a few odd members of the Haddlesey family in occasional records, e.g., in the register of marriages at Selby Abbey under date March 18, 1622: Edward Haddlesey and Alice Barstowe.

CHAPTER XII.

TEMPLE HIRST AND THE DARCIES—*(continued)*.

WE now return to Temple Hirst and the events associated with it after the Fitzwilliams became resident at East Haddlesey. In Chapter IX. we broke off our history of the Darcys at the death of John Darcy, who died in 1363 quite young. His mother, however, survived, and a younger brother named Philip, who took the title of Baron Darcy and Meinill from his mother. The Countess died in 1377—a very eventful date in English history. In 1376 the English Parliament —called 'the good' because of its patriotic spirit—passed the law of Præmunire and Provisors, forbidding presentations to benefices in England by the Pope, and the publication of any decree or Bull without royal permission asked and granted. The Pope strove hard to get this statute repealed, for it effectually arrested that ruinous process by which the Court of Rome extracted from England a revenue five times as great as that received by its own monarch. This patriotic and reformation movement was strengthened by the fact that the House of Commons asserted its right to have a voice in the administration of national affairs. So they took up the line of opposition to the powerful Duke of Lancaster, whose mismanagement of the French war had caused universal indignation, and also to the prelates, who wished to continue their extortions. The movement of ecclesiastical reform found an eminently capable leader in the person of John Wycliffe, one of Yorkshire's noblest sons, one of England's saintliest and most learned doctors. It would take up too much of our space to follow his grand career as confessor and apostle of truth in an age when its voice was almost entirely hushed. Let it suffice to say that his own indignant rebuke of the mistaken rejoicings of the monks at Oxford over his anticipated death —'I shall not die, but live to declare the evil deeds of the friars; truth is great, and shall prevail'—have been emphatically fulfilled in the results of his labours. His invincible courage, his burning eloquence, his convincing dialectics, his gift of God's Word to a hungering nation, and his clear exposition of the fundamental basis of evangelic truth, broke down the barriers with which falsehood and superstition had kept back the onflowing stream of the river of water of life across the dry places of England, and paved the way for that flood-tide of freedom and truth which reached its high-water mark in the glorious Reformation of the sixteenth century. It is important to bear in mind the deep hold Wycliffe's teaching had on the masses, so that his enemies said that every second man they met was a disciple of his. But it was not only the masses, but also the classes, of that day who learnt to love the truth of the Gospel as taught by the good parson of Lutterworth, to say nothing of Lord Cobham, who died for the cause, or the Earls of Salisbury, Neville, Latimer, and the powerful Duke of Lancaster. In the royal circle itself Wycliffe had zealous supporters —' the Fair Maid of Kent,' the widow of the Black Prince; 'the Good Queen Anne,' widow of Richard II.; and secretly the good Duke Humphrey, as well as many of the clergy, including David Gothraie, of Pickering, monk of Byland. The year 1377 was also the year of the death of Edward III. and of the accession of his grandson, Richard II., whose cruel death in the neighbouring castle of Pontefract is quite within the scope of a history of Haddlesey, inasmuch as Haddlesey was then, and is still, part of the Honour of Pontefract, and of the ancient possessions of the duchy of Lancaster. The boy-King Richard ascended the throne amidst a whirlwind of excitement, caused by the peasant revolt and the poll-tax troubles. The chief disturbance from these labour wars, however, was in the southern and eastern counties, for in the fourteenth century they were, as regards industrial movements, of much the same importance as the northern and midland counties of our day. The battle which raged in Haddlesey at the end of the fourteenth century seems to have been the attempt made by the Knights Hospitallers to deprive young Philip Darcy of Temple Hirst and Temple Newsam. The attempt failed, and the Court of King's Bench decided in his favour in 1380. But again in 1402 the Hospitallers opposed the succession of John Darcy, the son of Philip; and again they were unsuccessful. We must not dismiss our notice of this nobleman, who died at Temple Hirst, December 9, 1411, and was buried in Selby Abbey, without further consideration. 'A splendid altar-tomb, with an effigy all of alabaster,' was erected to his memory, and ought to have been cherished as one of the most valuable trophies in the keeping of its authorities. A very full and interesting description of the monument and its misfortunes appears in Part xlvii. of the *Yorkshire Archæological Journal*, with a carefully elaborated engraving of the tomb, of which, by the kindness of Mr. C. C. Hodges, of Hexham, and the courtesy of the editors of the *Archæological Journal*, I am enabled to give the readers of this volume the benefit. One can scarcely imagine that so precious a monument, in so many senses of the word, should have fallen a victim

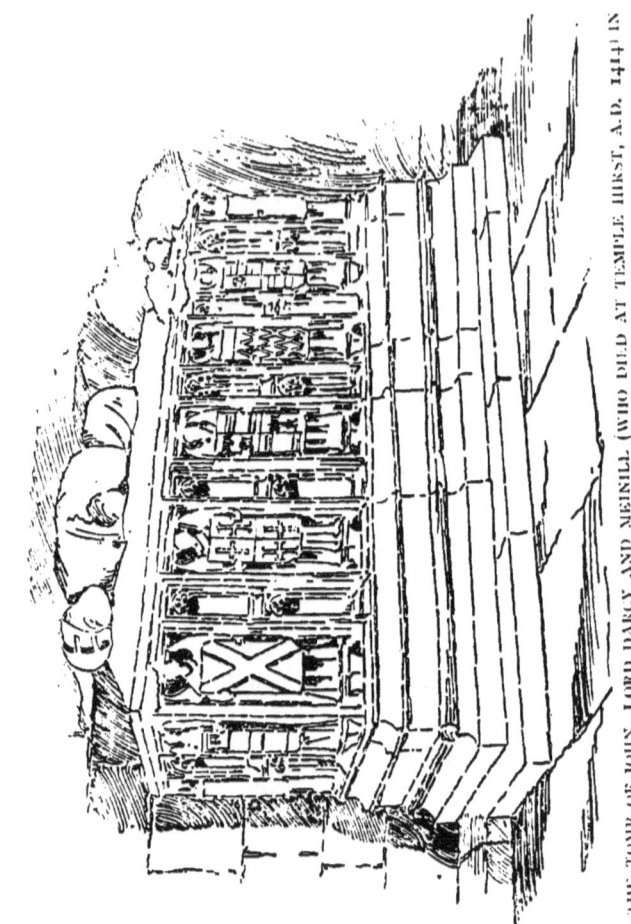

THE TOMB OF JOHN, LORD DARCY AND MEINIL (WHO DIED AT TEMPLE HIRST, A.D. 1414) IN SELBY ABBEY, BEFORE ITS RECENT MUTILATION.
Drawn by Mr. J. W. Twist, A.R.I.B.A.

to the untoward treatment which it has sustained. It is hard to understand on what pretence it was ever removed from its original site; and as to the difficulty of repairing so valuable a relic, I certainly think that a little of the zeal and liberality which displayed itself in a bazaar, yielding a net profit of some £1,500, might have been expended on the care of an object which ought to have been regarded as valuable as any part of the abbey treasures, and infinitely more unique than some of those modern embellishments which have been allowed to supersede monuments which no architectural legerdemain can reproduce. Our local interest in this tomb justifies my quoting two letters of Mr. Mill Stephenson, F.S.A., on the subject:

'To the Editor of the "Selby Times."

'SIR,

'The choir of the Abbey Church has just gone through the ordeal of a "restoration." Gravestones, as usual, have been swept into obscure corners to make way for marble pavements. One tomb—the interesting alabaster high tomb to one of the Darcy family, c. 1400, with recumbent effigy and rich in heraldry—has been wantonly and wilfully broken up, one can only suppose for the sake of the material, since the new credence-table is constructed from some of the fragments. The monument in question stood, previous to the restoration, directly under the great east window; for more than two centuries before this, and probably from its erection, it stood in the second bay of the choir. A drawing of this monument, taken in 1641, is still extant, and shows the effigy and all the shields of arms perfect. Now the mutilated trunk lies in the south choir-aisle, whilst the richly-panelled sides, adorned with the shields of the great families of Neville, Fitz-Hugh, Roos, Willoughby, etc., are placed under the east window like museum specimens. Such is the fate of one of the most interesting tombs in the church; the fragments remain for the present mute witnesses of the iconoclastic barbarism of the nineteenth-century restorer. The next step will be to consign these fragments to the obscurity of the lumber-room, where they will be lost for ever. The outlay of a small sum in the first instance would have repaired this interesting memorial of one of the greatest families connected with Selby and the neighbourhood. Notwithstanding that the mischief has now been done beyond repair, the fragments still remaining are worthy of the most careful preservation. In the neighbouring church of Brayton may still be seen a monument to the same family carefully and reverently preserved.

'I am, sir, yours, etc.,

'MILL STEPHENSON, F.S.A.

'Howden, March 28, 1892.'

'*To the Editor of the "Selby Times."*

'SIR,

'... With regard to the Darcy monument—or, as Mr. Tweedie prefers to call it, "*a* tomb"—when it stood under the east window it was plain to all people that it *was* a monument. To those conversant with our ancient monuments it told more, viz., that the figure represented a man in armour of the era known as the "camail period"—that is to say, in a mixed armour of mail and plate. The head, enclosed in a pointed bascinet, rested on a tilting helmet adorned with a crest of feathers—this latter still remains. To the bascinet was attached a camail, or gorget of mail, and over this was worn the famous Lancastrian collar of the SS. Traces of both camail and collar are still visible. The body was fully protected by armour, and over this armour was worn a jupon, or short sleeveless garment of silk, emblazoned with the owner's arms. If Mr. Tweedie will examine the trunk carefully, he will have no difficulty in finding which is the back or which the front, for just under the raised arm of the figure are still to be seen the cinquefoils and crosses which constituted the Darcy shield of arms. So far from the writer's own notes, taken in 1879, when noting the monuments in this and neighbouring churches. Traces of a lion at the man's feet then existed, but now seem to have disappeared, perhaps into the credence-table as one of the " shapeless fragments."

'Last year my attention was called to a valuable MS. containing notes on the heraldry and monuments in the Abbey Church, taken in the year 1641. In this is a sketch showing the monument, then standing on the south side of the choir, and giving the heraldry complete. The jupon bears the arms of Darcy and Grey, of Wilton. From this evidence, taken in conjunction with the shields on the sides, it appears that the monument is that erected to the memory of John Darcy, Lord Darcy and Meinill, who died 9th December, 1411, and by his will desired to be buried either in Guisborough Priory or Selby Abbey; this to depend in which neighbourhood he happened to die. His wife was Margaret, daughter of Henry Grey, Lord Grey of Wilton. His mother was a Grey of Heton; his grandmother the daughter and sole heiress of Nicholas, Lord Meinill, by Alice, daughter of William Ros, Lord Ros. His son Philip, Lord Darcy, married Eleanor, daughter of Lord Fitz-Hugh, and, dying without male issue, the barony of Darcy went into abeyance, where it still remains. The arms of all these great families are still to be seen on the fragments of the monument as now arranged under the east window.

'Mr. Tweedie says the monument was principally made up of cement. To a certain extent this was to be expected, for there is no doubt that considerable damage was done at the time of its former removal, but these "restorers" had the grace to erect it again as well as they could. Had this monument been again taken to pieces and recemented, it would have still remained a monument, and not a mere collection of fragments, as at present. Your readers may gather from this short account that the monument in question was erected to the memory of the head of one of the most powerful families in the neighbourhood, and even in its cemented condition was worthy of preservation as a monument.

'I remain, sir, yours, etc.,
'MILL STEPHENSON, B.A., F.S.A.

'Howden, April 9, 1892.'

This John Darcy died in 1411, having married Margaret, daughter of Henry Lord Grey, of Wilton, and it was from Philip's second son William that the last of the Darcys of Temple Hirst and Temple Newsam was descended. This last Lord Darcy was summoned to Parliament in 1509 by the title of Darcy of Temple Hirst. The original barony of Darcy had fallen into abeyance in the reign of Henry V. between heirs general of the eldest line, married to Conyers and Strangeways. The male line had been continued from John, the uncle of the co-heirs, and a new barony was created, as just stated above. This Thomas Lord Darcy was knighted by Henry VII., who made him Governor of Berwick, served Henry VIII. in the wars in Spain against the Moors, and was employed by him in offices of trust and honour, Henry making him a Knight of the Garter and Justice in Eyre of the forests beyond Trent.

But he sorely disliked any measures of revolt from the Church of Rome, and especially the suppression of the monasteries, as was being carried on under the direction of Cromwell the Vicar-General, though it should never be forgotten that the first movement for the suppression of the monasteries was due to Wolsey, encouraged by license of Pope Clement V., 1525.[1] And Wolsey and Lord Darcy were intimate friends, as the following letter will show, January 15, 1514. After certain requests, he says: 'Sir, when I went in my chief room and office within the court, ye and I *were bedfellows*, and each of us brake our minds to other in all our affairs, and every of us was determined and promised to do other pleasure if it should lie in either of us at any time. Sir, loving to God, now it lieth in your power to help and advance such of your friends as ye favour.' After this reminder he ventures to ask for the office of Marshal, and a discharge of a debt of £266 13s. 4d., as he is about to shift his poor plate, as his purse was never so weak. He concludes: 'Sir, every man will now seek to be your friend, and to be in favour with you; but yet in no wise forget not to cherish such as were your lovers and friends, and desired and was content with your favour and company, for your own sake only, when they reckoned nothing to have you to do for them.' Wolsey was at this time Bishop of Tournay in France, Lord High Almoner to the King, and Bishop of Lincoln, and soon after Archbishop of York; so that, with his residence at Cawood, no doubt Lord Darcy would renew his friendship with the companion of his youth. At all events, we may believe he would not neglect any opportunity in that direction. But the policy of which Wolsey was the author bore fruit in a direction little liked by his friend at Temple Hirst. Henry was not content that his favourite should suppress a few religious houses for his own special purposes. He saw an opening to replenish the royal exchequer, and so it came to pass, in the quaint language of Fuller, 'the dissolution of forty small houses, caused by the Cardinal, made all the forest of religious houses in England to shake, justly fearing that the King

---

[1] See 'Lives of the English Cardinals,' by Folkestone Williams, vol. ii. (Allen and Co., Strand, 1868), and Fuller's 'Church History.'

would finish to fell the oaks, seeing the Cardinal began to cut the underwood.'

Hence in 1536 a motion was made in both Houses of Parliament 'that, to support the King's states, and supply his wants, all religious houses might be conferred on the Crown which were not able clearly to expend above two hundred pounds a year.' The reason assigned for this measure was the grossly immoral lives led by the inmates of these houses, and the impossibility of reforming them, 'although continual visitations had been had for the space of two hundred years and more.' A clear income of £30,000 per annum, besides £10,000 worth of plate and furniture, was thus obtained ostensibly for the Crown, but only for a short time, as grants were made to the King's subjects, not so much, says Fuller again shrewdly, ' hoping that these small morsels to so many mouths should satisfy their hunger, but only intending to *give them a taste of the sweetness of abbey lands!*'

But the dissolution of these lesser houses awakened feelings of insecurity as regards the bigger, and so we find some of them not only shaking in their shoes, but also wagging their tongues in the way of rebellious protest. It was in Lincolnshire, 'one of the most brute and beastly of the whole realm,' in the flattering language of the irate monarch whose conduct they arraigned, that the rebellion broke out. Some thousands of people, made up largely out of the unpensioned monks and nuns turned adrift to beg, thieve, or starve, appeared suddenly at Louth in the end of September, 1536. On Sunday morning, October 1, people gathered on the green, and in the evening were led by Nicholas Melton, a shoemaker called Captain Cobler. The next day a crowd met in the market-place armed with bills, scythes, and staves, and the King's Commissioner barely escaped with his life. Similar scenes occurred at Caistor and Horncastle. But at the latter place Dr. Mackarel, the deposed Abbot of

Barlings, came armed with a banner embroidered with a plough, a chalice, the Host, a horn, and the five wounds of Christ. Here the insurgents formulated their demands, viz., 'the restoration of the monasteries, the remission of the subsidy, the clergy to pay no more firstfruits or tenths, the repeal of the Statute of Uses, the removal of villein blood from the Council, and the deprivation, etc., of Archbishop Cranmer, Bishops Latimer, Hiley, Longlands, and Brown.'

CHAPTER XIII.

THE PILGRIMAGE OF GRACE.

LINCOLN joined in the rebellion and became its centre. Sir Marmaduke Constable and Sir Edward Madyson meanwhile had been sent to the King at Windsor with the demands of the insurgents, and got the reply in which occurred the words already quoted as to the rude Commons of one shire finding fault with their prince, etc., ordering them by proclamation in Lincoln market-place to give up their arms and return to their homes. The appearance of an army under the Earl of Suffolk led many to withdraw, so that the 60,000 at Lincoln were reduced to 20,000, and when Suffolk entered the city he met with scowling faces, but no overt resistance. Indeed, the nobles and gentry and their labourers helped to restore order, and the towns one by one submitted. Abbot Mackarel and his canons were sent to London, and half of them set free after a short imprisonment. The Abbot himself and twelve others were hanged for the murder of the Chancellor of Lincoln. Baron Hussey of Sleaford was found guilty of high treason and fined with the loss of his barony, manor of Sleaford, worth £5,000 a year, and finally beheaded. Out of some 60,000, only a score were punished with death, and so ended in a fortnight the Lincolnshire Pilgrimage of Grace. But the spirit of revolt spread into Yorkshire, and in its development involved Lord Darcy of Temple Hirst, so that our parish was closely associated with the events of this religious war, and, indeed, some of its most significant passages took place on the very soil which we daily traverse.[1] The second outburst was much more formidable than the first, inasmuch as it embraced persons of greater weight, but who evidently entered more deeply into the aim and object of the revolt.

We must remember that the divorce of Queen Catharine and the religious changes which followed, although not caused by that event, produced very different sensations among the lower ranks in the Northern counties, and in those near and around London. In the home counties opinion was with the King. Here the cause of Spain and the creed of Rome were rejected, and the decrees which were to restore the Anglican Church to its independence and the English Sovereign to his supremacy had been arrived at long before the King and Parliament had embodied them in legal phrase. But it was not so in the North. The division of England into two Church provinces was very much of a reality in the time of the Tudor King. The two provinces had different customs, and in some things different law. York was a great capital. Monarchs had lived and fought and married and died within its walls. Parliaments had met there many a time, and a great many thought the King should again hold his Court and assemble his Parliament within this

[1] As regards Lord Darcy, it is important to note how strongly attached he was to the cause of the religious houses. For his generous benefactions to the friar-preachers at Beverley the Prior and brethren of this convent entered in a binding contract on August 29, 1524, to celebrate the anniversaries of the death of Lord Darcy and of his wife, the Lady Edith (? Elizabeth) in the most solemn and grateful manner. It is worthy of note, likewise, that Lord Darcy got special leave of absence from attendance in Parliament in 1535 because he foresaw the ruin of the religious houses, and was unwilling to give his vote therein.

ancient city. London was regarded as almost foreign to many a sturdy Yorkshireman. Yet, for all this, in all points of culture and foresight the Northern shires were much behind those of the South and West. Those instincts out of which rise a nation's greatness (with few exceptions), in the reign of Henry, had their root not alongside of the Humber and Tyne, but by the banks of the Severn and the Thames. Those silent changes in public opinion which were so welcome in the South, as seen by the reception of Wycliffe at St. Paul's and at Lambeth, by the Lollard Lord Mayor, Sir John Northampton, and in other forms, had no full counterpart in the shires of the North. In these parts men saw few travellers and read no books. They roamed through their native dales, they tented on their wolds, from youth to age; even in the nineteenth century there are men in some of the remoter districts of the North who have never gone beyond their nearest market town. Proud of their dogs, their horses, and their wives, they were at war with all outside their own special thoughts and customs. Coarse in manners and rude in speech, they were not so shocked by the moral shortcomings of their spiritual guides, the monks and friars, as Southerners were. While the laity of Kent rejoiced over the destruction of St. Augustine's, the friars of Jervaulx,[1] with their fine horses and good cheese, were looked upon as the peasants' best friends. Hence, when Darcy of Temple Hirst and Dacre of Gillesland, or 'the North,' spoke unfavourably of the changes being made in London, 'the common people took up the tale with a clatter of hoofs and pikes which echoed through the land.' It is possible, too, that Yorkshiremen had not forgotten Bosworth field. The White Rose had been worsted in conflict with the Red; and although it was true that Henry united in himself the two Roses, yet, as he was quarrelling with the Pope and

[1] More correctly Yore Vaux, or the valley of the Yore, or Ure.

making new laws, he might fight and fail, and then there might be a reversal of the position. A Yorkist prince might marry a daughter of the Red Rose. However, whatever were the motives which stirred the malcontents, it is a fact that the royal decree for suppressing monasteries met with violent resistance in the North, especially in Yorkshire. Among the more local causes of discontent was a report that some of the parish churches were to be removed so that no two should be nearer than five miles apart.

Robert Aske, a gentleman of middle age, was riding home from a hunting-party at his cousin Ellerkers, near Beverley, the end of September, 1536, when he was seized by a band of so-called pilgrims, made to swear their oath, viz., ' Ye shall not enter into this our Pilgrimage of Grace for the Commonwealth, but only for the love you bear unto Almighty God, His faith, and to holy Church militant, the maintenance thereof, to the preservation of the King's person, his issue, to the purifying of nobility, and to expulse all vilain blood, and evil counsellors against the Commonwealth, from his Grace and the Privy Council of the same, and that ye shall not enter into our said Pilgrimage, for no particular profit to yourself . . . nor slay nor murder for no envy, but in your hearts put away all fear and dread, and take afore you the cross of Christ, and in your hearts His faith, the restitution of ye Church, the suppression of these heretics and their opinions by all the holy contents of this book.' Having done this he was proclaimed their leader.

It was a strange choice. Aske was a London lawyer, totally unacquainted with the art of war. Yet here he was, on a Yorkshire wold, with a general's staff, in the midst of an excited crowd, most of them armed and mounted, clamouring to be led to London in defence of the King and holy Church. Aske began to think. Evidently he felt with those who had so suddenly elevated him to power. But he knew that if this rising of the commons was to succeed it must be led by the ancient lords of the soil, by the Percys of Wressil and the Darcys of Darcy and Temple Hirst. So he made up his mind to seek these men. Lesser men, Bulmers, Tempests, and others were coming into the camp, why not Percy? Henry Percy, sixth Earl of Northumberland, was the man of highest rank and power north of the Trent. He was the King's deputy, Warden of the East and Middle March, the fountain of authority in the border districts. Henry, the Earl, no doubt sympathized with the rebels. But he was thriftless and weak in body. He had never got over his love for Anne Boleyn, and he was mourning in his great house at Wressil, on the Derwent, her unhappy fate! When Aske and a body of riders rushed into the courtyard at Wressil, shouting 'A Percy! a Percy!' that redoubtable personage slipped into bed and sent out word that he was sick. Aske sent a fresh message—they wanted a Percy, the Earl if possible, but if not, his brothers, Sir Thomas and Sir Ingram. These young knights rose with alacrity. Henry protested feebly, and revoked the commission they held under him as officers in the East and Middle Marches. Catharine, their mother, widow of the fifth Earl, detained them with tears, as she foresaw their doom. But though they paused a moment, 'they soon leapt to horse, and, clad in flashing steel and flaunting plume, rode forward into camp, where the pilgrims received them with uproarious joy.' These very things were afterwards referred to as showing their deliberate choice. Some 30,000 pilgrims began their march towards London. York opened her gates after a brief parley. Then Aske advanced on Pontefract, the surrender of which by Lord Darcy gave him the command of Barnsdale up to Doncaster. Darcy 'captured,' at Pomfret was sworn and became a leader; also Sir John Bulmer and many more, although Aske still continued the captain. And here it will be convenient to recount other aspects of the rebellion. It is remarkable how much the Aske family were involved in it. Robert Aske, the captain, belonged to a younger branch which had settled at Aughton, and of which I am told an old man of the labouring class survives to-day. But the senior branch of the family was headed by William Aske, of Aske Park, near Richmond (now the seat of the Earl of Zetland). Alice, daughter of William Aske, married Cristofer Stapilton, of Wighill. He was a studious man, and of feeble health, and so in 1536 was at Beverley 'for change of ayer.' When the rebellion broke out, Cristofer and his second wife, daughter of Sir John Neville, of Chevet, were lodging at the Greyfriars' monastery, and the populace forced them to take the oath of alliance to the rebels, but he retired to his house at Wighill as soon as possible. But William, a younger brother, like Robert Aske, a young lawyer returning to town after his vacation, seems to have been drawn completely into the movement. His confession has furnished Mr. Froude with one of his picturesque chapters, from which and Mr. Chetwynd-Stapylton's article 'The Stapiltons of Wighill,' in *Yorkshire Archæological Journal*, I abridge. The first Sunday in October a proclamation was issued, 'Every man to Westwood Green (near Beverley) with such horse and harness as he had on pain of death and to take the oath.' After resisting, William Stapilton and his nephew, Sir Brian, reluctantly submitted; then the mob cried out, 'Master William Stapilton shall be our capitayne,' and so at length he became captain, with young Sir Brian and Richard Wharton and the Bailiff of Beverley as captains under him. On October 12 came a letter from Aske that he had raised all Howdenshire and Marshland, and would be at Market Weighton that night. All Holderness was up, they said, and they had taken Sir Christopher Helyarde and Ralph Constable and others; but Sir John Constable and his son, Sir William Constable, young Sir Ralph

Ellerkar, Edmund Roos, and Walter Clifford of Gray's Inn, and others of the King's servants had fled to Hull. Sir George Conyers and Ralph Evers had gone to Scarborough Castle. Leaving some to keep the array at Huntley beacon, Stapilton and others met Aske at Market Weighton to consider the intelligence from Hull and Lincolnshire. The Hull messengers were detained, while Nicholas Rudstone, young Metham, Robert Hotham and Stapilton rode to Hull. The citizens refused to join. On their return it was agreed to attack the town. Stapilton was now in command of about 9,000 men, and maintained strict discipline, but with difficulty. On October 20 Hull surrendered to the rebels. News of the advance of the Lord Steward against Aske led them to set out for Tadcaster, where they spent the night. At midnight they had orders to be at Pomfret the next morning. Many thousands assembled there, including thirty-four peers and knights, who met in the castle hall, while the Archbishop held a convocation in the church. A council met 'to set forth their wards.' The eastern ward was given to Sir Thomas Percy, with whom was Ellerkar, Sir William Constable, Rudstone, and the captains of Holderness and Stapilton with his Beverley men, who were to muster at Wentbridge on the Doncaster Road; Lord Darcy and Sir Richard Tempest and the western, *i.e.*, I suppose, West Riding, men, the middle ward; and Neville, Latimer and Lumley to keep the rearward with Aske. It appears that Aske was at Temple Hirst on October 19, as he wrote letters on this date to Nicholas Tempest and Sir Stephen Hammerton to attend meetings in York. However, we learn from the report of the Lancaster herald, sent by the Earl of Shrewsbury to make a proclamation, that Aske, with Lord Darcy, the Archbishop of York and others were at Pontefract on October 20. This herald gives a graphic picture of the scene which met him as he attempted to read the King's proclamation at the market cross. Aske sent for him to wait upon him at the castle, and he tells us he passed through three wards, each guarded by many in harness, very cruel fellows, and a porter with a white staff in his hand, and the castle hall full of people, where the herald was made to wait the pleasure of the rebel chieftain. When the herald was admitted to the presence of Aske, he says the latter kept his countenance as a great prince. 'He asked to see the proclamation, and read it openly without reverence to any person, and said he should not need to call any council to answer the same, for he would of his own wit give me the answer, which was this: Standing on the highest place of the chamber, and assuming the highest state, he said: "Herald, as a messenger you are welcome to me and all my company, but as for this proclamation coming from the Lords, it shall not be read at the market cross, nor in no place amongst my people, which be all under my guiding, nor for fear of loss of lands, life or goods, nor for the power which is against us doth now enter into our hearts with fear, but are all of one accord, with the points of our articles clearly intending to see a reformation or else to die in these causes."' After further words, in which the herald fell on his knees before Aske, and the Archbishop of York rebuked him, telling him he had no right to fall on his knees to any but the King, Aske dismissed the herald, first commanding Lord Darcy to give him two (5s.) crowns whether he would or not, and then led him by the arm outside of the castle and declared he was to have a safe conduct and his horses returned to him under penalty of death.

Meantime Aske and his followers move on to Doncaster. At the bridge they came to a halt. The Duke of Norfolk, a great soldier and able counsellor, the hero of Flodden Field (at which, by the way, one of our Haddlesey connections, Sir Brian Stapleton, of Carlton, was present), was there to meet him. 'Aske was strong in horse, Sir

Thos. Percy, glittering in steel and *bearing St. Cuthbert's banner*, was followed by five thousand mounted men. In all, 12,000 horse waited the signal to advance. The Duke, though weaker in numbers, kept a firm front to the north, waiting for his reserves to come in; negotiating with the chiefs, especially Darcy.'

Froude says (' History of England,' vol. iii., p. 127): ' Lord Darcy of Temple Hirst was among the most distinguished of the conservative nobility. He was an old man. He had won his spurs under Henry VII. He had fought against the Moors by the side of Ferdinand, and earned laurels in the wars against Louis XII. Strong in his military reputation, in his rank, and in his age, he had spoken in Parliament against the separation from the See of Rome; and, though sworn like the rest of the peers to obey the law, he had openly avowed the reluctance of his assent.' He then adds that, although the King trusted Lord Darcy, he was at heart with the rebels, and, as a proof, did nothing to resist their design, but shut himself up in Pomfret Castle without fuel or provisions and only twelve followers. Describing the further progress of the rebellion under Aske as its chief, with Lord Darcy and Sir Robert Constable as next in rank and influence, the historian states ' that regular posts were established from Hull to Temple Hirst, from Temple Hirst to York,' etc. He also relates an attempt of the Duke of Norfolk to win over Lord Darcy to betray Aske in the following terms: He (*i.e.*, the Duke's messenger, Percivall Cresswell) arrived at Temple Hirst on Friday, November 10, 1536, shortly before dinner. Lord Darcy was walking with Aske himself, who was his guest at the time, and a party of the commons *in the castle garden*. Next morning, after they had heard Mass in the chapel, Darcy admitted this messenger to his presence, and dismissed him.

Lord Darcy, later on, was invited to wait upon the King, but pretended he was too aged (over eighty) and too unwell to visit London. He, however, advised Aske to go, under conditions, one of which was that he should send a swift messenger to Temple Hirst if the monarch broke faith; and so Lord Darcy, though too sick to pay obedience to the summons of his King, was well enough to stand by the side of his friend in the hour of danger. Indeed, the attitude of Lord Darcy in this wretched business of the Pilgrimage of Grace is fertile in material for serious reflection, and contains lessons of most valuable thought, not merely as regards this particular epoch of English history, but for our own. Let us try and realize the state of things in our parish in the early days of November, 1536. The rebels under Aske are induced, by the plausible offers of the Duke of Norfolk, to lay down their arms, at least temporarily. Lord Darcy's castle at Temple Hirst becomes the council chamber of the contending parties. In that park, which Darcy had fenced in for himself by royal license, steeds rush to and fro bearing missives from the Duke to Darcy. One of these was a proposal that Darcy should tell the Duke of Aske's whereabouts, with a view to surrender him. So Darcy says to his friend : 'Shall I give thee up ?'

However strongly one's sympathies may go with what we may call the reforming tendencies of Henry and his chief adviser Cromwell at that time—and certainly my sympathies are with the measures, if not exactly the men who carried out the measures and the methods by which they were carried out—yet it is impossible not to be deeply touched with the position of such a man as Lord Darcy. He had everything to lose and nothing possibly to gain by siding with Aske and his party. A man of Darcy's experience must have known that after a very short struggle the rebels would be overmatched and that frightful retribution would follow the suppression of the outbreak. Why, then, did he hesitate ? I do not think it was from either cowardice or treachery. No, it was a far different cause. He had not learnt those principles of patriotism which was evinced by a later son of the house of his neighbours at Carlton, viz., that, when the claims of the Pope and the King come into collision, then duty to the King must take precedence of that to the Pope (see speech of Thomas Stapleton, Lord Beaumont, in House of Peers on debate of Ecclesiastical Titles Bill, 1851). Lord Darcy was evidently under the influence of the doctrine that the Pope was above the King. He, in common with Aske and his followers, thought that the interests of religion were in jeopardy, and they came forward with a reckless disregard of every other consideration to defend 'holy Church.' That they were mistaken does not detract from the chivalry of their conduct; but it does supply a very much-needed warning for us in this nineteenth century. Under the blinding influence of personal ambition and the degrading slavery of party exigencies, we find men hoary in years, boasting of their Parliamentary experience and political sagacity, ready to tear down the last small relic of protection against Papal aggression erected by our forefathers; and others, in their forgetfulness of all the teachings of our marvellous national history, aiding and abetting this criminal proceeding with a trustfulness and a docility which would be delightful if it were not so unspeakably dangerous. It is strange that men who can rave about the perils of sacerdotalism, where sacerdotalism is an odious parasite, yet have no fear of it where it is enthroned and fortified by the most terrible enactments which superstition could devise; and claims, which laugh to scorn either popular rights or royal prerogatives. Although the book which political Nonconformists profess to revere teaches them to 'Fear God and honour the King,' yet we find these parties giving their most infatuated support to schemes which practically set aside the Divine injunction! And although the words I have quoted are the words of that

Apostle whom the Church of Rome, by abusing the *metaphoric* language of early Church writers, claims as the first Bishop of that historic Church and 'Prince of the Apostles,' still she regards them not, but, instead of teaching men to honour the King, adds the neutralizing comment, ' only when he obeys the Pope '!

Here, then, is the secret of Lord Darcy's seeming treachery and disloyalty, and one cannot refuse the expression of regret that under the influence of this unscriptural and unpatriotic sentiment he should have pursued a course which dragged him from his home at Temple Hirst and brought him to the dishonoured death of a traitor on Tower Hill. The crisis, however, did not culminate at once. The pardon proclaimed by the King at Windsor on December 9, 1536, led to the disbanding of the rebel forces, Aske himself going to the King, by whom he was very favourably received. But in the meantime dissatisfaction was felt at the delay in carrying out some of the promises made by the King. Meetings of the disaffected were held at 'Temple Hyrst' on January 17, 1537, at which it was said that Lord Darcy, Nicholas Tempest, and others 'persevered and continued in their treasons subsequently to the King's pardon.' Also that on January 28 of the same year various letters and correspondence were mutually sent and received at Temple Hirst. A special commission was addressed to the Duke of Norfolk and Sir Thomas Tempest, Knt., Sergeant-at-Law, in April, 1537, and on May 3 following a precept sent to the Sheriff of Yorkshire commanding him to return a grand jury of fifty gentlemen to meet at York Castle on May 9 following. Norfolk wrote to Cromwell in answer to instructions from the King, and Cromwell from Sheriffhutton on May 8 : '. . . . Doubte ye not, my lord, but that the matter shall be found according to the King's pleasure.' Among the grand jurors' names were the two foremen (for the jury was divided into two bodies), Sir Christopher Danby and Sir James Strangways, and among other jurors were Sir Thomas Metham, Sir Nicholas Fairfax, Henry Ryther, John Aske, eldest brother of Robert; and in the other set Sir Henry Everingham. The relationship of some of the jury to the prisoners has been noted, but Nicholas Tempest was cousin to Dousabella Tempest, wife of Lord Darcy.

On Wednesday, May 9, 1537, the prisoners, Sir Thomas Darcy, 'late of Temple Hyrst, co. York, Knt.; lord Darcy, otherwise Thomas Darcy; lord Darcy, late of Tempyl Hyrst, Knt.;' Sir Robert Constable; Sir Francis Bygod; Sir Thomas Percy; Sir John Bulmer; Margaret Cheyne, wife of William Cheyne, Esq., late of London (Lady Bulmer);[1] Robert Aske, late of Aughton;

[1] Mr. Hepworth Dixon ('Her Majesty's Tower,' fifth edition) gives us such a racy picture and stirring story of this remarkable woman that I think I may be excused for borrowing largely from it. She supposed herself married to Sir John Bulmer, whose troop having been disbanded by the Lord-Lieutenant (Lord Surrey), he returned to his eyrie, Eston Nab, on the Cleveland Hills, called Wilton Castle, in a sore spirit. But the news which wandering friars brought of the conflicts between King and Pope gave him fresh hopes of finding work for his sword. So, stirred by his cousin William (third Lord Dacre of the North), he took up the tale of sedition and joined the Pilgrimage. Urged to this more by hate than love, as the Duke who was coming to oppose the Pilgrims was the very man who had broken him as a soldier and branded him as a coward. So he goes forth, attended by his son, his brother, and his faithful Madge. Now she, too, had her grudge against the Duke. Norfolk was her kinsman, and she and others thought he could have done more to save her father, Edward, Duke of Buckingham, from Wolsey's malice. At the second outbreak a fire was lighted on Eston Nab, and Madge cried, 'Now is the time; up and join them!' Another idea was that they should descend from their wild retreat, raise Guisborough, seize the Duke, and carry him by force to Wilton Castle. But while they were dreaming of this bold attempt the officers were at hand, and in a few hours Sir John and Madge also were marching South. They pleaded guilty and were condemned to die. Madge met the most terrible fate

James Cokerell, late Rector of the Parish Church of Lythe, co. of York, formerly Prior of Guisborough; William Wood, late Prior of Bridlington; John Pykering, late of Lythe, clerk, and John Pickering, late of Bridlington, of the order of Preaching Friars (at Beverley ?), who were greatly mixed up with the Pilgrimage; Adam Sedbergh, Abbot of Jervaulx; William Thriske, late Abbot of Fountains. A true bill being found, Lord Darcy and his companions were hurried to London for further trial. They were lodged in the Tower, the Constable there being directed on May 14 to bring the prisoners before the Lord Chancellor, Sir Thomas Audley, and his fellows at Westminster.

On Wednesday, May 16, Sir Brian Hastings, the High Sheriff of Yorkshire, was ordered to send to the same place by Thursday, May 17, twenty-four gentlemen ' of the visne (voisinage, neighbourhood) of Tempylherst, Brydlyngton, Flamborough, Aughton, Baschehall, and Wilton, co. York,' who had no affinity with the prisoners, to act as jurors. Most of the prisoners were dragged on a hurdle from the Tower to Tyburn, and there hanged and quartered.

Lord Darcy was executed on Tower Hill June 20, 1538, and afterwards buried at St. Botolph's Church, without Aldersgate. His feelings during the trial are thus given by Froude:

'On the 9th of May, 1537, Darcy was the subject of examination. Careless of life, and with the prophetic insight of dying men, he turned, when pressed with questions, to the Lord Privy Seal: " Cromwell, it is thou that art the very special and chief causer of all this

of all. The wild daughter of Buckingham was sentenced to die by fire, and being carried in a cart to Smithfield, she was placed in the centre of a pile of faggots, and on the very spot where so many noble Lollards had been burnt her passionate life was licked up by the flames.

rebellion and mischief . . . and dost daily earnestly travail to bring us to our ends and to strike off our heads. *I trust that ere thou die, though thou wouldest procure all the noblemen's heads within the realm to be stricken off, yet there shall one head remain that shall strike off thy head."* '—
—' History of England,' vol. iii., chap. xiv.

'On the 22nd of May the King desired the Duke of Norfolk to make due search of such lands, offices, fees, farms, and all other things as were in the hands and possession of the Lord Darcy, Sir Robert Constable, Nicholas Tempest, and all the persons of those parties lately attainted here, and certifye the same to his Grace, to the entent he may conferre them to the persons worthy accordingly, and likewise cause a perfect inventory of their lands and premises to be made and sent up with convenient speed.'

The following, extracted from Additional MSS. 6,155, in the Record Office, London, probably was in obedience to the King's order :

' Court Roll of the Manor of Temple Hirst.—Names of copyholders composing the court held Apl. 19th, 1540, are as follow : the heirs of Sir Gregory Hastings, do. of Sir Thos. Metham, do. of Radulphus Hopton, do. of John Cresaker, do. of Thos. Gascoigne, Wm. Tarrald, Charles Drunnfeld, Kt., Rd. Baxter,[1] Rd. Hartelay, John Mawdesley, John Templar, Willm. Bolton, Wm. Mastall, Wm. Womersly, John Kynge, Senr. and Junr., Wm. Hoyle, George Norman in Haddlesey, and about twenty others for Kelyngton, three by the name of Alleyn and one Thos. Hassard. The court levied fines to the amount of 44s. 11d. for the admission of new tenants to the manor.'

Among the documents preserved in the same file of MSS. as that from which the preceding extracts are taken is the will of Agnes Hassard. It begins :

[1] The Baxters of Hirst still survive in this parish. In 1596 John Baxter of Hirst was married to Mary Harrison of Gribthorpe.

'In the name of God, Amen. The last day of October, the year of our Lord God a thousand fyve hundreyth and xxxixth. I, Agnes Hassard of Kellyngton, vydow, sycke in body and howle in sowll and off gude memorye, ordines and makys thys my testament coteyning my last will in manr foloyinge.

'Ffyrst I bequeyth my sowl to Almyhty Gode, or Lady Saynt Marye and to all the Holy Copany in Heyven: and my body to be buried win the churche-yarde of Saint Edm. of Kellyngton.

'Item, I bequeyth to the *high altar for tithes negligently made* iiijd. Item, I bequeyth to the Rode lyght iiijd. Item, I bequeyth to the seypurchur light iiijd.'

Then she goes on to make about twenty other bequests to different persons of corn, cattle, clothing, etc. We select the following as the most remarkable:

'Item, I bequeyth to Pr. Richd. More, Vicar of Kellyngton, 2 linen sheets. To Agnes Grenfylde one brown gowun. To Janet Reyn my best gowun and *my hatt that she bought wt two church ewes.* To Arthur Green and Agnes his sister eyther of them one speyninge calfe. To Xpfer Grenfyld my three best kyrtels with the sleeves belonging to the same. To Jane Willinson my violet kyrtell. To James Grenfyld my wayne, my plough and yoke and teymes with all thereto belonging, with vj oxen, iij stocts,' with the remainder of her property, and appoints him her 'full executor to fulfill thys my last wyll and to do for my sowll at syght of my overseers. These I make my overseers: Pr. Rd. More of Kellyngton; Pr. John Jaffrason, and Robert Grenefyld, to se that thys my last will be fulfilled according as my mynde was and as my especiall trust ys in them.

'Witness hereof: Richard Wettworth,
Priche Clarke,
James Langton.'

Below is written in Latin in another hand that the will was proved at Temple Hirst in the presence of John Nevill, Knight Seneschal there.

The will of William Fauge of Campsall, dated March 14, 1538, is also with this file of MSS., and was proved before Sir John Nevill at Temple Hirst.

Temple Hirst with Temple Newsam, after the rebellion of Lord Darcy, seems to have been granted in 1544 by Henry VIII. to Lord Lennox and Lady Margaret, his wife, and subsequently falling into the hands of the Crown, were bestowed by James I. on his cousin, Esme Stuart, second Duke of Lennox and Richmond, who had married the only daughter and heiress of Sir Henry Darcy. His extravagance led to the alienation of Temple Newsam, which became the property of Sir Arthur Ingram.

The 'List of Court Rolls of some Yorkshire Manors, 1572-73' (*Yorkshire Archæological Journal*, vol. x.), gives us another glimpse of the state of things at Temple Hirst. We translate from the Latin, as these can be seen in the authority just noted :

Temple Hirst, 1572.—View of frankpledge at the court of our very noble lady Countess of Lennox, held there 9 of Oct., 14th year of Q. Elizth. :

Free tenants' total fines, xxij*d*. Thos. Metham, Kt. (4d.) ; the heirs of Hugh Hastings, Kt. ; the heirs of Elizth. Savell, excused ; Geo. Darcy, Kt., for lands *formerly Tempest at Gateforth;* John Baxter, Senr. ; Wm. Caverde (or Saverde), for lands in Thorpe formerly Darralls ; Roger Wentforth, by right of his wife, for lands lately Dransfield, in Walding Stubbs, fine iiij*d*. ; John Skelton, right of his wife ; Joan Gascoigne, widow, fine 2d. ; Wm. Myleson, excused ; Rd. Brearley, excused ; Edmund Watkinson ; Wm. Tayleyor, excused ; John Seynter (or Santerre) ; Robt. Lovedey, excused ; Thos. Baxter, for land in Carlton, excused ; John Baxter, excused; Jane Stockall, widow; Henry Freer, fine iiij*d*.; Thos. Cowper; Edmund Lambie, fine iiij*d*.; Wm. Allanson and John Moore, fine iiij*d*., are free tenants who owe service to this court.

Customary tenants: Joan Stokall; John Barret, fine 4d.; Henry Lande; Robt. Loundey; *Joan Hassard* (perhaps a relation of Agnes, see p. 168); Edmund Holton, fine 4d.; John Templeyerde, fine 4d.; Wm. Womersley; John Jackson; Edmund Frobisher; Henry Barker; John Risby; John Chapman; Thos. Redhouse, fine 4d.; John Allan, excused; Robt. Tomson; Wm. Fenny; Rd. Allan, fine 4d.; Rd. Tayleyor, fine 4d.; Henry Hodgson; Christofer Leche; Wm. Wardtham; Henry Allan; Wm. Pagett, right of his wife; Robt. Wayde; Robt. Arnerde, fine 4d.; Wm. Babthorp, miles; Agnes Tather; George Laciter, by right of his wife, excused; John Leche; Christofer Allan, dead; John Aubie; Thos. Sayle, fine 4d.; Rd. Ellis, excused; Wm. Thorpe, Robt. Cowper, and Rd. Wright are customary tenants, etc.

Inquisition of twelve men are sworn, and Alice Tather does homage and is admitted as tenant of fourth part of two houses and a fourth part of an acre of land which Edmund Tather surrenders.

The will of Wm. Stockall is proved, and administration granted to his widow Jane, and Edmund and Anne Stockall exors. Also the will of Isabella Hodgson, late of Kellington. Henry Hodgson also surrenders a messuage and a bovate and half of land and pasture, with belongings, in Kellington, for the use and enjoyment of Robt. Hill and Elizth., his wife, for a term of 21 years, from the feast of St. Martin next, at a yearly rent of 28s. 4d., to be paid half-yearly.

Two cases of affray and assault between Charles ffarer and Peter Saynter are dealt with by fines, etc.

Wm. Stokall and Joan, his wife, who held a messuage and six acres of land and meadow, etc., in Temple Hirst in common, asked permission of the court that the reversion owing to the death of the wife should be allowed to his son and nearest heir, ten years old, which was granted in a fine, vijs. vj$d$.

Temple Hirst.—View, etc., 15th year of Elizth, 1573:

A jury of twelve sworn. A kind of County Court action takes place between Rd. Crabtree, who sues Agnes Peper for 15s. (*pro uno quarterio et dimidio brasii*). Defendant pleaded she only owed 12s. 6d. The jury decided in her favour.

George Laciter and Joan, his wife, paid a fine of 6s. 8d. for license to let third part of one messuage, one cottage, $4\frac{1}{2}$ acres of meadow, one close called Hogge Ridding, and one called foal hagg, with appurtenances in Temple Hirst to Christopher Lech for a term of six years, etc.

The aforesaid George Laciter, clericus (probably Vicar of Darrington), and Joan, his wife, in full court before the Steward, Joan herself appearing alone (her husband died in 1571), and being examined, surrendered another third of the above property to Robert Tomson, his heirs and assigns in perpetuity.

Charles ffarer was charged and fined xij$d$. for felling by his servants and carrying away growing woods of the lady of the manor without her license.

Henry ffreer, a tenant of the court for a cottage at Camelforth in the jurisdiction of this court, having died since the last meeting of the court, Henry, his son and heir, was admitted, etc.

The above documents are very instructive as showing how justice was administered in this parish some three hundred years ago, and how persons in those days who had disputes to settle or crimes to punish betook themselves, not to the court-house, Selby, but to the manor-house at Temple Hirst; *i.e.*, the ancient preceptory.

CHAPTER XIV.

THE DARCYS AFTER THE PILGRIMAGE OF GRACE.

IN consequence of this confiscation of the property of Lord Thomas Darcy, Temple Hirst is to know the Darcys no more as owners and residents. Still, this ancient family are not annihilated, and we will devote a little more space to recount briefly their after-history, so far as it is connected with local interests.

George, the eldest son of Lord Darcy of Temple Hirst, was betrothed to Dorothy, daughter of Sir John Melton, according to Rev. Joseph Hunter's 'South Yorkshire,' vol. ii., 1831 edition, from which we chiefly borrow the remainder of our statements concerning this family. She died on September 21, 4 and 5 Philip and Mary, 1557. In the inquisition taken at Doncaster on October 17 following, we find what lands she brought to her husband: The manors of Killom, Swine, Aston, *Carleton*, Owstwick, and Hatfield, co. York; with 40 messuages, 60 cottages, 4,000 acres of arable, 500 acres of meadow, 3,000 acres of pasture, 100 acres of wood, 2,000 acres of moorland, and £5 rent, with the appurtenances in Killom, Swine, Aston, Aughton (in Rotherham), Harwick, Waleswood, Brookhouse, Whiston, *Carlton* (in Royston, I presume), Catwick, Austwick, and Hatfield; and a certain pasture called Melton Lees, and an acre of land in Hooton Roberts, with the advowson of the church appendant.

This would be a very seasonable addition to the fortunes of the house of Darcy, which, though of right ancient and noble descent, had been weakened by heiresses and confiscation.

Ten years after his father's death George Darcy was restored in blood. He was a much less conspicuous man than his father. While his father was living (1535) he served the office of Sheriff of the county of York. In 1556 he had a commission from Queen Mary to raise what forces he could on an apprehended insurrection in the North and expected invasion from Scotland. The latter years of his life were clouded by the misconduct of his younger son, George Darcy, who, in one of those feuds which were rarer in the sixteenth century than in the preceding, had assaulted and slain his neighbour, Lewis West, a son of Sir William West, at Rotherham fair, on Whitsun Monday, 1556. (Under the head of Aughton, p. 173, the author states that Lewis West lived at Wales, near Aughton.) The feud was between the whole family of Darcy and the whole family of West, but the chief actors were the two sons of Lord Darcy and the two sons of Sir William West. Neither the origin of the feud nor its end is given, but a long ballad written by a contemporary writer, of which a copy is preserved in the Ashmole Library, No. 6,933, vol. xlviii., p. 55, blames John and George Darcy, the sons of Lord Darcy.

The first document (apart from the ballad just referred to) which mentions this painful transaction is a letter by the father of the Darcys, preserved in the memoirs of the Foljambe family. This letter, written from Aston twenty-one days after the fight (May 28, 1556) states that the eldest son is 'sore hurt,' and offers to surrender himself to Sir James's keeping, or Lord Darcy will provide bail. On November 11 a compromise was made as regards John Darcy, but exempting George from its provisions. Later on George took sanctuary at Westminster, but was publicly whipped and did penance in a white sheet, etc., on December 6. But on February 10 of the next year he was arraigned at the bar of the King's Bench and challenged to combat, but what happened afterwards is left in oblivion. The father, Lord George Darcy, died September 23, 1558, and was buried at Brayton Church, where a handsome tomb of marble with ten shields was erected to his memory. This tomb has happily escaped the treatment awarded to that of his ancestor in Selby Abbey, and through the courtesy of the late Vicar, the present Bishop of Beverley, Suffragan of York and Archdeacon, we are able to present our readers with an engraving thereof. Around the tomb is the following inscription :

'Here lieth LORD GEORGE D'ARCY and LADY DOROTHEA, his wife, daughter and sole heiress of John Melton, who died 23rd day of September, 1558, on whose souls may the Lord have mercy. Amen.'

Whether it was the painful memories of his son's disgrace which led the father to choose Brayton as his burial-place rather than Aston, his chief seat, is difficult to say; but as Lord George Darcy was at one time the owner of Gateforth House estate, having sold it to Mr. Burke, whose grandson, the famous old Humphrey Burke, was writer of the Court letters in the time of Queen Elizabeth, he may have wished to be laid at Brayton, in the near vicinity of the place where he had spent his boyhood with his famous father, K.G., etc.

He was succeeded at Aston by his son John, who lived there during the long reign of Elizabeth. The care of Doncaster was entrusted to him during the rebellion of the two Northern earls (Northumberland and Westmoreland) in 1569. This movement was for much the same

TOMB OF LORD GEORGE DARCY, SON OF THOMAS, LORD DARCY, OF TEMPLE HIRST, IN BRAYTON CHURCH, BEFORE ITS RECENT ALTERATION.

objects as the Pilgrimage of Grace (mustering at Durham, they burnt the Bible and celebrated Mass in the Cathedral), and threatened to be still more formidable had it not been for the prompt measures adopted by the Queen in sending Lord Sussex, Sir Ralph Sadler, and others into the North. In 1573 Lord Darcy seems to have gone into Ireland with the Earl of Essex, and in 1584 Sir Ralph Sadler speaks of him as 'living besides Sheffield,' and receiving with much joy and comfort letters from the Queen. He died in 1592 at Aston, and was buried there. His only child, Michael, predeceased him, but left a son named John, who became the fourth Lord Darcy of his line, and was called ' John, Lord Darcy the Younger, and sometimes 'the good Lord Darcy.' He enjoyed the estate of Aston above thirty-two years. He spent his life chiefly as a private individual, seeking the happiness and religious welfare of those around him. Gervase Markham challenged him to a duel in 1616, but Lord Darcy declined, and Markham was censured by the Star Chamber (Harleian MSS., 3,638, 6,807).

One of the four wives of this Lord Darcy was remarkable for her patronage of Puritan ministers. This was the daughter of Sir Christopher Wray, the widow, first, of Godfrey Foljambe, Esq., and, secondly, of Sir William Bowes, and who was living at Walton, the house of the Foljambes, when she married Lord Darcy. She was the great patron of Carte,[1] Barnard, and Rothwell,[2] all celebrated names in the history of Northern Puritanism.

[1] ' Mr. Cart, near Sheffield' (says Oliver Heywood), 'a great scholar, a good man, a good preacher, a Nonconformist, dyed in beginning of Sepr., 1674. This is a great losse, being an useful man in these parts' (vol. i., p. 306).

[2] Rothwell was one of Mr. Frankland's pupils at Rothwell, and became minister at Poulton le Fylde June 7, 1693; afterwards at Tomley, near Wigan, and Holcombe Chapel, near Bury, about 1712. He died February 8, 1731. At Holcombe the congregation numbered 570, of whom twenty-three had county votes.

One of the divines supported or patronized by her probably drew up the 'Memorial of the Happy Life and Blessed Death of the Right Hon. Religious Lady, Isabel Lady Darcy of Aston,' which was in the library of Thoresby, the Leeds antiquarian.

Among Hopkinson's MSS. are several poems relating to this Lady Darcy, who is happily described in one of them as belonging to the class of 'Virtue's true people, with honour's gold enchast.'

Two of the shortest I transcribe:

> 'Virtue, religion, prudence, piety,
> Munificence and hospitality,
> Honour, the Graces, Truth and equal right,
> Living with her—yea, living by her sight,
> Are banished, vanished, fled, decayed and gone,
> Since her decease, that gave them life alone.'

Again, p. 164, 'Upon the Day and Time when she died, Jan. 27th, Sunday, about noon,' A.D. 1622:

> ''To wreath their wrath the Fates espied their time,
> .   .   .   .   .   .
> And on the Sabbath; then they held it best
> To waft her hence to her desired rest;
> That such a nurse to God's most sacred word
> Might keep eternal sabbath with the Lord.'

After the death of this lady Lord Darcy married his third wife, viz., Mary Bellasis, a daughter of Lord Fauconberg. The year 1624 was one of great affliction to Lord Darcy. In April he lost his only son, aged twenty-two; in June the younger of his two daughters; and in September his wife at the age of nineteen, after giving birth to a son, who died in infancy and was buried at Aston. Only one daughter by his first wife remained—Rosamond. She was baptized at Aston February 9, 1606. She died in 1628, just as her marriage with Lord Brook had been arranged. But, notwithstanding these domestic trials, Lord Darcy seems to have taken an active part in superintending the drainage of Hatfield Chase, in conjunction with Viscount Wentworth, Lord President of the North (Stovin MSS., *Yorkshire A. and T. Journal*, vol. xxvi.).

The fourth wife of Lord Darcy was one of the co-heirs of the Wests of Firbeck. By his will, dated January 23, 1633, he appointed her sole executrix. He leaves Mr. William Fletcher, preacher of Aston, £13 6s. 8d. (Mr. Fletcher was presented by Lord Darcy to the living in 1631); Mr. Thomas Burney, assistant to Mr. Fletcher, £10; to John Angel, his godson, minister at Leicester, £10 per annum out of the manor of *Swillington*, and £20 in money. There is a funeral sermon by this John Angel for Lord Darcy. Aston was settled on this lady, as she continued to reside there after the death of Lord Darcy (1635) until her death in 1669, as did her second husband, Sir Francis Fane, till his death in 1680.

No issue remaining from the last Lord Darcy, the representation of himself and Dorothy Melton rested in the issue of Henry Saville of Copley, Esq., and *Ann Darcy, his wife,* the only sister of Lord Darcy; but they seem to have been entirely passed over in the disposition of these estates, which, after having been held by the Dowager Lady Darcy and her husband for forty-five years, passed to the male heir of the house of Darcy, the descendant and representative of Sir Arthur Darcy, a younger son of *Thomas, Lord Darcy,* and brother of George, Lord Darcy, who married the heiress of Melton. This branch of the family had been enriched by the marriage with a co-heir of the Baron Conyers of Hornby Castle, at which place they resided till, on the death of Sir Francis Fane, Aston became theirs, and afforded them a more convenient and agreeable residence. Soon after Conyers Lord Darcy became possessed of Aston he was advanced to the rank of Earl of Holderness.

Pedigree of the Noble Family of Darcy of Aston.

Thomas Lord Darcy, beheaded 1538, =Dousabel, dau. of Sir Richard Tempest.

Children:

- **George, Lord Darcy**, died Sept. 23, 1558, =Dorothy, dau. and heiress of Sir John Melton of Aston.
- **Sir Arthur Darcy**=Mary, dau. and co-h. of Sir Nicholas Carew of Beddington.

Children of George, Lord Darcy:

- **John, Lord Darcy**, son and heir, aged 28 A.D. 1558; bur. at Aston Oct. 19, 1602. =Agnes, dau. of Thomas Babington, of Dethick.
- **George.**

Children of Sir Arthur Darcy:

- **Elizabeth**=Bryan Stapleton of Carlton.
- **Thomas Darcy**
- **Elizth.**, dau. and co-h. of John, Lord Conyers of Hornby.
- **Clara.**
- **Mary**=1. Hen. Babington. 2. Hen. Foljambe.
- **Agnes**=Sir Wm. Fairfax of Gilling.
- **Edith**=Sir Thos. Dawney of Cowick.[1]
- **Dorothy**=Sir Thos. Metham.

The pedigree is continued by Hunter, p. 165, but the only point of interest is that the

- **Conyers, Lord Darcy**, who received that title 17 Chas. I., and died 1653. =Dorothy, dau. of Sir Henry Belasis, of Newborough.
- **Henry Darcy**, Esq. =Mary, heiress of Wm. Scrope, Esq. See escutcheon in St. Olave's, York.[2]

Conyers, Lord Darcy and Earl of Holderness, died June 14, 1689, and was buried at Hornby. =Grace, dau. and heir of Thos. Rokeby, Esq., of Skiers.

Conyers, Earl of Holderness, died in 1692. =Frances,[3] 3rd wife, dau. of William, Duke of Somerset, widow of Lord Molyneux.
=Elizabeth, 4th wife, dau. of John, Lord Freshville of Staveley, widow of Philip Warwick, Esq.

- Ursula=Sir Christ. Wyvill, Bart.
- Elizth.=Sir Henry Stapylton, Bart.
- Grace=Sir John Legard.
- Margaret=Sir Henry Marwood.
- Ann, died unmarried.

---

[1] In 1603 James I. grants the manors of Temple Hirst and Greenlagh to Sir David Fowleys (the ancestor of Viscount Downe) and his heirs. Temple Hirst was valued at £64 17s. per annum, and Greenlagh at £53 7s. 4d.

[2] On the north side pillar hangs up a wooden frame whereon is this escutcheon depicted : Azure, three cinquefoils and semée de crosslets argent for Darcy, impaling azure a bend or for Scrope, and this inscription : 'Here lyeth interred the bodies of Ye Right Honble. Henry Darcy, Esq., 3rd son of the Right Honble. Conyers, Lord Darcy Menhill and Conyers, who departed this life ye 28th day of April, 1668, anno ætatis suæ 57. And Mary Darcy, his wife, daughter and heiress of William Scrope of Heighley Hall, Esq., who departed this life ye 17th April, 1667 ; who had issue 10 children. Now they both rest in Christ, waiting for the blessed resurrection of the Just.'

[3] There is some confusion here. Compare the pedigree from Burke, p. 113 ante.

A John Darcy died unmarried April 21, 1624, aged twenty-two, and was buried in Westminster Abbey. Another John Darcy, eldest son of the second Earl of Holderness, died June 7, 1688, before his father and grandfather, and was buried in Westminster Abbey.[1] The fourth and last Earl of Holderness died May 16, 1778, aged fifty-nine, and was buried at Hornby. He married Mary, daughter of Sieur Francis Doublet, a Dutch noble, and from him the Darcy and Holderness peerage became vested in the Duke of Leeds. (See Burke's Peerage and Hunter, vol. i., p. 144.) Sir Conyers Darcy was a P.C., and M.P. for Richmond, co. York.

Robert, fourth and last Earl of Holderness, was Lieutenant of the North Riding, Ambassador to Venice and Holland, in 1751 P.C., Secretary of State in 1761, in 1765 Warden of the Cinque Ports and Governor of Dover Castle, also Governor to William IV. and his brothers.

The Earls of Holderness, who resided much at Aston, rebuilt the house, partly because of fires, and especially one which nearly destroyed the whole fabric, and consumed, it is thought, a MS. history of the family of Darcy.

In 1771 the last Earl of Holderness sold Aston to Mr. Verelst, late Governor of Bengal. The property still belongs to his eldest son, Harry William Verelst, Esq., although the patronage of the Rectory belongs to the Duke of Leeds.

In the east window of Aston Church is a shield of the arms and quarterings of Darcy, viz. :

1. Darcy, azure, semée of cross crosslets, three cinquefoils argent.

---

[1] This John Darcy was associated with Thomas Osborne, then Earl of Danby, and William Cavendish, Earl of Devonshire, in the surrender of the city of York to the Prince of Orange, A.D. 1688. (Baine's 'Yorkshire, Past and Present'). This fact, coupled with those we have recently read of the Darcys of Aston, seem to show that the later generations of the family had no sympathy with the cause which cost their ancestor of Temple Hirst his life and estates.

2. Bertram, gules, an inescutcheon and orle of cross crosslets, argent.

3. Tempest, argent, a bend between 6 martlets, sable.

4. Azure, a chief, or. (Note.—In this place we generally find among the Darcy quarterings: azure, a fess between three fleurs-de-lis for Skelton.)

5. Melton.

6. Lucy.

7. Hilton, argent, two bars azure, on the uppermost a fleur-de-lis, or.

8. Darcy, crest, a bull passant, sable, as may be seen in the arms of the present Duke of Leeds.

CHAPTER XV.

THE STAPLETONS OF CARLTON AND BARONS BEAUMONT.

IT is now time we gave some account of another branch of the Stapleton family, associated more or less with the history of this parish for seven or eight hundred years—a family which, unlike the other great houses of which we have been writing, still holds its titles, although not all the lands which it once had in our parish and neighbourhood.

To avoid useless repetition, we commence our pedigree of this branch of the great Stapleton family with

Bryan Stapleton, jun.=Elizabeth de Insula, heiress of Sir William Aldeburgh
(m. 1371). of Harewood.

William of Aldeburgh (the old town), near Boroughbridge, built on the site of the Roman Isurium, had summons to Parliament as a baron from 44 Edw. III. to his death in 1388. Marrying the heiress of the last Lord Lisle (Insula) of Rougemont, opposite Harewood, he purchased that castle and manor from Lord Harewood in 1365 for £1,000. His arms, with the predestinarian motto, 'Vat sal be sal,' or, as the Beaumonts of our day have it, 'Che sara, sara,' are still to be seen over the chapel window of the castle, also over one of the entrances to Carlton Towers. By the death of his widow and only son in 1391 his two daughters became heirs to his estate. A few scattered notices of Elizabeth, who married Bryan Stapleton, seem to imply that she had embraced the doctrines of Wycliffe, like many in her station in these parts at that time; *e.g.*, her mother left her a ring inscribed 'Jesu, be my help;' Sir Robert Ross of Ingmanthorpe, a French work called 'Sydrak,' in 1392. She had legends of the saints from his son in 1399, when she is first called Lady Elizabeth Redman. It would seem she was not on good terms with her father-in-law, who left her a table with a coronation of the Virgin in enamel and a medal of Our Lady in 1396 on condition that she behaved well. In 1413 she had a ring from Sir Henry Vavasour of Haselwood. She seems to have had two sons by Brian Stapleton, who died in 1391; viz., Sir Bryan, who married Agnes, daughter of Sir John Goddard, and John of Flamborough.

Taking the last first, there is a curious entry in Patent Roll 14 Rich. II., part 2: 'Grant to John Stapulton, varlet of the Duke of Lancaster, at the request of the Duchess, Jan. 9th, 1391.' Confirmation of recent grant of 'officium tronagii ville nostra di Kyngeston super Hull' to John Stapulton, at request of Constance, late Duchess of Lancaster, June 30, 1398 (Patent Roll, 22 Rich. II., part 1). I take it that 'officium tronagii' means a collector of tolls, probably market tolls, arising from the use of a weighing machine.

With regard to Brian, he succeeded at his grandfather's death in 1394, being quite young. In May, 1416, it is said he 'remained' about the King, so that he may have left England the year before, when Henry laid siege to Harfleur and won the splendid victory of Agincourt. In the commission of May, 1416, we find the names 'of the Earls of Northumberland, March and Salisbury, with Brian Stapilton, Thos. Rokeby, and other chevaliers.' Some of the prisoners taken at Agincourt were awarded to Sir Brian Stapleton. At the end of July, 1417, Stapleton seems to have been in the company of Lord Salisbury with five lances and eighteen archers. Salisbury, after taking the castle of D'Anvillers, joined the King before Caen. The English marched out of Caen on October 12, taking Courcy, Argentan, Seiz, Verneuil, and Alençon in succession; made a treaty with the Duke of Brittany at the latter place November 16. It was in this month, October 13, that Sir Brian met his death. He was only thirty years of age. He was buried in the church of the Friar Preachers at York, 1417.

Sir Brian left in charge of his widow: Elizabeth, born in 1404; Joan, afterwards wife of Sir William Ingleby; Isabella; and Brian, heir of Carlton, born November 6, 1413, so he was only four years old at his father's death. He was baptized in Carlton Church (*ecclesia villæ de Carlton*). The first time it is mentioned, the license for this place of worship is given in Coucher Book of Selby Abbey, vol. ii., pp. 132, 133. License for Carlton Chapel by Henry IV., November 20, 1410: 'Henricus, Dei Gracia Rex Angliæ et Franciæ et dominus Hiberniæ, etc. . . . . de gracia tamen nostra speciali et pro viginti marcis quas dilecti nobis Johannes Gybonson et Johannes Herdyng de Carlton juxta Selby nobis solverunt in banaperio nostro concessimus et licenciam dedimus pro nobis et her, quantum in nobis est, eisdem Johanni et Johanni quod ipsi (one as cantarist, the other as chaplain), etc., at the principal altar of the chapel of the Blessed Mary in town of Carlton, near Selby, for our own health while we live and for our soul when we die (pro anima nostra cum ab hac luce migra verimus), or for the soul of our dearest consort Mary, late Countess of Derby, and for the health of Brian de Stapilton and the aforesaid J. G. and J. H. while they live, and for their souls when dead, or the souls of their relatives and benefactors, on the days appointed by the aforesaid John giving and confirming for this purpose, one messuage, seven cottages, 126 acres of plough land, 20 acres of meadow, 4 acres of wood, and 20s. rent, with all appurtenances in above-named town of Camylford (Camblesforth) . . . that they may give to aforesaid chaplain for him and his successors, to have and to hold, etc. Witness myself at Westminster 20th day of November in 12th year of our reign.'

He marries in 1451 Isabel, daughter and heiress of Sir Thomas Kempston, Kt. By this marriage the Stapiltons acquired the manors of Rempston and Hingham, Notts. Sir Thomas Kempston was half-brother of Sir Robert Plumpton's wife, *Alicia Foljambe*, the heiress of Kynalton. On June 24, 1452, was born the first child of this marriage, young Brian the fifth, and baptized in the Chapel of Carlton, as it is now called (*in capella villæ de Carlton*). Mr. Chetwynd-Stapylton gives a circumstantial account of the christening in the *Yorkshire Archæological Journal*. The same year Brian, the father, was returned to Parliament as one of the Knights of the Shire with Sir William Gascoigne, of Gawthorpe Hall, son of the Chief Justice. The Parliament was strongly Lancastrian. Brought up in the guardianship of the Duke of Bedford, we might suppose that Sir Brian would be an adherent of the same cause, but the orders he received from the Duke of York to go with his father-in-law and Sir John Melton to seize young Henry Holland, Duke of Exeter, out of sanctuary at Westminster, indicate a leaning to the other side. They brought him to Pontefract, but he was released on the recovery of Henry. The Yorkist cause was popular, it is said, in all the towns and manufacturing districts owing to the misgovernment of the Lancastrian nobles, though the superior title to the throne of Edward may have also contributed to win support. We have no record of Sir Brian's taking part in the famous fight at Towton on Palm Sunday, March 29, 1461. But the second Viscount and Baron[1] Beaumont was one of the prominent supporters of the Lancastrian party on that fatal field. He was taken prisoner, and though his life was saved, he lost his title and estates until restored 7 Hen. VII., A.D. 1492. Sir Bryan himself died in 1467, having a few months before been admitted into the Guild of Corpus Christi at York. His son, Brian the fifth, who succeeded him, was a minor. He married Joan, sister and heiress of Francis, Viscount Lovel, and *niece of the last* Viscount Beaumont of Towton Field celebrity.

The Beaumonts were always Lancastrian.[2] John de Beaumont, the sixth Baron, had been advanced by Henry VI. to the dignity of Viscount. He was the first who bore that title in England by reason of his descent from the Viscomtes of Maine. The Lovels also were steadfast Lancastrians. John, the eighth lord, who married Beaumont's sister, held the Tower of London for King Henry when Warwick landed from Calais in 1459. He died in 1465, and his son, Francis Lovel, then a boy of nine, was put in charge of Delapole, a Yorkist. This Delapole was restored to the dukedom of Suffolk in 1463.[3] So Lovel joined that party, and attaching himself

---

[1] The barony of Beaumont, it is interesting for Haddlesey folk to remember, dates from 1309, the year when Baron Stapleton got license to *rebuild* their ancient chapel.

[2] 'So when the Duke of Lancaster landed at Ravenspur in 1399 he was joined by Lords Willoughby, De Ros, DARCY, and Beaumont.'—Smollett, Hist., vol. iv., p. 207.

[3] As regards this dukedom of Suffolk, it was associated with the Stapiltons before this date, for the charter of John, Duke of Suffolk, enrolled on Close Roll 16 Edw. IV., has this record: 'The honourable and my most dradde lady and mother, Alice, Duchess of Suffolk,' says in her will that she bought the manor of Norton-under-Hampden, co. of Somerset, for £200, of Lady Catherine, then wife of Sir Miles Stapleton, and now wife of Ric. Harcourt, Knight.'

to Richard, Duke of Gloucester, was in the Scotch expedition of 1482 created a Viscount in 1483 and a Knight of the Garter. At Richard's coronation he bore the Sword of State before the King, and was made Lord Chamberlain, etc. He was almost the only one of Richard's adherents who survived the last charge on Bosworth Field. His end was tragical.

But to return to Brian Stapleton who was about the same age as his brother-in-law, Lovel, and followed his career. At twenty-three Sir Brian Stapilton was made Knight Banneret at Sheriff Hutton, 1483. In 1484 he has the Archbishop's license to marry Alice, relict of Sir William Nevill of Calthorp, 'in the chappel of his manor of Carlton, the banns being once asked between them in their parish churches.' On the 23rd of the same month he has a license from the King ' to fulfil certain vows and pilgrimages at Compostella, in Spain, accompanied by Richard Holt and a chaplain.' He died intestate 1496, aged only forty-four, and was succeeded by his eldest son, Brian Stapilton the sixth, who has license to enter on his father's estates in 1497, though not yet of age. He must have been in favour at Court, for he was made a Knight of the Bath in 1503, when Henry, Duke of York (afterwards Henry VIII.) was created Prince of Wales. He was also at the battle of Flodden Field in 1513 in company with Sir George Darcy of Temple Hirst, and the tournament of the Cloth of Gold in 1520. He married, first, Elizabeth, grand-daughter of John, sixth Lord Scrope of Bolton, who in a memorandum attached to his will, dated July 3, 1494, confirmed a promise to his son (the seventh lord) towards the marriage of his daughter Elizabeth to a gentleman cleped Stapilton (then aged eleven), 'cccc marks in iiij yeres. It to stand good.' After her death Sir Brian married Joan, daughter of Thomas Basset, Esq., of Rutland, and died in 1547, leaving children by both wives. The eldest son, Richard, succeeded to

Carlton, and married as his first wife Thomasin, daughter and co-heiress of Robert Amadei, goldsmith, Master of the Jewel House to King Henry VIII. He died in 1550 at TEMPLE HIRST, January 11; buried at Snaith. He was succeeded by Brian Stapleton, who married as his second wife Elizabeth, daughter of Lord George Darcy of Aston. In 1585 he was Sheriff of Yorkshire, and died December 13, 1606—'head of that noble house;' buried at Snaith. There were sons of this marriage—Richard, Miles, died young; Thomas, Brian, George; Robert of Temple Hirst, baptized at Snaith June 6, 1575; married Mary, second daughter of Sir Robert Dolman of Gunby, who died December, 1623.

Sir Brian Stapleton, second son of the above, was killed in the abortive action of the Royalists near Chester, 1644. The Carlton line resumes itself in Richard Stapleton, eldest son of Brian, who died in 1606. His second son, Gilbert of Carlton, 'a recusant,' married Helen, daughter of Sir John Gascoigne of Lasingcroft and Bamborough, co. York, Bart. From this marriage was born Richard Stapleton, born 1620-21, and died *s.p.* 1670; Gregory, a monk at Douay, who gave up his birthright to *his brother Miles*, born October 19, 1626; created a Baronet March 20, 1662. Bought Drax and Berrickhill. His first wife was Elizabeth (Mary), daughter of Robert Bertie, Earl of Lindsey, K.G., etc., slain at Edgehill. She died in 1683-84, and was buried at Snaith. Sir Miles's second wife was Elizabeth, daughter of Sir Thomas Longueville, Bart., of Woberton, Bucks. She died 1706, and was buried at Snaith, aged seventy-nine. Anne Stapleton, sister of Sir Miles, born at Carlton 1628; married Mark Everington, Esq., of Ponteland, co. Northumberland. She left a son, Nicholas Everington, born 1660, who took the name of Stapleton. *He was of Quosquo* Hall, sole executor of Sir Miles Stapleton's will; died December 7, 1716, and was buried at Carlton, aged fifty-six. His first wife was

Mary Scrope[1] of Danby, who was buried at Carlton 1695. His second wife was Mary, daughter of Thomas Sandys of Worcester. They married in 1699, and she died 1755, aged fifty-four. From this marriage was born Nicholas Stapleton, *alias* Everington (died 1750), married Winifred White, who died 1761, aged forty-seven. The third son of this marriage was Miles Stapleton of Clints and Drax, buried at Carlton October 24, 1808, aged sixty-six. He married as his second wife Mary, daughter of Willoughby, Earl of Abingdon, who died 1826. They left a son, Thomas Stapleton of Richmond and Carlton, under the will of Lady Throckmorton in 1839. He was born April 28, 1778, and died July 6, 1839, aged sixty-one. He married, first, Maria Juliana, daughter of Sir Robert Causfield Gerard, Bart., November 3, 1802. She died at York February 9, 1827. There was issue of this marriage: Miles Thomas Stapleton of Carlton, one of the co-heirs of the barony of Beaumont, and as such summoned to the House of Lords October 16, 1840. He was born June 4, 1805, and married September 9, 1844, Isabella Anne, eldest daughter of Lord Kilmaine, and died August 10, 1854; buried at Carlton. By the second wife (of Thomas Stapleton, who died in 1839), Henrietta Lavinia, second daughter of Richard Fitzgerald Austen, Esq., there were several children : first, Bryan John Stapleton, of the Grove, Richmond, and D.L. of North Riding, Yorkshire, late Captain 4th West Yorkshire Militia, born January 6, 1831, and married June 24, 1857, Helen Alicia,

---

[1] It was this lady who presented the pair of silver candlesticks to York Minster in 1673, and about the lighting of which there was the extraordinary mistake in Archbishop Benson's judgment on the prosecution of the Bishop of Lincoln. In this judgment it was stated that lighted tapers were to be placed in these candlesticks at *every* service instead of 'at *evening* service from All Saints' to Candlemas.' Such an error is the more remarkable because it had been corrected in the Second Report of the Ritual Commission.

only daughter of J. T. Dolman, Esq., Souldern House, Oxon, M.D., a former claimant of the barony of Stapleton. They have a numerous family. Another descendant of this second marriage is Henry Edward Chetwynd-Stapylton, of London, to whom the readers of the *Yorkshire Archæological Journal* are much indebted for very valuable papers on the Stapleton family in all its branches, as well as on the Knight Templars of Temple Hirst, etc.

Henry Stapleton succeeded his father, Miles Stapleton, as ninth Lord Beaumont. He was born August 11, 1848. He was a Knight of the Order of St. John of Jerusalem, Knight Grand Cross of the Order of the Holy Sepulchre, Lieutenant in the Life Guards, and by virtue of his descent from Louis VIII. of France styled cousin by the French kings. He married July 20, 1888, Violet, only daughter of Mr. Wootton Isaacson, M.P. for Stepney, and died January 23, 1892. He is succeeded in the title by his brother, Colonel Miles Stapleton, born July 17, 1850, who married Ethel, daughter of Sir Charles Tempest, November 7, 1893.

Considering the close connection of this family with our parish, and the kindly interest it has shown in the well-being of the neighbourhood, we can but wish that no adverse circumstances may be allowed to banish the Stapletons of Carlton from the magnificent house which under humbler architectural conditions has been the home of so many generations of that ancient and distinguished family, however true may be their motto, 'Che sara, sara!'

CHAPTER XVI.

THE FITZWILLIAMS AT EAST HADDLESEY.

WE now resume the story as it belongs more particularly to the centre of the parish. The church and the Fitzwilliams claim our attention. All through the troublous period of the religious disturbances during the latter part of the reign of Henry VIII., up to the beginning of the Civil War time of Charles I., we have traces of the Fitzwilliam connection with our parish. The following table may serve to show this more easily:

```
      Sir William de Fitzwilliam ─┬─ Maud, dau. of Ralph, Lord Crom-
  of Sprotborough, Hathelsay, Knight │  well of Tattersall, etc.
  of the Holy Sepulchre.             │
                                     │
             Sir John Fitzwilliam ─┬─ Eleanor, 1st wife, dau. of
          of Emley and Sprot-      │   Sir Henry Green.
          borough, died 1418.      │
                                   │
         John Fitzgerald ─ Margaret, dau. of      Nicholas ─┬─ Margaret, dau. of
  of Sprotborough, died at │ Sir Thos. Clarell.            │  John Tausley.
  Rouen 1421.              │                               │

  Sir William Fitzwilliam ═ Elizabeth, dau.   Ralph Fitzwilliam ═ Joan, dau. of
  s. 1421; died at Hathel-  of Sir Thos.      of Hathelsay, Cap-  │ Rd. Bolton
  say 1474.                 Chaworth.         tain of Salvaterra, │ of Hathel-
                                              Aquitaine, 1441.    │ say.
```

a

The Fitzwilliams at East Haddlesey.

John Fitzwilliam, = Margery, dau. of John Clervaux
eldest son ; died in 1542 ; buried | of Croft ; living in 1516.
at Birkin.

John Fitzwilliam = Elizabeth, dau. and heir of Chris-
of Haddlesey, eldest | topher Damory of Crockwell
son. | Grange : living 1540.

| John Fitzwilliam = Eliz. of Aldwick, grandson and heir, aged nine at death of his grandfather, who died at Hathelsay 1474. He died himself 1512. | 1. John, died beyond sea March 10, 1562-7, *s.p.*
2. Hugh, the antiquary.
3. Ralph, *s.p.*
4. Anthony.
5. Ralph, a merchant ; died in Spain. | 6. William, went to Ireland ; d. 1567, *s.p.*
7. George, travelled in Africa, etc.
8. Nicholas, born at Haddlesey; d. in London 1562, *s.p.*
9. Thomas, born at Haddlesey: d. in 1567, *s.p.* | Elizabeth, born at Plumtre. Ann, born at Haddlesey. |

CHAPTER XVII.

HADDLESEY CHURCH: ITS CLERGY AND ENDOWMENTS.

THE clergyman next in succession to Ralph Levet seems to be John Thackeray, appointed in 1584. But we are not sure as to his patron, and the same remark applies to his successor, James Sibbald, M.A., of the University of Aberdeen, and Master of the Grammar School, Snaith.

To turn again to the ecclesiastical history of Haddlesey, allusions occur in certain documents which seem to imply that chantry chapels were added on to the main building. The word 'triptite,' used by John Hathelsey, may refer to three foundations. There is nothing unusual in this circumstance, but if these were apart from the chapel of St. John the Baptist in East Haddlesey, they seem, like the income bequeathed to the chaplain, to have disappeared. As regards both these points, the following quotation from the Patent Roll, 4 Jas. I. (1607), paragraph 13, is interesting and instructive: 'Concession was made in consideration of good faith and accepted service by Oliver Cromwell mil.[1] of portions of 2 houses and sundry lands nuper (late) of the *Chantry of St. John the*

---

[1] Sir Henry Cromwell, father of this Sir Oliver, was called 'the Golden Knight' from the largeness of his gifts. He received Queen Elizabeth at Hinchinbrook in August, 1564.

Evangelist in Haddlesey. It will be remembered that the original *chapel* was dedicated to St. John the *Baptist*.' The Sir Oliver Cromwell mentioned in the above gift appears to have been the nephew of the Lord Protector Cromwell put to death by Henry VIII., as desired by Lord Darcy previous to his own execution, and the uncle of Oliver Cromwell, who was one of the chief instruments in putting to death a successor of Henry's on the English throne. 'The accepted service,' which procured Oliver Cromwell of King James's day his title and share of the endowments of the church at Haddlesey, seems to have been a very sumptuous entertainment provided for the King on April 23, 1603, at Hinchinbrook House,[1] near Huntingdon, as he was on his way from Scotland to take possession of the English throne. Although the entertainment exceeded in costliness any offered before by a private subject, Sir Oliver added thereto a gift of horses and hounds for his Majesty's use. Indeed, his liberality was so great that he was compelled to sell Hinchinbrook in 1627 to Sir Sydney Montague, father of the first Earl of Sandwich.

Again, the year after we read that 'concession was made on the petition of Roger Aston, mil., to Roger Aston, Kt., and John Grymesdiche, gentleman, of half a house and garden *in East Hathelsey nuper of the chantry of the Blessed Virgin*, Hathelsey, and the Duchy of Lancaster.'

Also, A.D. 1611, we find that certain lands in East

---

[1] Hinchinbrook House was originally granted by Henry VIII. to his Minister, Sir Richard Williams, who assumed the name of Cromwell (*English Illustrated Magazine*, May, 1888). Before this it was a nunnery, to which the nuns of Ettesley, in Cambridgeshire, are said to have been removed by William the Conqueror, who is, therefore, the founder of the priory of the Benedictine Order dedicated to St. James. Lord Cromwell was succeeded by his son Gregory. See 'Life and Times of Sir Ralph Sadleir.'

Hathelsey were assigned to Edward Bates of London, haberdasher, and Henry Ellwers, also of London, gentleman. At this time, likewise, the manor of East Hathelsey, with the free rents, late Sir Leonard Dacre's, attainted, were conveyed to Thomas Granage. Again, the above-mentioned manor, together with those of West Haddlesey and Birkin, with court-leet and view of frankpledge, were in the year 1615 conceded to William, Lord Cavendish (Pat. Roll, 12 Jas. I., paragraph 26). The same year also we find that *Edward Bates* (see above) obtained the following additional grants of land in Hathelsay, viz.: six acres in the occupation of William Watson for 2s. 6d.; also a tract called 'Irnespurland,' 'tenanted by one' William Cowper (a frequent name), 18s. per annum and three acres more called Selby Row. The above word 'Irnespurland' sets one asking where and what this land could be. Knowing that on February 12, 1426, Robert Lacy of Gaytford bequeathed two acres of 'priest land' between John Strensall, Vicar of Brayton, and Hugh Sherley, priest of Haddlesey, I guessed that 'Irnespurland' might really be a corruption by some transcriber of the word 'two priests' land,' and my conjecture is strengthened by the circumstance that the trustees of this gift were William Pall, Vicar of Riccall, and John de Riccall, priest (see Morrell's 'History of Selby,' p. 314), while in the *Selby Times* of January 24, 1890, appears an advertisement offering for sale 'all that close of land, formerly in *two* closes, called the Beast Lands, *otherwise Priests' Lands*, etc.' So the probability is that Mr. Robert Lasey, although living at Gaytforth as a 'domicelli' (? 'domicellus'), indicating, possibly, office under a nobleman, or relationship to one of those Lacys who were feudal lords there, was yet owner of property in his own right at Riccall, and out of his estate there made a bequest to the priest at Haddlesey, which, like some other gifts for a similar purpose, had been alienated from the church to which they were given. The appropriation of Church property to laymen for secular uses is an old disease, although it has broken out with greater violence in our own day.

But we are now approaching a period in which there was to be even greater ecclesiastical changes than these acts of petty spoliation. Haddlesey was to be powerfully influenced by these coming events. In the meantime we have to record what was not, perhaps, a very usual event —the marriage by license at Haddlesey of John Methley of Birkin to Joan Scruton of Haddlesey in the year 1612. Let us hope that their married life was one of peace and prosperity, notwithstanding the period at which they pledged 'their troth either to other.'

In thirty years after this date we find the framework of the organization of the National Church violently dealt with. When Charles I. came upon the throne and opened the Long Parliament, things looked most promising for continued peace and maintenance of the institutions of the country, but there had been changes in theological opinions going on which would bear fruit presently. Under Elizabeth all the leading clergy, including the bishops, held distinctly Augustinian views of doctrine, while they were strongly attached to Episcopacy and to the liturgy and offices of the Church as established at the Reformation period; but under Charles I. a number of the clergy, of whom Laud was a conspicuous example, became Arminian in their theology, so that when Bishop Morley was asked 'what Arminians held,' he wittily replied, 'The best bishoprics and deaneries in England.'

Well, this change of religious opinion was partly in consequence of a greater respect for mediævalism than was felt by the divines of the Elizabethan era, and in many cases it degenerated into formalism and ceremonialism, which showed itself in habits of increasing worldliness, which the 'Book of Sports,' issued by James I., and afterwards by his son, accelerated, and also accelerated the spirit of dissatisfaction which, later on, resulted in such terrible suffering for both King and country as makes one feel that Englishmen should never forget nor cease to be on their guard against conduct which may lead to any like results again. It is said that Laud kept a ledger in which he recorded what he supposed was the theological and ecclesiastical bias of all the clergy, as a guide to the King in his exercise of his patronage. 'O' and 'P' were the letters at the head of the two lists. On the one—*i.e.*, Orthodox—all favours were showered; on the other—the Puritans—there were nothing but frowns.

In 1633 Charles unwisely endeavoured to impose an episcopal government on Scotland, with accessories especially distasteful to the people of that land. The consequence was an outbreak which did not limit itself to the north of the Tweed. So that an agitation in Parliament began against the English Church, the cowardly legal murder of Strafford, the removal of the Bishops from the House of Lords in 1642, and the confiscation of their private as well as their public incomes shortly after. In 1643 committees were appointed in all the counties for sequestrating the incomes of benefices (although tithes were ordered to be paid as heretofore), and for inquiring into the lives, doctrines, and conversation of all ministers and schoolmasters. However, through the kindness of Mr. Kershaw, the obliging librarian of Lambeth Palace Library, I am able to give original and authentic details of the action of the Commissioners in this parish and neighbourhood.

Taken from the 'Parliamentary Surveys,' vol. xviii., p. 247, in the Lambeth Palace Library:

'Anno 1650.

' BIRKIN.

'Wee finde for the Parish of Birkin a Parsonage or Rectory presentative with cure of Soules, the gleabe, Tythes and proffitts thereof, worth about one hundred and sixtye pounds per ann.

'Mr. Everingham Cressye is Rector of the said parsonage, and hath the advowson of the Rectorye, who receiveth the proffitts, and hath for his Curate one Mr. David Barnes, a painefull Mynister, to whome he alloweth ffiftye pounds p' ann. for his Sallarye.

'Wee finde one Chappell onelye for the said parish, called Hadleseye Chappell, in w^{ch} *Chappellrye* are these Townes (viz.), Hadlesey West, East Hadleseye, and two Hirsts. It is three myles distant from the Parish Church and onely twelve pounds p' ann. maintenance belonging . . . wch is received by one Mr. Bryan Ffisher, who supplyeth the cure there and is laborious therein.

'Wee think fitt that the said Chappell of Haddlesey be made a Parish Church, and the said Mr. Cressey to have the advowson thereof, and ffurther that one third parte of the value of the said Parsonage be added for Mayntenance of a Mynister there, the other two partes to goe to the Mayntenance of a Mynister att the mother Church of Birkin.'

With regard to Mr. Everingham Cressy, Rector and patron of Birkin in 1650, he seems to have been related to Adam de Everingham, who was summoned to Parliament from 2 to 9 Edw. II. This Adam de Everingham was nephew of John de Everingham of Birkin, whose lineal descendant and heir general, Eleanor Everingham, married in 1547 to Gervas Cressy, and was great-grandmother of Everingham Cressy of Birkin, referred to in the above document; but as there is a little romance in the story, I mention further that Dorothea, his daughter and sole heiress, became the wife of Archibald Primrose, Earl of Rosebery, and so was great-grandmother of the present Prime Minister of Great Britain!

'By the Trustees for the better maintenance and incouragem^t of preaching ministers and for uniting of parishes. *March 4th*, 1655.

'*Haddlesey and Birkin.*—Whereas the Rectory of Birkin in the county of Yorke is of the yearly value of one hundred and threescore pounds, and whereas there is within the said p'ish the chapelry of Haddlesey, having in it the townshippes of East Haddlesey, Temple Hurst, and Hurst Courtney, which said Townshippes are three miles distant from the said p'ish church, and the yearly sum of twelve pounds is the only maintenance for a minister of the said chappele *over and above what profits may be allowed out of the said Rectory* and by a Survey of the said p'ish and chappelry taken by virtue of a commission under the great seal of England, in pursuance of an *Act of Parliament* intituled an Act for providing maintenance for preaching ministers and other pious uses, appeareth upon consideration thereof and of the petition of severall of the parishioners of the said p'ish *within the Chapelry of Haddlesey* aforesaid. And after hearing partys on all sides concerned, these Trustees think fit, and it is ordered by consent of Everingham Cressy, Esq., patron of the said Rectory, *David Barnes, Incumbent* of the said Rectory, and the inhabitants of the said Rectory, that the said townshippes of East Haddlesey, West Haddlesey, Temple Hurst, and Hurst Courtney, and all messuages, lands, tenements, and hereditaments within the said townshippes, and the precincts and limitts thereof bee and stand severed and divided from the said parish church, and made one distinct parish, and that the same be from henceforth deemed and adjudged one distinct p'ish, to be endowed as well with all former pensions and salary as due and payable to the minister of the said Chappellry, as with the tythes and the profitts of the said Rectory from time to time *arising, accruing, incoming,* and growing out of the townshippes, Hamletts, and precincts of East Haddlesey (West Haddlesey, see back), Temple Hurst, and Hurst Courtney aforesaid, and that the chapele of Haddlesey, bee the meeting-place for the said inhabitants of the townshippes so to be divided as aforesaid. And that there be from henceforth one rector and incumbent of the said Rectory and parish, and to be from time to time presented, nominated, and appointed to the Church of Haddlesy, hereby appointed as aforesaid by the patron of the said Rectory and Church of Birkin aforesaid, to be from time to time maintained out of the aforesaid pensions, salarys, tythes, and profitts arising as aforesaid, without any further charges upon the public revenue. And that the first fruits of the said Rectory of Birkin and Haddlesey, amounting to thirty-six pounds, shall from henceforth be p'portionately divided between the incumbent of Birkin and the incumbent of Haddlesey; that is to say, the incumbent of Birkin and his successors shall pay for the first fruits of the said Rectory of Birkin the sum of twenty-two pounds tenne shillings, and the incumbent of Haddlesey and his successors shall pay for the first fruits of the said rectory of Haddlesey the sum of thirteen pounds tenne shillings, and that the Tenthes of the said Rectorys be divided p'portionately between the respective incumbents of Birkin and Haddlesey and their successors; that is to say, the incumbent of Birkin and his successors shall pay two pounds five shillings a year for the tenths of the said Rectory of Birkin and the incumbent of Haddlesey and his successors shall pay one pound seven shillings a year for the tenths of the said rectory of Haddlesey. All which we humbly testify to his Highness the Lord Protector and Counsell.

'Given under our handes the day and yeare aforesaid.

'Jo. Thoroughgood, Jo. Pocock, Ri. Yong, Edw. Hopkins, Ri. Sydenham.'—Parliamentary Surveys, p. 51.

'*July* 21, 1656.

'*Haddlesay and Birkin*.—The Trustees having the 4th of March, 1655, resolved upon the dividing of the Chappell of Haddlesay from the P'ish Church of Birkin in the County of York, and making the same a distinct p'ish of it selfe, and ordered the reporting thereof to his Highness and the Counsell for their approbation therein, which hitherto is not obtained, notwthstanding which the Trustees are informed that by colour of the said resolution of these trustees and report, several of the inhabitants of Haddlesay interrupt the interest of Mr. David Barnes, incumbent of Birkin, with the said chappell of Haddlesey, detaining from him the tithes of the said chapelry, the Trustees do hereby declare that the said David Barnes ought not to be interrupted in the quiet enjoyment of the tithes of Haddlesay aforesaid until upon approbation of his Highness and Counsell the Trustees shall have made and perfected the said division under their handes, and seals to be inrolled in Chauncery, and doo therefore leave the said Mr. Barnes to his quiet poss'ion and injoym^t of the p'fitts of the said Chappelry of Haddlesay, and doo recommend it to all whom it may concern to give him all due assistance in his enjoyment of the premises against all opposers.

'Jo. Thorowgood, Rd. Hall, Ri. Young, Jo. Pocock, Ri. Sydenham.'—Vol. 991, p. 139.

'June 13th, 1658.

'Instrument for severing the township of East Haddlesey (and West), Temple Hurst, and Hurst Courtneye, and making the same a distinct parish from Birkin.—Augmentation of Church Lands, Lambeth Palace Library, MSS. 1015, p. 38.

'*Haddlesey, in ye County of Yorke.*—'Thomas Pickard Clerke. Admitted ye 27th day of October 1658 to the Rectory of Haddlesey in ye County of Yorke. Upon a presentation exhibited the 15th day of the month from Everingham Cressy Esqre the Patron and certificates from Thos. Calvert,[1] George Wilson,[2] Rob. Hall, Thos. Belasis.'[3]—Vol. 999, p. 121.

In consequence of this appointment, then, Brian Fisher, who is represented as fulfilling his duties as a 'laborious preacher' at Haddlesey, on what was equivalent to £60 per annum of our money, to the great discontent of the inhabitants, *who wished to give their tithes to him* instead of to Mr. Barnes, who succeeded Mr. Everingham Cressy as Rector of Birkin in 1654—we now find Mr. Thos. Pickard duly installed as Rector, with all the profits of the ecclesiastical revenues arising out of the four townships which

[1] Thos. Calverts, a famous Puritan preacher, born at York, B.A. of Sidney Sussex College, Cambridge. Having been episcopally ordained, he was chaplain in the family of Sir Thos. Burdett, Bart., at Foremark, in Derbyshire; Rector of Christ Church, York, in 1838. In 1644, after the surrender of York to the Parliamentarians, the Rev. Thos. Calvert, with three other ministers, were appointed to be the four city preachers, with suitable stipends. In 1662 Mr. Calvert was deprived of his benefice. He was a man of universal learning and greatly respected; among his friends were Matthew Poole and Christopher Cartwright, both, like himself, natives of York. He died in 1679, and was buried in the church of his native parish, All Saints' Pavement, York.—Davies' 'Walks through the City of York.'

[2] Wilson of Monk Frystone.   [3] Possibly of Danby Wisk.

were to form the parish as to-day. How long Mr. Pickard remained at Haddlesey, and what was his career, or even his classification among the parties, so varied at this time, it is impossible to say. As his name is not to be found in any Nonconformist list, not even that of Dr. Calamy, which mentions Mr. David Barnes, Rector of Birkin, as one of the 2,000 expelled by Act of Uniformity in 1662, notwithstanding my laborious search in scores of volumes, public libraries, questions addressed to editors of likely literature, and privately to eminent writers in this kind of historic research, such as Dr. Grosart, Dr. Stoughton, and others, I am inclined to think that he was one of those who, while not caring to run counter to the ordinances set up by Cromwell, which forbade the use of the Prayer-Book and substituted the Directory for the Liturgy, yet secretly preferred things as they had been to things as they were. At all events, it is noteworthy that so staunch a Churchman as Mr., afterwards Bishop, Bull was appointed to the rectory of Luddington, near Cirencester, *the very same year as Mr. Pickard was appointed to Haddlesey.* Mr. Bull had been ordained privately deacon and priest on the same day by Bishop Skinner of Oxford during this troublous period when he was only twenty-one years of age; his contemporary, the afterwards celebrated Bishop Jeremy Taylor, was also ordained at this time, when only nineteen. Whether Mr. Pickard belonged to this class it is impossible to say with any degree of positiveness, but it is not forbidden to think that he may have been such. Had he been one of the expelled for conscience' sake after the Restoration, we think it likely his name would have been preserved in some form, especially as the Pickards are so numerous a tribe in this part of Yorkshire.[1] That he was removed from

[1] Apropos of this statement, I find from the registers of St. Mary's, Hull, published in *Yorks Archæological Journal,* vol. xii., that Mr. Christopher Pickard was minister of that church up to December 9,

Haddlesey when Mr. Stone, who was appointed Rector of Birkin on May 15, 1654, was dismissed at the restoration[1] of Robert Thornton to Birkin in 1664, is highly probable. Apart from the feelings of irritation which would naturally exist in the mind of Mr. Thornton in recollection of his barbarous treatment, there would be that intelligible but not intelligent spirit of overturning everything done during the Commonwealth, whether good or bad. Again, no doubt Mr. Thornton would consider that the new arrangement about the income of his benefice,

---

1656, when he was buried; that on March 30, in the previous year, his son William is said to have been born, but I think, as he is called 'Mr. William,' there is an error, and buried is meant. Whether the Rector of Haddlesey was one of this family is an interesting question. I find also from the *Yorkshire Post* of November 18, 1893, that Elyas Pickard was appointed Vicar of Thorp Arch September 18, 1668; he died, and was succeeded by John Gibson, January 2, 1672. The present Rector of Thorp Arch, the Rev. W. H. Jackson, kindly supplements the above by telling me that whilst he has no record of the induction of E. Pickard, yet that his predecessor was inducted March 11, 1624, and was buried March 20, 1667. And he further adds from the parish registers that Faith, daughter of Mr. Elias Pickard, Vicar of Thorp Arch, was baptized March 5, A.D. 1670. So it seems there were Pickards holding Church preferment in Yorkshire after the Restoration.

[1] 'The restoration of Robert Thornton the second to Birkin,' brings us to another tangled web in our story. Quoting from Forest's 'History of Knottingley' and other accepted authorities, the Birkin Rectory stands thus: 1612, Robert Thornton, May 27; 1654, Wm. Stone, March 4; 1655, David Barnes; 1662, September 30, Robert Sorsby, S.T.B., who had been appointed Precentor of York Minster September 2, 1661, and who held that office to the day of his death, August 15, 1683, and was buried in the north aisle of the Minster choir under a blue stone; he was descended from the first master cutler of Sheffield, and an ancestor of a family now spelling their name Sorby, and who are well represented in Haddlesey parish. As Robert Thornton was restored to Birkin March 30, 1664, I take it that Mr. Sorsby had been put in by the Puritan party. On his gravestone at York he is said to have been educated at Cambridge, at *Emmanuel College*, which was a notable seminary of the early Puritans.

which had been made without his consent being asked, was one to which he was not obliged to conform. So we come to a very dark period in the history of our parish —the zeal of its early inhabitants, backed up by the munificence of the Stapletons and Hathelseys of the fourteenth century, all disregarded, and their bequests, so far as untouched by previous spoliation, carried off to the credit of the revenues of Birkin. And Haddlesey so recently constituted in a way befitting its claims as recognised by the treatment of its sister church at Sprotborough, a twin creation ecclesiastically disestablished and disendowed. And although the chapel as a building was not destroyed, yet that its services were insufficient in number may be readily granted when we recall what I have been told by persons only recently taken from us, of a *monthly* afternoon service as all that was allowed even within the last sixty years, and a *yearly* administration of the Holy Communion even up to the time when the present writer took charge of the parish. However sad, therefore, it can be scarcely considered surprising that Churchmanship in Haddlesey twenty years ago was of the most tepid character, and as small in quantity as poor in quality. But I must not anticipate too much, nor forget that during the Civil Wars the inhabitants of this parish played their little part in defence of their King and Church, although the latter had not done all for them it might reasonably have been expected to do. So we find an indignant letter from General Cromwell, a facsimile of which I am able to present to my readers through the kindness of Miss Davison, of Haddlesey House, the owner of the original document. What was the effect of this peremptory epistle we have no record. But I fear that the absence of proprietors complained of by Oliver Cromwell in 1648 continued throughout the century, for in 1690 I find only one gentleman's seat mentioned, that of a baronet at Temple Hirst; so that the old house of the Templars was at that

7

which had been made without his consent being asked, was one to which he was not obliged to conform. So we come to a very dark period in the history of our parish —the zeal of its early inhabitants, backed up by the munificence of the Stapletons and Hathelseys of the fourteenth century, all disregarded, and their bequests, so far as untouched by previous spoliation, carried off to the credit of the revenues of Birkin. And Haddlesey so recently constituted in a way befitting its claims as recognised by the treatment of its sister church at Sprotborough, a twin creation ecclesiastically disestablished and disendowed. And although the chapel as a building was not destroyed, yet that its services were insufficient in number may be readily granted when we recall what I have been told by persons only recently taken from us, of a *monthly* afternoon service as all that was allowed even within the last sixty years, and a *yearly* administration of the Holy Communion even up to the time when the present writer took charge of the parish. However sad, therefore, it can be scarcely considered surprising that Churchmanship in Haddlesey twenty years ago was of the most tepid character, and as small in quantity as poor in quality. But I must not anticipate too much, nor forget that during the Civil Wars the inhabitants of this parish played their little part in defence of their King and Church, although the latter had not done all for them it might reasonably have been expected to do. So we find an indignant letter from General Cromwell, a facsimile of which I am able to present to my readers through the kindness of Miss Davison, of Haddlesey House, the owner of the original document. What was the effect of this peremptory epistle we have no record. But I fear that the absence of proprietors complained of by Oliver Cromwell in 1648 continued throughout the century, for in 1690 I find only one gentleman's seat mentioned, that of a baronet at Temple Hirst; so that the old house of the Templars was at that

Forasmuch as I am informed that there is belonging to the Township of West Hudd'sfey in the County of Yorke & soo k great quantityes of land, which usually by reason of the owners not living thereupon is wholly freed from all charges of quartering soldiers. I doe therefore hereby require all officers, as quartermrs and others, togeyer with the Constables of the said towne that they charge the said lands equally with the Inhabitants, afwell by sending soldiers to the stewards & tennants thereof, as to such Gentlemen & others as hid for &c. the said towne & ye having lands there: That so the burthen may not singly lye upon a few pharlar Inhabitants to their utter undoing. But yt every man may beare his proportion answerable to the lands he enioyeth &c. Given under my hand and seale at Knottingley this 27 of No. 1648

To all Quartermrs & other whome this may concerne

O Cromwell

date the only house of a resident gentleman, unless it be that East Haddlesey was overlooked, a question we leave for our next chapter.[1] In the West Riding assessment, A.D. 1584, *i.e.*, some sixty years before the Civil War, I find East Hadlesaye returned at vs, West do. vis viii*d*, Hurste xs, Byrkyn vis viii*d* (*Yorkshire Notes and Queries*, vol. vii.).

[1] The diary of James Tetwell tells us, however, of William Moore, of good family, who married the widow of a Mr. Walker, she being the daughter of the Rev. Ralph Oates, Rector of Kirk Smeaton.

CHAPTER XVIII.

THE HOUSE OF ANCASTER.

OUR last chapter dealt with the period of the Civil Wars and the Commonwealth. It is fitting, then, to introduce in this place another illustrious family which owned at one time large estates in this parish, including the Hall at East Haddlesey, close to the church. It is not easy to say exactly when the noble family of Bertie, afterwards Duke of Ancaster, became first connected with Haddlesey; but Sir Miles Stapleton, Bart., of Carlton and Drax, first married Elizabeth, second daughter of Robert, first Earl of Lindsey, who fell whilst leading the King's troops as Commander-in-Chief at the battle of Edgehill in 1642. This nobleman was so enthusiastic a Royalist that he reproached the Earl of Essex and other officers of the Parliamentary army for their rebellious conduct, even as his life's blood was oozing away on the bed of straw in a poor cottage near Edgehill. His eldest son, Montague Lord Willoughby, who was with his father at the battle of Edgehill, and allowed himself to be taken prisoner that he might attend on his wounded father, succeeded as second Earl of Lindsey. He lived to the restoration of Charles II., who made him a Privy Councillor and Lord-Lieutenant of the counties of Lincoln and Oxford in

1660, and in 1661 Knight of the Garter. Also at the coronation of this monarch he claimed to act as hereditary Lord Chamberlain, which claim was allowed. His death took place at Camden House, Kensington, in 1665, when he was fifty-eight years of age.

He was succeeded in the title by his eldest son, Robert. He married, first, Mary, daughter of John Massingberd, of the East India Company, London, and by her had an only daughter, Arabella, married to the Earl of Rivers. By his second wife, Elizabeth, daughter of the famous Philip, Lord Wharton, he had five sons, of which the second, Peregrine Bertie, was Vice-Chamberlain to William III., and also Queen Anne. Robert, the eldest, became first DUKE OF ANCASTER, October 1, 1714, and died in 1722; he was succeeded in his title and estates by his second son, Peregrine, second Duke of Ancaster. Queen Anne made him her Vice-Chamberlain when not quite sixteen years of age, *i.e.*, in 1702; and in 1714-15 he was summoned to the House of Lords by writ as Lord Willoughby of Eresby. In 1724 his Grace was appointed Lord-Lieutenant of the county of Lincoln and Keeper of the Rolls of both county and city, and in 1734 Lord-Warden and Justice in Eyre of all his Majesty's parks, chases and forests north of Trent. He died in 1742, having married Jane, daughter and co-heiress of Sir John Brownlow, of Belton, Bart. Her Grace died in 1756, leaving five sons and five daughters. Peregrine, the second son, succeeded his father as third Duke of Ancaster. He had the courtesy title of Marquis of Lindsey, and married in 1735 Elizabeth, widow of Sir Charles Gunter Nicol, Knight of the Bath, and daughter and heir of William Blundell, Esq., of Basingstoke. This lady died childless in 1743, and the Duke married in 1750 Mary, daughter of Thomas Panton, Esq., Master of the Horse to George III. The Duchess was appointed Mistress of the Robes to Queen Charlotte in 1761; there were three sons and three daughters of this marriage. *This* Duke of Ancaster was the owner of a large estate in the townships of East and West Haddlesey, and Lord of the Manor. He had a residence here called Haddlesey Hall, close to the church; and the fields which now extend from the north side of the river below the Dam, up to Hall Garths, are called in the parish map 'Hall Ings.' This estate was sold before his death (about 1777) to William Cockell, William Toutill, and the trustees[1] of John Sawyer, who lived at Haddlesey Hall, and about whom we shall have more to say later on. The last and fourth Duke of Ancaster died childless in 1789.

It would have been sad if a family with such a brilliant record should have been thus ingloriously extinguished, and therefore it is pleasant to know that the title of Earl of Ancaster has been lately revived (1893) in the person of Lord Willoughby of Eresby, who had previously succeeded to the office of Great Chamberlain of England, and as such has the chief control of her Majesty's Palace of Westminster. He is the descendant of the Berties who were previously the heirs of Aubrey Veer, or 'De Ver,' who held the office in 1100, nearly eight hundred years ago!

But high official rank is not the only thing which gives interest to the family of Bertie. One member of the family was honourably conspicuous for the great interest displayed in the advancement of the Gospel during the

[1] These trustees are mentioned in Act of Parliament, A.D. 1789, as 'Wm. Cockell, Wm. Toutill, John Hemingway, John Henfrey, and Francis Sawyer, who were also lords of the Manor of Haddlesey aforesaid, but all rights were given up.' The date of the deed of sale between the most noble Peregrine, Duke of Ancaster and Kesteven, Lord Great Chamberlain, P.C., and William Cockell, of Pontefract, surgeon; John Sawyer, the younger, of East Haddlesey, and William Toutill, of Smithalls, gentleman, of the other part, is dated September 30 and December 2, 1776.

dark period of Queen Mary's reign, viz., Katherine Willoughby, Duchess of Suffolk. She was the only surviving child of William, ninth Lord Willoughby of Eresby, and his wife Dona Maria de Sarmiento, a Spanish lady related to the Counts of Salinas Danaya y Rivadeo, and with most of the royal and noble houses of Europe. Katherine was born at Parham, March 22, 1519. Her father died on October 27, 1526, and was buried at Spilsby, Lincolnshire; so his little daughter in her eighth year became tenth inheritor of the barony of Willoughby de Eresby. When ten years of age, King Henry granted to his favourite and brother-in-law, Charles Brandon, Duke of Suffolk, 'the custody of the person and marriage of Katherine Willoughby.' Strange to say, towards the end of the year 1534, when only fifteen years of age, she was married to Charles Brandon as his fifth wife, her husband being about fifty years of age !

It is needless to remark that Katherine Willoughby was never consulted about this arrangement. It is said that next to the hard task of Katherine of Arragon, the Queen of Henry VIII., came this of Katherine Willoughby; bound for life to a man devoid of principle, she yet so demeaned herself that even calumny itself could bring no reproach upon her name. Her position was one full of painful perplexity and heart-sickening discouragement. Poor humanity may ask, Why should such things be? and what could be the good of such a fiery furnace for this young girl-wife ? But, strange as it might seem, she was at school, qualifying for the Master's service in a high degree in the not distant future. She was now learning how unsatisfying were the world's best things— wealth, rank, fame. And when her heart had discovered all was vanity, a loving voice would breathe into her ears, 'Come unto Me!' For the present she was as a frail bark on the raging sea, seemingly abandoned to destruction. But no, the eye of the Good Shepherd was following her even in the trackless deep, and would in His own time take her to the arms of His protecting care.

We have already said that the youthful Duchess acquitted herself in her household with great prudence. On only one point does she seem to have been indiscreet. Her wit (probably inherited from her Spanish mother) occasionally got the better of her judgment. Among the Duke's friends was Stephen Gardiner, a man whose crafty, dissimulating character excited the intense dislike of the straightforward and ingenuous Duchess, so she made him sometimes the butt of her satire. At a large supper-party given by the Duke, he proposed, in the spirit of rough joking then customary, that each lady should select to lead her to the banqueting-hall the gentleman she loved best, excepting her husband. So Katherine, then about twenty years of age, walked up to Gardiner, and said, 'As I may not sit down with him I love best, I take him whom I love worst!' Gardiner neither forgot nor forgave that speech, and fifteen years afterwards, when opportunity occurred, he showed it.

As to the rise and progress of spiritual enlightenment in the heart of the Duchess it is not easy to speak, but two things may be noted which no doubt contributed towards its development. First, shortly after marriage Katherine appointed as her chamberlain Alexander Seaton, a learned Scottish friar who had fled from Scotland on account of his preaching the doctrine of justification by faith in Christ in opposition to the Roman doctrine of good works; secondly, by her intercourse with, and sort of daughterly affection for, Bp. Latimer, who was select preacher at Court in the Lent following her marriage.

On September 18, 1535, the Duchess gave birth in London to a son, who was named Henry, after the King, who stood sponsor for the heir to the dukedom of Suffolk. A second son was born, probably at Grimsthorpe, in September or October, 1537. For a time the Duchess remains quietly at Grimsthorpe while great agitations are taking place in the religious state of England. The Protestant party were known either as Lutherans or Gospellers, corresponding to the *old-fashioned* High Church party of our day and the Evangelicals. Nearly all the leading Reformers except Bilney and Latimer were Lutherans at first. Edward VI., Katherine Parr, Lady Jane Grey, and others, lived and died Lutherans. Katherine, Duchess of Suffolk, was a Lutheran for about twelve years. Gardiner remembered his grudge against the Duchess, but, serpent as he was, he did not attack her openly. His object was to get Ann Askew to betray other Gospellers, and she was asked ' if she knew anything against the *Duchess of Suffolk*, the Countesses of Sussex or Hertford, Lady Denny, or *Lady Fitzwilliam*.' Her cautious reply was, ' If I should pronounce anything against them, I should not be able to prove it.' So the firmness of this Christian martyr protected her friends and benefactresses. However, trouble of another kind was in store for the Duchess of Suffolk: her husband died at Guildford Place, after a short illness, in his sixty-first year, leaving her a widow at twenty-six !

King Henry honoured his favourite with a magnificent funeral in St. George's Chapel, Windsor. Katherine's eldest son, Henry, now became Duke of Suffolk. He, with his brother Charles, remained with their mother at Grimsthorpe for eighteen months. On May 18, 1546, King Henry authorized the widowed Duchess to retain forty persons in her service. One of these was Richard Bertie, her gentleman usher, son of Captain Bertie, of Hurst Castle, who was a descendant of Philip Bertie, who settled at Bersted, in Kent, early in the twelfth century.

Stephen Gardiner urged the King on July 8, 1546, to issue a decree that no one should be allowed to have in his possession any copy of the New Testament, as was permitted by Act of Parliament, 1543. The Duchess knew that this decree was specially aimed at her. The arrest of the old Duke of Norfolk, a nominal Protestant, and of his son, whose Countess was well known to be a Gospeller, would not add to her quietude of mind. Surrey was beheaded, and his father only escaped the same fate by the death of the King on the day before that appointed for his execution. Henry died at 9 a.m., January 28, 1547. He was speechless when Cranmer arrived; but when asked by him to give some sign of his trust in the merits of Christ only for salvation, he wrung the Archbishop's hand. Before this he had expressed regret for the judicial murder of his Queen, Ann Boleyn. The death of Henry and the accession of his son to his blood-stained throne gave new hope to the Gospellers, which included now Cranmer and Somerset, while Bonner and Gardiner had gratuitous lodgings in the Fleet prison. The Duchess sent her eldest son to Court under the protection of Somerset, and her younger, a boy of ten, to St. John's College, Cambridge. In her own county of Lincoln, where she reigned as a queen, she entered heart and soul into the work of reformation, abolishing all the monuments of superstition and idolatry in the churches, reforming the clergy, supplying every church with a large copy of the English Bible, and exhorting bishops and clergy to promote the reading of the Holy Scriptures, and of teaching the young the Lord's Prayer and Ten Commandments, etc., in English. In 1549 the Duchess sent her eldest son to France, where he learnt the language and many other accomplishments, and when about eighteen years old joined his brother at Cambridge. About the same time the Duchess herself resided at Cambridge to be near her sons and to minister to the last days of her old friend Martin Bucer. In October and November, 1550, the Duchess entertained Latimer at Stamford, who preached before her. But in February of the next year she returned with her boys to Cambridge. She also renewed her devoted care of Bucer, who was called home on February 28, 1551, and buried on March 2 in St. Mary's Church, Cambridge. But a yet greater than any previous trial was now about to befall her. On July 9 the sweating sickness, as it was called, broke out in London, and quickly spread to the provinces. Only about five per cent. of those attacked died, but in those cases where the attack was mortal the end came with terrible speed. When the disease reached Cambridge the Duchess sent off her sons in haste to Bugden in Hunts, the Bishop of Lincoln's palace. They reached Bugden on the 13th, in the afternoon. A little after midnight the eldest was seized by the fearful sweat. The mother summoned her physician in haste, but all remedies were in vain, and between seven and eight o'clock on the following morning Henry Brandon, the young Duke of Suffolk, 'was taken to the mercy of God.' The younger son had sickened before his brother's death, and died within half an hour. The poor mother was overpowered with grief. She went from Bugden to Grimsthorpe, and received many letters of condolence from her friends. Her heart was too much bruised to reply for two months. When she did 'to Master Cecil,' she related how her sharp and bitter 'trials had been used of God for her good.' She founded four scholarships at St. John's, Cambridge, 'in perpetual remembrance of her two sons. The Duchess must have spent a weary winter at Grimsthorpe, and continued there probably over the next year. But in the summer of that year she seems to have recovered her spirits, from the tone of a letter in which she writes to Cecil, sending him the present of a buck, at the capture of which she seems to have been present.

Her restored cheerfulness seems to have been partly due to a private reason. The lonely splendour in which

so much of her life had been passed was to continue no
longer. Although Richard Bertie was relatively socially
inferior to the Duchess, yet his education, attainments,
personal character, and religious sympathies would make
him in many ways her equal, to say nothing of his possible
descent from a very ancient family of patrician origin,
suggested by the three battering-rams in the family arms,
which connects the Berties with Leopold de Bertie, Constable of Dover Castle in the reign of Ethelred. During
the six months succeeding her second marriage probably
she and Mr. Bertie spent their time at Grimsthorpe. At
Christmas, 1553, their first child was born, a daughter
named Susan. Towards the end of March the Sheriff of
Lincoln appeared at Grimsthorpe Castle with a warrant
from Stephen Gardiner, Lord Keeper of the Great Seal,
for the apprehension of Richard Bertie, Esq., of that place.
No bail was to be allowed. The Sheriff, however, allowed
bail, and Mr. Bertie was to appear before Gardiner on
March 23, Good Friday, which he did, and again the
next day, when he met Mr. Sergeant Stamford, his
companion in the service of Lord Wriothesley, who
spoke highly of his early friend. By a wonderful providence Mr. Bertie escapes, and gets leave to go beyond
the seas, ostensibly to collect debts owing from Charles V.
to the late Duke of Suffolk. Early in June, 1553, Bertie
crossed from Dover to Calais, with no intention of returning while Mary reigned. The Duchess followed on
the last night of the year 1554. She was accompanied
by one gentlewoman and six of 'the meanest of her
servants,' because others were not to be trusted with her
secret. They took with them the little Susan, just a year
old. But the way of escape was full of risk and alarm.
I dare not linger over the details, but commend my
readers to Miss Holt's narrative in her story of 'Good
Soldiers of Jesus Christ' ('Christian Armour,' vol. i.),

from which I have borrowed much. After many perils, Katherine stepped on the Dutch shore, and forgot her fears and fatigues as her hand was grasped by that of her husband, who had been long waiting for her on the coast. They stayed a short time at Xanten, but as there was a Walloon minister named Perusell at Wesel, to whom the Duchess had formerly shown kindness, she requested him to obtain permission from the Burgomaster of Wesel for them to settle in that town. Before, however, Perusell's reply could be had, the fugitives were obliged to leave Xanten. On the road they were attacked and pillaged by highwaymen, and drenched to the skin by rain and hail, so that in a most pitiful plight they only caught sight of the lights of Wesel between six and seven o'clock of a winter's night. But then their troubles were not over. They could not find Mr. Perusell nor speak the German language, which seemed at first the only one understood in Wesel. At length the Duchess, overcome with fatigue, anxiety, and the weather, broke down, and they took refuge in the porch of St. Wilbrode's Church. Here they seem to have got rested and refreshed with a little food. By another special providence, at length they find Mr. Perusell, who with his friends gave them a cordial and Christian welcome. This time their troubles were over. Mr. Bertie hired 'a very fair house in the town,' and here, on October 12, was born the youngest child of Katherine Bertie, the future Lord Willoughby de Eresby, and who, because he was given by the Lord to his pious parents in *terra peregrina*, they named Peregrine. The name has been carefully cherished, and handed down by succeeding generations, so that the third Duke of Ancaster, owner of Haddlesey Hall, as well as many of his ancestors, have preserved the name in recollection of this marvellous history and providential preservation of one of the noblest ladies of her time, as well as most illustrious of the progenitors of the house of Ancaster. Peregrine Bertie married Lady Mary Vere, daughter of John, Earl of Oxford, and became a worthy son of such noble parents. The Berties, after other vicissitudes, spent their later days in peaceful retirement at Grimsthorpe, the Duchess dying in 1580, and Mr. Bertie two years later.

CHAPTER XIX.

EAST HADDLESEY (*resumed*).

AMONG the resident families of this parish, from the early part of the seventeenth century with a continuous succession, occurs the Bromleys. In the absence of any family pedigree accessible to me, I am obliged to assume that the first notable member of that family was John Bromley, who signalized himself by 'a pension of £6 13s. 4d. yearly to the Church at Haddlesey, payable out of his land at East Haddlesey.' I further assume that this gentleman was the father of Joseph Bromley, who died December 13, 1723, aged eighty years. This gives the year of his birth 1643, and if so, Mr. John Bromley probably showed his zeal for the interests of religion early in the seventeenth century, after the spoliation of the revenues of the Church by King James, as mentioned in a previous chapter; so that Mr. Bromley's payment, which continues to this day, formed a part of the slender income of the minister of Haddlesey when the Ecclesiastical Commissioners of the Commonwealth made their report, as previously noted, of Haddlesey as a chapelry worth £12 a year, and having for its minister 'Mr. Brian Fisher, a laborious preacher.' Mr. Joseph Bromley's son of the same name predeceased his father, if he departed this life on the 5th

December, 1712, as the gravestone seems to say. But as Mary, his wife, died May 22, 1769, aged seventy-six years, I think that the figures on the stone are not to be relied on. It is strange that his age is not stated, as in the case of all the others. The next mentioned is Benjamin Bromley, who died August 9, 1816, aged fifty-five years. This gives 1761 as his year of birth, and supposing Joseph the second to have been his father, it may suggest 1762 as the likely date of his father's decease, and so implies that the figure which now reads like 1, has had a portion effaced. Ann, the wife of Benjamin Bromley, died May 15, 1842, aged seventy-five. So it appears she was six years junior to her husband when married, and outlived him twenty-six years. This Benjamin and Ann Bromley had a son named John, born in 1801, who died April 28, 1884, aged eighty-three. His wife Sarah was born in 1816, and died October 27, 1884. They had a son John, who died February 15, 1858, aged nine years, and left two sons, Benjamin and Joseph, them surviving.

While still among the tombs, I will give some further gleanings out of our churchyard, where 'the rude forefathers of the hamlet sleep.' The Crawshaws, of East Haddlesey, are a family dating nearly as far back as the Bromleys. On the south side of the ancient portion of our churchyard is a stone on which is inscribed: 'Here lyeth interred the body of Robert Crawshaw of East Haddesley, who departed this life November 19th, Anno Dom. 1727, aged 67 years.' So here we have one who began to live just as Charles II. began to reign. On the same stone, also, we read: 'Here lyeth also the body of Dorothy, wife of the said Robert Crawshaw, who died the 2nd day of March, 1739, aged 84 years.' So this good woman was born, under the Protectorate of Cromwell, five years before her husband, as well as outlived him twelve years. Again: 'Here lieth the body of Sarah,

ANCIENT HOUSE OF THE BROMLEYS.

wife of Richard Crawshaw,[1] who departed this life June 17th, Anno Dom. 1763, aged 63 years.' 'Here also lieth the body of Richard Crawshaw,[2] who departed this life March 26th, Anno Dom. 1766, aged 66.' The Crawshaws seem to have been originally South Yorkshire people. The signature of John Crawschagh, of Calborne, to a deed dated November 11, 1399, is mentioned in *Yorkshire Archæological Journal*, vol. xii. In 1613 the name Crawshaw occurs among the freeholders at Woolley, and in 1663-66 Joseph Crawshaw is recorded as paying tax for eight hearths at Woolley (*ibid.*).[3] In Aldborough Churchyard is buried Elizabeth, wife of Jonathan Crawshaw, of Longthorpe; she died November 10, 1857, aged seventy-seven years. Also Jonathan Crawshaw, husband of the above, died November 24, 1864, aged eighty-two (*ibid.*, vol. ix.).

SAWYERS.

We now come to the gravestones of the Sawyer family. Near the south corner of the vestry we read: 'Here lieth interred the bodies of three daughters and one son of Mr. John Sawyer, of Chappell, Haddlesey, by Ann, his wife. Mary, died Sept. 18th, 1768, aged 2 years; Ann, died April 23rd, 1770, aged 8 years; Margaret, died April 24th, 1770, aged 5 years; Richard, died April 26th, 1770, aged 2 years. Here lieth also the body of the said Mr. John Sawyer, who died Nov. 24th, 1789, aged 51 years. Also Ann, the wife of the said Mr. John Sawyer, who died March 31st, 1792, aged 62 years.'

[1] Richard Crawshaw and his wife Sarah were married at St. Peter's, York, November 11, 1746 ('Diary of James Fretwell').

[2] A Richard Crawshaw, 'poet and saint,' is mentioned (*Yorkshire Archæological Journal*, vol. vi.) in the seventeenth century in Swaledale.

[3] Thomas Crawshaw and Martha Hobson were married in Silkstone Church, February 10, 1689-90. In a letter dated April 5, 1699, Thomas Crawshaw is mentioned as a tenant of Mr. Wortley, of Wortley, near Sheffield.

The above stone evidently refers to 'John Sawyer *the Younger*, of East Haddlesey,' as he is designated in a document from which I have before quoted; but there is a more ancient stone which refers to his mother and to the second wife of his father, John Sawyer (the elder), as follows: 'In hopes of a happy resurrection lies here interred the body of Frances, the wife of John Sawyer, of Haddlesey, who departed this life the fifth day of Sept., 1745, aged 47 years.' So she was born in the eventful year 1698, and was with her husband a contemporary and neighbour of the first Mr. Joseph Bromley, also of Mr. John Davison, of West Haddlesey, of which we shall have more to say later on. The gravestone of Mrs. Frances Sawyer continues: 'She had issue 6 sons and daughters, and having been virtuous and affectionate towards her husband, tender and indulgent over her children, Provident in her family, well disposed and charitable among her neighbours, her death was much lamented.'

'Also interred the body of Jane, the wife of the above John Sawyer, who departed this life March 6th, Ann. Domini 1755, in the 44th year of her age.' The following lines by a parishioner will come in here not inaptly:

HADDLESEY CHURCHYARD.

Tread softly o'er the graves, for each green sod
Hath been the place where mourners' feet have trod;
In whispered accents let your voices rise,
The air around has drank their heavy sighs.

A plot of ground where oft deep silence reigns,
From early morn till dusky evening wanes.
A place of sepulture in verdure drest,
Where all the worn and weary are at rest.
The years go by—a few more knolls are spread
Where lay the ashes of the silent dead.
And so, through creeping time are gathered there
The friends, the kindred who our love did share.

E'en as we muse, resounds the solemn knell—
The deep vibrations of the Passing Bell ;
Another soul has parted from the clay—
Earth-bound no more, it wings its flight away.
Pause we to meditate—the place—the hour
Approve the force of deep reflection's power.
A grassy mound, a heap of silent stones,
On which is writ the name of that which owns :
Is this the end of all our hopes and fears ?—
The eager plottings and the strife of years ;—
The quick resolves that vanished in a day,
And like the mists of morning passed away ?
No ! to the pious soul a glorious thought
Pervades each moment with sweet comfort fraught—
And through the discord of its earthly woes
A strain of music softly ebbs and flows ;
The voice of Jesus calling 'midst the din,
' Courage, faint soul ! look thou the prize to win.'
These rays of sunshine, and the clear rich lay
Of yon sweet bird upon the hawthorn spray—
The lovely flowers—the green boughs overhead
Foretell the morn when these our loved ones dead
Shall burst their bonds and soaring, change for this
Dark house of death, a realm of endless bliss.

June 23rd, 1890. J. S.

Here, I think, I may interpolate that in 1774 a canal was cut by the Aire and Calder Navigation Company (authorized by Act of Parliament, 1698) from the river Aire at Haddlesey, so as to form a junction with the Ouse at Selby. This company carried on a flourishing trade, so that the dividends on its original capital of £11,300 were at the rate of £70,000 per annum during the years 1824-27. In 1826 a good deal of the local traffic between Haddlesey and Selby was diverted by the cutting of another canal giving a direct approach to Goole from Knottingley. In all these developments of water communication Haddlesey has carried off a very small portion of profit, while Goole has become a seaport at the cost of Selby, and has now a considerable population.

CHAPTER XX.

THE DAVISONS OF HADDLESEY HOUSE (ANCIENTLY BEGHBY HALL).

THE earliest record I have is of an indenture of a fine in which Thomas Davison and Ann Spofforth are plaintiffs, dated 1668. I rather think that the family of which the Morritts of Rokeby are now the representatives were the possessors of what we may call the Haddlesey House estate early in the sixteenth century, who probably succeeded the Methams. At all events, the will of Thomas Morritt, of West Haddlesey, was proved on April 20, 1596, and on August 21 next year an indenture of release was executed between Thomas Metham, of Metham, Esq., and his son, on the one part; Thomas Jempson, otherwise Morritt, and John Jempson, otherwise Morritt, of West Haddlesey, of the other part; and there are other transactions with regard to real property in which the Morritts' names occur up to 1679, 1680, 1686, 1770, 1772, 1774, and even as late as 1776. In the first-mentioned year, 1679, Robert Morritt, of Ryther, clerk, is mentioned in an indenture of demise. This gentleman was probably Rector of Ryther, and I believe the Morritts still own property in the parish of Ryther. Spofforths and Scholeys also figure among West Haddlesey proprietors at this time. But as

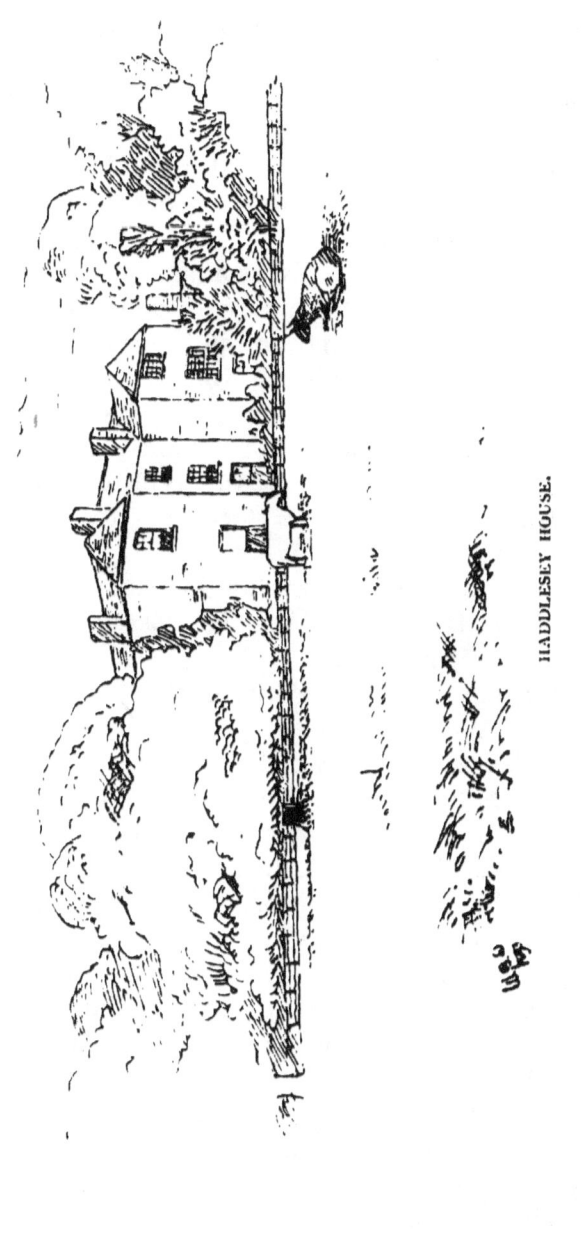

HADDLESEY HOUSE.

the Davison estate grew these other names disappear. The will of John Davison, of West Haddlesey, yeoman, was proved November 25, 1723; also that of Ed. Davison, of same place, gentleman, May 15, 1752; and April 13, 1761, that of Wm. Davison, of same place, gentleman. He was brother of Ed. Davison, and seems to have succeeded to his brother's property only on March 31, 1761. Still, his name appears in a deed of partition dated April 23, 1763, between Robert Baxter, of Hirst Courtney, gentleman, of the first part; Joseph Baxter, of Hirst Courtney, yeoman, of the second part; the above Wm. D., of W. H., gentleman, and Wm. Davison, of the same place, *yeoman, of third part;* so there is a little confusion here.

April 20, 1780.—There was an indenture of feoffment between Wm. Davison, of West Haddlesey, yeoman, and John Davison, gentleman.

January 12, 1781.—Grant from the Crown to John Davison, of West Haddlesey, gentleman, of two annual rents payable to the duchy of Lancaster.

April 20, 1782.—Isabella Davison, of West Haddlesey, spinster, is mentioned in connection with the tithes of South Elmsall. In 1797 Mr. John Davison, of West Haddlesey, bought a large portion of Mr. John Sawyer's estates in East Haddlesey.

1802, February 26 and 27.—John Davison, Esq., is mentioned in an indenture, and in 1814 the same gentleman is spoken of as a deforciant in an action by Wm. Dickon, the elder, of Beale. At this time also he had property in Kellington, Kellingley, Beale, Moorhouse, South Empsall and Carlton. It was between this date and that of our next that Haddlesey House, the only family residence left in this parish, was considerably enlarged. By the kindness of the owner of to-day we are able to give a view of the house as it now is.

Under date of December 31, 1821, is an indenture

of demise of Thos. Wood Davison, Esq., of West Haddlesey; November 27, 1823, Sarah Wood Davison, Mary Wood D., Hannah Sophia Wood D., and Elizabeth Wood D., spinsters, are mentioned as the surviving daughters of the said T. W. D.

May 27 and 28, 1830, Geo. Ed. Wood Davison, Esq., is mentioned as a party to an indenture. And on June 4 and 5 same year there is an indenture between Sarah Wood Davison, widow of the said Geo. Ed. Wood Davison, and others.

July 6 and 7, 1838, are indentures between the said G. E. W. D. (now styled clerk) and Sarah W. D., the younger, Mary W. D., the Rev. John Bowman, of Burcough, near Ormskirk, clerk, and Hannah Sophia, his wife; and the Rev. Geo. Thomas, of Tarleton, and Elizabeth, his wife, and others. And so we are brought down to present times. The Rev. G. W. Davison married Mary Brougham, third daughter of the late Joseph Skelton, Esq., of Loweswater, and the widow of late J. L. Brougham, Esq., of Askrigg, Yorkshire, in the year 1853, and in 1856 a daughter was born, who succeeded to a portion of her aunt's and father's estates after protracted litigation in 1877. An address was presented to Miss Davison by the Rector and the tenants of the Haddlesey House estate on the occasion of her coming of age and taking formal possession of her property, August, 1877, when appropriate rejoicings were indulged in. The Rev. G. E. W. Davison, who died in 1860, is still remembered by some as a kind landlord and one interested in the moral welfare of his neighbours, as a proof of which he suppressed the license of a public-house on his property. His widow survived him a good many years, a portion of which she lived at Haddlesey House. Her remains were laid beside her own kindred amid the beautiful lakes and hills of Cumberland, A.D. December 2, 1891. She was seventy-five years of age, and left only two children—Major Brougham by her first marriage, and Miss Davison by the second.

Before resuming the general history of the parish as a whole, it may be well to give a glance at the east end. The township of Hirst Courtney is mainly the property of the late Lord Beaumont, and of Charles Weddall, Esq., of West Bank, who is also lord of the manor of that township. An Act of Parliament for enclosing the commons was passed in the thirty-ninth year of King George III. The acreage is 588. There is a tithe rent of charge *commuted*[1] at £139, payable to the Rector of Haddlesey. The township of Temple Hirst has an area of 710 acres. At the enclosure in 1793 forty-seven acres

---

[1] We say 'commuted' at £139, but worth this year (1894) only £103 2s. 5½d.; such has been the depreciation of tithe rent-charge, owing largely to the fact that its value was based *on cereals alone*, and the value of those cereals, especially wheat, are so reduced in value by a *one-sided* Free Trade, which gives to foreigners all the profits of our markets, while leaving the cost of keeping them open to the British taxpayer, whose income is reduced, by this falsely-called Free Trade, from 30 to 40 per cent. It may be useful to recall first of all that tithe proper was levied, not only on corn, but also grass-lands; further, that it included animals and poultry; and, in the case of Hirst Courtney, Easter dues and moduses of every kind were included in the Commutation. Secondly, that at the time of the Commutation

Wheat sold at	7s.	0¼d.	per bushel. To-day	3s.	11d.
Barley "	" 3s.	11½d.	the prices are	3s.	4d.
Oats "	" 2s.	9d.		2s.	3¼d.

not one item of the same value, and consequently the tithe value is reduced, although, had it been based on the value of cattle, eggs, poultry, butter, and fruit as well as cereals, there would not have been such an unfair depreciation of tithe rent-charges. Doubtless the results of commercial changes never entered the minds of our legislators in 1836, but unless all sense of justice is extinguished, one might hope that our legislators would devise some plan for alleviating an undesigned hardship to that class of the community whose duties and services are not diminished by the very large reduction of those revenues which were supposed to be sacredly set apart for their maintenance.

of land was to be allotted in lieu of tithes. The Templar preceptory and farm attached was the property of the Denhams early in the eighteenth century. Elizabeth Denham left a benefaction of £40 yearly to be distributed among the poor of this township and those of East Haddlesey, but no record can be found of the gift ever being received within the present century. From the Denhams, I think, the Temple passed to Major Briggs, of York, who sold it to the father of Riley Briggs, Esq., of Osgodby Hall, the present owner. Earl Sheffield is the chief proprietor of the remainder of this township, and lord of the manor.

CHAPTER XXI.

FROM DARKNESS TO LIGHT.

WE now resume the general history of the parish as broken off at Chapter XVIII. We had travelled down to the eve of the Restoration of Charles II., and we shall have to record that, however good that event might be in a national aspect, *parochially* it brought harm instead of good, so far as we can gather, for we have but little information to aid us. However, for the next 200 years Haddlesey is deprived of its ecclesiastical independence, and becomes simply dependent on the Rector of Birkin for such fragmentary services as are to be had in its ancient parochial chapel. This brings us, then, to mention that the Rev. Robert Thornton was admitted to Birkin Rectory in 1612, married Alice Hymsworth at Arksey in January, 1613, ejected in 1650, succeeded by David Barnes in this year either as Rector or curate, for there is some doubt as to whether Mr. Everingham Cressy was Rector from 1650 to 1654. However, Rev. William Stone was Rector from 1654 to 1664,[1] when the Rev. Robert Thornton was restored, and he died Rector of Birkin in 1665. He was followed by Robert Thornton the second (his son), who died January 29, 1697-8, aged seventy-four, and was followed

[1] See also note, p. 205, *ante*.

by his son, William Thornton.[1] He married Abigail
Rudston, June 8, 1697, and died September 10, 1718,
aged forty-nine years. The Rev. William Aslabie, of
whom we know little, was Rector from 1718 to 1741,
when he was succeeded by the Rev. Thomas Wright,
chaplain to King George II. He wrote the refusal of a
bishopric from Birkin. His wife was Elizabeth Wright,
daughter of Thomas Hill, of Chipping Wycombe, Bucks
—born April 27, 1711, married February 22, 1742-3,
died February 23, 1783—and I take it that it was through
this marriage that the advowson of Birkin ultimately
devolved to the late Venerable Thomas Hill, Archdeacon
of Derby, who made it over to the trustees of the late
Rev. Charles Simeon before his death in 1875. The
inscription on this lady's tablet in Birkin Church was
written by the lamented poet-laureate William White-
head. Mr. Wright was succeeded in 1788 by the Rev.
George Alderson, who was forty-seven years Rector
and nineteen years previously curate, making a total
ministry of sixty-six years.[2] Stories of this gentleman's

[1] These Thorntons, it is interesting to remember, were of the family
afterwards immortalized by Sir James Stephens in his *Quarterly
Review* essays on 'The Evangelical Succession' and 'The Clapham
Sect.'

[2] It was at this time (1789) the enclosure of the common lands in
this parish took place, 29th and 30th years of his Majesty George III.
At the same time the rectorial tithes (with certain exceptions) were
exchanged for land in the townships of East and West Haddlesey and
Temple Hirst. Other minor adjustments of landed property between
other owners took place, and the roads leading from Birkin to Carlton
were either laid out or improved. As ignorance in some quarters
prevails with regard to the provisions of the award issued by the
Commissioners appointed to carry out the provisions of the aforenamed
Act of Parliament, I may state that a body of 'five of the owners or
occupiers of the greatest number of acres within the said townships,'
of which the Rector of Haddlesey is an *ex-officio* one, were appointed
to carry out the direction of the Commissioners; and, further, that the
authority of this award is not affected by the recent Local Government Act of 1894.

career still linger. His mismanagement of the glebe land was most disastrous to his successors. He allowed some four acres of the Haddlesey marsh to be taken for the making of the new turnpike road from Doncaster to Selby, and another seven acres to be robbed of its top soil, and so permanently deteriorated, without a penny compensation; and thus he caused the benefice to be robbed permanently of a considerable portion of its income. This happened in 1833-4, when a new iron bridge was erected over the Aire, consisting of three spacious arches, by the Butterly Company. For several years coaches ran along this road several times a day, so that, as with other rural districts, we were better off than under the railway *régime*, with stations distant and trains at infrequent and inconvenient hours. According to the *Yorkshire Weekly Post* of October 5, 1890, the last coach which ran over this road was the Edinburgh Mail, driven by Tom Holtby. In 1842 it passed through Haddlesey for the last time, and closed its career in front of the Black Swan, York. Among its proprietors stands the name of the Rev. George Alderson.

Mr. Alderson died in 1835, and was succeeded by the Rev. Valentine Green. His incumbency was inaugurated by the rebuilding of the ancient church erected by Baron Stapleton in 1312. In 1836, according to a black board which was suspended at the east end of the church, for there was no chancel at that date, 130 additional sittings were provided, eighty of which, in addition to a hundred previous, were to be free for ever, the Incorporated Church Building Society having made a grant in aid subject to those conditions. So that there ought to have been a total of 230 sittings. It has been a great puzzle to myself and to others to discover what was the area allotted to each worshipper to verify this provision. The site and its surrounding graveyard is the only link between the present structure and that which it superseded. And although it would be ungrateful not to recognise the advantages of its enlarged accommodation, its solidity of workmanship, and the general fitness of its internal arrangements, yet I must say I wish there had been some part of the old building worked into the new, if it had only served as a chancel, a vestry, or a porch, and, moreover, that the new had somewhat more of an ecclesiastical character imparted to it. Its severe plainness gives, especially at this time of day, when it may be that too much importance is attached to architecture in certain quarters—its severe plainness, I repeat, gives one an idea of coldness and indifference to the claims of religion, which is as unjust to the memory of those no longer amongst us, as it is out of harmony with modern notions, when we find that even those whose forefathers repudiated steeples and other architectural adornments, now vie with the most æsthetic amongst us by the erection of structures which far exceed in costliness and architectural adornment many a parish church.

I am told that there was some interesting carved work in the old building, which was cast out among the common lumber of decayed gate-posts and rotten boards in the yard of the village carpenter; but the most grievous thing of all was the getting rid of the ancient bell, which the late Rev. Stephen Cattley Baker, curate in 1837, Vicar of Usk at his death, 1892, tells me had a curious inscription, which I have endeavoured to reproduce, but in vain.

He also told me of the hanging of the present bell, which unfortunately superseded instead of supplementing its venerable predecessor of some 600 years before. Mr. Baker writes, August 13, 1890: 'I find it noted in my diary that on October 12, 1839, we dedicated the new bell; weight 2 cwt., cost £17. I and my brother and Messrs. Wm. and Rd. Prince, with J. Holmes, the "wreet," fixed it. I first rang a vigorous peal on it. It came to

HADDLESEY RECTORY.

Haddlesey on September 29, and I therefore gave it the name of Michael.'

In spite of the enlarged church and the new bell, perhaps as a consequence, I find a Wesleyan chapel was built within some hundred yards of the church in 1839. One of the chief originators of this building told me he was sorry that it had been erected. However, the spirit of Wesley was no doubt more carefully attended to in avoiding collision with Church services at that date than in our own day, and the infrequency of those services made it easy to open the meeting-house when the church was closed. I feel Churchmen are most to blame, who left so many gaps in the way of service for others to fill. This may explain that another chapel was built at Temple Hirst in 1842, to be followed by another in West Haddlesey in 1856 at a cost of £130. Three chapels and a church in a parish of less than 600 population hardly conduce to the spiritual prosperity of any place, because such minute subdivisions greatly enfeeble organized effort. One vigorous central congregation, with offshoots for outlying hamlets worked from a common centre, with a *corps d'esprit* arising from unity, would be an immense encouragement to many a faithful pastor in rural parishes. Such an one longs to do much more than he is allowed for the spiritual life of his parishioners, but he is defeated and discouraged by these miserable subdivisions of what at the best is but a little flock. Oh, that good men would look this question in the face, not in the spirit of competing sectarianism, but in the freer, grander, and more Christlike spirit of the highest interests of humanity and the glory of God!

To show, however, that those responsible for Church work at Haddlesey were not indifferent to its claims for more effective pastoral care, I have pleasure in noting that the patron, the Ven. Thomas Hill, Archdeacon of Derby, procured an Order in Council in July, 1855, reconstituting the parish of Haddlesey substantially on the basis of a previous Order in Council, June 13, 1658.

The chief provisions of this order are—firstly, that it should take effect after the next avoidance of the rectory of Birkin; secondly, that the ancient chapel or church of Haddlesey should be the parish church of the new benefice; thirdly, that the new parish and benefice should be subject to the same ecclesiastical jurisdiction as the rectory of Birkin, and that the incumbent of the new parish should have exclusive care of souls within the

HADDLESEY NATIONAL SCHOOLS, 1875.

limits of the same; fourthly, that two churchwardens should be annually chosen in the customary manner, and at the same time when churchwardens are usually appointed, and that every person so chosen shall be duly admitted, and shall do all things pertaining to the office within the said parish; fifthly, that all such part or parts of the glebe lands, tithe rent-charges, or other payments or compositions, for or in lieu of tithes belonging to the rectory of Birkin as are situate, and arise, and accrue, and are payable for or in respect of all the lands and hereditaments situate and being within the said townships or places of West Haddlesey, Chapel Haddlesey, Temple Hirst, and Hirst Courtney, belong and be attached to the separate benefice of Haddlesey; sixthly, that all fees and payments for churchings, marriages, burials, and other ecclesiastical offices solemnized and performed within the said proposed separate parish and benefice of Haddlesey, and all such other ecclesiastical dues, and offerings, and emoluments usually payable to the incumbent of a parish or benefice as shall arise within the said separate parish or benefice of Haddlesey, belong to the incumbent thereof; seventhly, that the patronage or right of nomination of or to the said benefice of Haddlesey shall be vested in the said Thomas Hill, his heirs and assigns for ever.

With regard to this last clause, the Ven. Archdeacon Hill some years ago, out of concern for the spiritual welfare of the inhabitants of Haddlesey and Birkin, made over his rights of patronage, with a munificent disregard of all private interests, to the trustees of the late Rev. Charles Simeon.

By the death of the Rev. Valentine Green, on December 2, 1873, the preceding arrangements came into operation, and opened up, as we humbly and fervently pray, a new era of spiritual prosperity and moral and intellectual progress to the people whose interests have been aimed at in their promotion. The author of these pages was admitted to the rectory of Haddlesey in January, 1874.

CHAPTER XXII.

FURTHER PAROCHIAL DEVELOPMENT.

A RESIDENCE for the minister of the parish, restored to its ancient constitution, was completed in 1875. The national schools were finished and opened on Whit-Monday, May 17, 1875. A special service was held in the church, when the Hon. and Rev. G. Y. Saville, Rector of Methley, preached, as representing the governors of the Wakefield charities, one of the landowners contributing to the work. Mr. Joseph Munby, of York, agent to the Davison estate, represented another subscriber. The Rev. H. J. Browne, Vicar of St. James's, Selby, and the late Mr. T. M. Weddall, were also present, with many friends, who assisted at the public meeting and tea held in the new buildings.

In 1870 a sale of work to inaugurate a fund for enlarging and improving Haddlesey Church was held in the schoolroom, September 12 and 13, and was very successful, realizing more than £100. About this time also a valuable gift of Communion plate was made to the church by the family of the late Rector.

In 1878 the church was enlarged by the addition of chancel and vestry; about fifty additional sittings were thus obtained. Urgent repairs were made, and an effective heating apparatus, supplied by Porritt, of Bolton, took the place of a cracked and useless stove.

In 1884, Miss Davison, of Haddlesey House, presented a handsome stone font, nicely carved, to the church. Up to this time there had only been a wooden font, provided by the present Rector, as on his coming to the parish a basin on the Communion-table seemed to be the only provision for baptizing!

The next event to record is one of very special interest, as marking the progress of our parish—I mean the consecration of an additional half-acre of land added to our churchyard by Archbishop Thomson, July 6, 1886. The cost of the site was borne by Miss Davison and the Rector, the fencing on the south and west was paid for by Mr. S. Brocklebank and Mr. Oxley Hartley, while the wall on the east was repaired and improved by the governors of Wakefield charities, and a new iron railing and dwarf wall all along the street side of the churchyard was erected by subscriptions from other landowners, the farmers throughout the parish doing the team work necessary to level, and drain, and lay out the new ground. The Archbishop was accompanied by Archdeacon Crosthwaite, and gave a very impressive address on the subject of the consecration as well as to the candidates, whom he confirmed at the same time. It is a time ever to look back upon with gratitude to the Giver of all good.

After the cost of the preceding important work had been met, our attention was again called to the yet unfinished enlargement and improvement of the parish church, which the greatly improved condition of the churchyard seemed to make more urgent than before, inasmuch as the site of the church was now so much better fitted for those structural additions which would improve its appearance. A series of efforts were made to commemorate the Queen's Jubilee by beginning the erection of the church tower. However, it was not before 1890 that these efforts were to find a realization. In May of that year a contract was signed for the erection of the church tower and spire, with entrance porch and other internal alterations for the rendering of the church more convenient to the congregation, and more fitting for its high and holy functions. On August 1 Lady Beaumont, of Carlton Towers, laid the corner-stone of the tower in the presence of the Bishop of Beverley, the Rector of the parish, churchwardens, building committee, contractor, and many of the parishioners and neighbouring clergy and laity, including the Rev. Canon Barnes-Lawrence, Rev. W. H. Cleveland, Major Eadon, Joseph Todd, Esq., J.P., etc.

On April 28, 1891, the Bishop of Beverley kindly came over again to celebrate a thanksgiving service in commemoration of the completion of the work thus begun the previous year, and to hold a confirmation in the enlarged church. Looking back on the twenty years which have passed since the parish began its new career of restored and enlarged ecclesiastical life, we have to record a sum of something like £5,000 as expended in supplying the parish with a residence for the clergyman, schools for the young, an enlarged and greatly improved church and churchyard for all classes of the parishioners. And when it is remembered that some of the landowners have contributed but little to this outlay, and that not all of the parishioners have done their part, although it is true that some, both among landowners and parishioners, have helped generously, it is a matter of deep thankfulness to Almighty God in the first place, and to kind-hearted personal friends, some of them strangers to Haddlesey, on the other, that so much has been accomplished. What we long for is not only improved machinery for spiritual work, but also greatly augmented results in the way of souls brought to know and love the

Lord Jesus Christ. We can say gratefully and yet humbly that we do believe the Lord has condescended to shine upon us at intervals during these last twenty years. The great day alone will declare how far we are right in this conjecture, but we feel sure that He who is faithful to His promises has not withheld His blessing from the sanctuary and its ordinances. One thing we may touch upon in passing as an incidental encouragement at least—I mean the results of the last census. Nearly all country parishes have witnessed a diminution of their inhabitants; not so with Haddlesey. In each of the four townships comprising this parish there has been an increase, and in the centre township a remarkable one, so that our population now is close on 600. Let us hope that there may be an increase in godliness, for it is true that righteousness is the only guarantee for prosperity. To show the greatly increased appliances for spiritual culture since 1874, I may mention that we have on an average four church services weekly where there used to be only one, to say nothing of day and Sunday schools, Bible-classes, Band of Hope, Temperance Society, and other institutions. It may interest some to know that there have been 320 baptisms, 70 marriages, 95 confirmees, and over 200 burials during the last twenty years. These figures have each their special lessons. As regards the baptisms, not all have been brought to the Bishop to be confirmed by him, as was promised; and, again, among those confirmed, only a small proportion have fulfilled their vows as good soldiers of Jesus Christ. With regard to the marriages, some are still amongst us, others have gone far away; wherever they may be, we hope they are trying 'to please God both in body and soul.' And then to refer to the last item of burials. How solemn the thought that, whether men come up to God's house or not in the days of health and strength, yet the time must come when they shall be brought to that house and laid in its graveyard! What need for us, then, to seek grace so to use all means of grace in health and strength that when our bodily strength decays our spirits may soar away to that blessed company who keep perpetual Sabbath in the presence of God! It is to this climax that all human history is ever tending, and all earthly records are but as the beating waves of time, intended to speed our way into the ocean of eternity. That Jesus may be our Guide, and heaven our resting-place, is the prayer of the writer of these pages.

If not too great a descent from the high thoughts and aspirations just expressed, I may be allowed to supplement an omission. In 1864 a railway-station was opened in this parish, giving us communication north and south. In 1890 we were favoured with a post-office in the central village of the parish. Fifty years ago the inhabitants of Haddlesey had to travel to Selby to get a letter, and, if it came from London, to pay elevenpence for it before they could call it their own! So times have changed, we hope, for the better, but not as much for the better as some of us could wish—or, rather, we do not find that everyone takes advantage of these social improvements, so we can sympathize with those who feel that in some respects our ancestors had the advantage of us. Certainly, village life at the beginning of the century had some features which we look for in vain. There was more contentment and quiet happiness in all classes than now. The spirit of restlessness which marks our age is an enemy to some of the highest interests of mankind. The spirit, too, which is always hankering after changes in legislation, as well as in personal circumstances, brings but little gain. If there was more public spirit and less self-seeking in rural communities, there might be a much higher standard of morality, intelligence and social wellbeing. If our legislators would remember these things instead of harassing the people with untried nostrums of Local Government, there would be what, after all, should be the aim of all legislation, a spirit of self-help and care for the rights and feelings of others, which alone can make us either self-respecting or respected by others.

One benefit from the study of the past is the removal of that spirit of conceit which makes us forget what we owe to those who have gone before. Another benefit to be desired is that of endeavouring to imitate the virtues of our progenitors while we endeavour to improve on their failings. The record of the past achievements of those who lived on the same soil as we now tread should awaken in us the desire to show our respect for their memories by following whatever good example they may have left behind them, so that in the coming time of resurrection and reunion we may have a joyful assurance that, by the grace of God, we have endeavoured to be faithful stewards in His service, and inheritors of that glory which He has promised to those who have proved themselves His faithful soldiers and servants.

INDEX.

A.

Accho, 33
Adam of Newmarket, 11, 14
Agincourt, 184
Ailsus or Alricus de Hausay, 40
Aire River, 2, 3, 105
  ,, iron bridge over, 235
Airemin, 3, 100, 123
Alba, Bishop of, 52
Aldersgate Church, St. Botolph, 166
Aldeburgh, Sir William, 183
Alderson, Rev. George, 234
Alencon, 185
Almanthorp, Robert de, 20
Amadei, Robert, 189
Ancaster, Duke of, 208
Antioch taken, 29
Apelton, 100
Aregrim, 13 *note*
Arengrimus, Roger, 13
Arundel, Earl of, 115, 118
Ascalon, 31
Aske, Robert, 156-165
Aske, William, 158
Aston, 178-185
Athelingflete, 100
Auvergne, 51

B.

Badlesmere, Lord, 114
Baker, Rev. S. C., 236
Balcock de Hausey, 17
  ,, Alan and Hugh of the Temple, 46
Baldwin, King of Jerusalem, 31

Baildon, Mr. Paley, 125
  ,, lands in, 125
Baliol, Edward, King, 107
Bannockburn, Battle of, 91-96
Barington, Viscountess, 50
Barkstone Ash, Division of W. R. York, 1, 45, 102
Barlow, John de, 122 *note*
Barnes, David, 203, 204
Bassett family, 36, 43, 45, 109, 114, 188
Baxter, John, 135
  ,, ,, marriage of, 167 *note*
  ,, Richard, 167
  ,, Robert, 229
Baxter family, 169
Beauchamp, Earl of Warwick, 109
Beaumont, Viscount, 187
  ,, Lord, 107, 117, 163, 187-191
Becket, Thomas à, 7
Bedford, Duke of, 186
Behal in Hausey, site of, 15, 17, 19
Bella-qua, Bellew family of, 16, 80
  ,, Hamon, 18
Bentley, John de, 110
Berkeley, Lord, 115
Bernard of Clairvaux, 31
Bertie, Richard, 216
Berwick-on-Tweed, 102, 103
Beverley, 101, 156
Birkin, parish of, 1, 74, 75, 205 *note*, 234

Index. 249

Bishopthorpe, 101
Blake of Catton, 138 *note*
Blanke, Humbert, 51
Bordarii described, 38
Boroughbridge, battle of, 104
Bosworth Field, battle of, 188
Bounty of Queen Ann, origin of, 28
Brayton parish, 1, 20; Richard le Clerk, 122; Poll-tax, 133, 134
Brayton Bargh, 2
Bridlington, Prior of, 166
Bristol, 109
Brittany, Duke of, 117
Brittayne, John, Earl of, 95
Bromley family, 219, 220
Brotherton, Prince Thomas de, 111
Bruce, Robert, King of Scotland, 90, 95
  ,, David, King of Scotland, 118
Bruges, city of, 10, 122
Brus, 39
Bubwith, 100
Buckingham, Duke of, 165 *note*
Bull, Bishop, 204
Bulmer, Sir John, 157, 165
Burstwick, 100
Burton, 100
Burton, Mr. Thomas, History of Hemingborough, 136
Bygod, Sir Francis, 165
Byland Abbey, 144
Byrne, 16, 44, 61
Byrkin, Adam de, 90
Byrom, 106

C.

Caerphilly Castle, 114
Caistor, 151
Calder River, 2, 3
Calf Enge, 46
Calthorn, William de, 123
Camblesforth, 4, 186
Camelford, Robert, 46
Carlton, by Snaith, 19, 45; Church, 185
Castleford, 3, 104
Catwick, Rector of, 141
Cavendish, Lord William, 196

Cawood, David de, Abbot of Selby, 43
Chapel of Hirst Templars, 14, 57, 58
Chaplain at Hirst of the Templars, 62
Charters, 11, 16, 39-45
  ,, lost, 59
Chaworth, Patrick de, 109
Cheyne, William and Margaret, 165
Clarell, Sir Thomas, 86
  ,, Sir John, 87
Clement, Pope, 53; death of, 69
Clermont, Council of, 28
Clergy and Patrons of Haddlesey, 81-88, 194, 199, 203, 230, 234
Clifford, Lord, 103
Cobcroft, 15
Cockell, Dr., 210
Constance, Duchess of Lancaster, 184
Conisburgh Castle, 49
Constable, Sir John, etc., 158
  ,, Sir Robert, 161
Conyers, Baron, 180
Copmanthorpe, 49
Cottarii described, 38
Cowick, 108
Crawshaw, 220, 223
Crecy, battle of, 118
Crepping, Sir John, 51
Cresaker, John, 167
Cressy, Everingham, 199
Cromwell, General, 206
  ,, Lord, 166, 195
  ,, Sir Oliver, of Hinchinbrook House, 195
Crumbwell, John de, 105
Crusaders, 28, 35
Cyprus, King of, 29

D.

Damory, Roger de, 107
Danby, Sir Christopher, 165
  ,, Earl of, 181
Darcy pedigree, etc., 116
  ,, Sir John, 116, 118, 148, 181
  ,, Thomas, 149, 172
  ,, Lord, 113, 180
  ,, Meinill, 145, 148
  ,, Lord Philip, 144

Index.

Darcy, Lord George, 174, 189
  ,, the Good, 177
  ,, his wives and successor, 177-181
Darrington Manor, 80; Vicar of, 171
David, King of Scotland, 115
Davison family, 224-231
  ,, Roger, 63
  ,, Sir Thomas, 180
Dayville, Robert de, 18
Derby, Countess of, 185
De Spenser, Earl of Winchester, 103, 109
De Vesci, Lady Agnes, 107
Devonshire, Earl of, 181 *note*
Dolman, J. T., Esq., 191
Dominicans, 11
Doncaster, 96
Dover, 109
D'Ossatt, Cardinal, 137
Drax, 1; Vicar, 138
  ,, Abbey, 110
  ,, Prior, 41
Duffield, South, 136-140
Duffield, 107
Duke of Lancaster, Henry, 120, 187 *note*

E.

Edward II., Coronation of, 89
  ,, Christmas at York, 90
  ,, holds a Parliament at York, 96, 102
Edward II. stays at Haddlesey, 98, 102
Edward II. at Beverley, 101
  ,, burial of, 117
Edward III., 121, 144
Eggboro township, 57
Emma, wife of John de Curteney, 20, 21
Endowments of Church, 73-78, 81, 194-197, 233, 234
Ergum, William de, 125
Estker or Karr or Carr, 40, 43
Etton, Ivo de, 67
Etymology of Haddlesey, 5, 6
Euermu, Walter, 40
  ,, William de, 40
Everingham, Lord Robert, 44
  ,, Sir Adam, 81, 99, 199

Everingham, Sir Henry, 165
Everington (alias Stapleton), Nicholas, 189
Exeter, Duke of, 186

F.

Fairfax, Sir Nicholas, 165
Farrer, Charles, 170
Fauconberg, Lord, 178
  ,, Walter de, 39
Fauge, William, 169
Faxflete, 100, 101
Felton, Sir John, 124, 130, 131
Felton, Robert de, Baron, 133 *note*
Fenwick, 11
Ferrers, Lord, 114
Ferry over the Ayre, 105
Finchden, Chief Justice, 127
Fishlake, 65
Fitz-William, William, 11, 82-85
  ,, Sir John, 87, 124-129; pedigree of, at Haddlesey, 192, 193
Flamborough, 166
Flodden Field, battle of, 188
Foljambe, Godfrey, 177; Henry, 180; Alicia, 186
Folliotts, 11
Fountains Abbey, 11
Fountains, Abbot of, 166
Fowleys, Sir David, 180 *note*
Freer, Henry, 170, 171
Frobisher, Edmund, 170

G.

Gaiteford, 36, 41, 43
Galfrid de Poterlawe, 15, 17
Gardiner, Bishop, 212
Garter, Order of, 120
Gascoigne, Richard, 86
  ,, Sir John, 189
  ,, Sir William, 87
  ,, Thomas, 167
Gateforth, 4
  ,, House, 174
Geoffrey Fitz Stephen, Master of the Templars, 48
Gloucester, Earl of, 107
  ,, Duke of, 187
  ,, Abbey of, 117
Goddard, Sir John, 184
Godfrey of Bouillon, 30

Goole, 107
Gothraie, David, monk of Byland, 143
Gournay, Thomas de, 114
Goushill, Ralph de, 113
Gowdal, John de, 17
Gower, Lord William de, Braose, 104
Grace, Pilgrimage of, 153-167
Granage, Thomas, 196
Grantvill, Hawise de, 18
Gray, Walter, Archbishop of York, 74, 75
Green, Rev. Valentine, 235
Greenfield, Archbishop of York, 51-68, 96
Grey, Lord Henry, 145
Grimsthorpe Castle, 212, 216
Gryce, Thomas, William and Oswald, 86
Grymesdiche, John, 195
Guiseborough Priory, 166
Gypton, Peter de, 14

H.

Haddlesey, 1, 17, 36-46, 99-101
Haddlesey, West, 3, 45 ; Poll-tax returns, 134
Haddlesey, East, Chapel of St. John the Baptist rebuilt, 45, 46, 75-81, 106
Haddlesey, East, corn mill, 46 ; Poll-tax returns, 132-134
Haddlesey Hall, 133, 134
Haddlesey family, pedigree of, 138-141
Haddlesey Hall, South Duffield, 137
Hall Garth, 132
Hambleton Hough, 2
Harcla, Sir Andrew, 104
Harewood, Earl of, 183
Harfleur, 184
Haringworth, Lord Zouch, 112
Hassard, Agnes, her will, etc., 167, 168
Hastings, Lord John, 113
Hastings, Ralph, 6-10
„ Richard, 7
„ Sir Brian, 166
„ Sir Gregory, 167
Hatecrist, Henry, 11
Hatfield Hall, 108

Hathelsay, John de, Sheriff of York, 77, 78
Hathelsea, 6, 99, 108
Hausee, town of, 15, 17, 41
Hausey, Alan de, and Richard, his son, 14
Hausey, Middle, 41-43, 46
„ Roger, son of Hugo, 17 ; son of Goodrich, 42
Hausey, town of, 41, 122
„ Wood of, 41
Heck, Henry de, 17
„ Hilard, 20
Hemingborough, 137
Hennebon, siege of, 117
Hensall, 1, 62
Hereford, Earl of, 104
Hill, Venerable H. T., 234-236
Hirst Courtney, 21
Hirst, derivation of name, 24
„ Inquest of lands, etc., 60-65
„ Inventory of goods, 55-60
„ Poll-tax returns, 132
„ Temple, 49-51, 65, 66
„ Court Roll, etc., 167-171
Hodges, Mr. C. C., 144
Holderness, Earls of, 180, 181
Holland, Sir Robert, 63
Holm, William de, etc., 17, 21 note
Holt, Miss E. S., 108
Holt, Rev. Richard, 188
Hopton, Ralph, 167
Horncastle, 151
Howden, 101
Humber, 3
Hunter's South Yorkshire quoted, 85, 172

I.

Ingleby, Sir William, 185
Ingram, Sir Arthur, 169
Inventories of Templar property, 55-65
Isabella, Queen, 100, 112

J.

Jaffa, 30
Jean d'Acre, 8, 32-34
Jerusalem, siege of, 30
Jervaulx, Abbot of, 166
John de Curteney, 18, 20, 21, 24, 61

Joppa, 32
Jordan de Insula, 18, 19

K.

Keighley, 3
Kellington, 1, 8, 50, 53, 133
 „ Church, 61, 62
 „ Henry, Clerk of, 13 *note*
Kellington, Ralph, Deacon of, 43
 „ William, Vicar of, 168
Kenilworth, 111
Keteley (Isle of Axholme), 18
Kirk Smeaton, 62, 207
Kirkby's Inquest, 44
Kirkstall Abbey, 10
Knottingley, 106 ; letter of Oliver Cromwell from, 206

L.

Lacy, Edmund de, 11 *note*
 „ Henry de, 8, 12, 61, 76
 „ Ilbert de, 10
 „ Robert de, 10
 „ Roger de, 10
Lancaster, Earl of, Thomas, 63, 104, 106
Landrik, Hugo de, 15
Lasci, Earls of Lincoln, 15
Latimer, Bishop, 212-214
Lathun, Robert de, 106
Laverock, John, 12 *note*
Leeds, 3
 „ Duke of, 182
Leland quoted, 2
Lennox, Lord and Lady, 169
Lindsay, Earl of, 189, 208
Llandaff, Bishop of, 117

M.

Malham Cove, 2
Mallynson, John, of Gateford, 43
March, Earl of, 184
Matthew de Maluvir, 9
Maulever explained, 9 *note*
Melton, Archbishop, 103
Metham, Sir Thomas, 124-126, 129-131, 167
Mickelmarsh, 41
Middleton, Thomas de, 133
Milford, Ralph de, 44
Molay, James de, 52
Monasteries dissolved, 149-152

Montzone, Lady, 110
Monument of Lord Darcy and Meinill in Selby Abbey, 144-49
Monument of Lord George Darcy in Brayton Church, 174
Morley, Bishop, 197
Morrit of Rokeby, at W..Haddlesey, 226
Mowbray, Roger de, 18
 „ John de, 63
 „ Philip de, 90
Mowbray, Barons, 39, 105
 „ Sir Geoffrey, 107
Myton Bridge, battle of, 103

N.

National Schools built at Haddlesey, 240
Neville, Sir John, 110, 158, 169
Newcastle, city of, 109
Newmarket, Adam, son of Lord John, 14, 15 ; charter of, 14
Newmarket, Sir Henry, 12 *note*
Nocton or Notton, 118
Norfolk, Duke of, 160
Normanton, William de, 14
Northampton, 110
 „ Earl of, 118
Northumberland, Earl of, 157, 184
Novo Mercato, 11

O.

Origin of Knights Hospitallers, 24, 68, 144
Order of Knight Templars, 48
Osbert of Bayeux, 40
 „ Schirburne, 42
Osbert, priest of Birkin, 75
Osgotcrosse Wapentake, 60, 133
Osmundthorpe, 18
Otho de Barkestone, 42
Ouse, River, 4

P.

Paganel, Philip, 110
Paganis, Hugo, 30, 34
Paris, City of, Templars persecuted in, 52, 53
Parishes, origin of, etc., 74
Pembroke, Earl of, 94, 115
Percy, Earl, 157

Peter de Birkin, 11
Peter of Amiens, 27
Philip, King of France, 53
Pickard, Rev. Christopher, 204
  ,,   ,, Elias, 205
  ,,   ,, Thomas, 203
  ,,   ,, William, 205
Pilgrims or Palmers, 26
  ,, of the Cross, 28
Pirou, Robert de, 12
Plague, The, 122
Pocklington, 101
Poll-tax returns, 133-135
Pollington, Ydannia de, 43
Pontefract, 1, 25, 106, 111, 157, 159
Pontefract, Prior of, 10, 11
  ,,   Honor of, 129, 161
  ,,   Castle of, 141
  ,,   siege of, 157, 160
Pope Urban II., 27, 28 and *note*
  ,, Clement V., 53
Potterlawe, 8, 12 *note*, 50 *note*, 119
  ,, inquest at, 60
  ,, site of, 15, 16, 57, 58
Præmunire and Provisors, Statutes of, 142
Preceptory, plan of, etc., 66
Prestdaghter, Johanna, 133
Presteson, John, 133
Property of the Templars in Yorkshire, 48
Ptolemais, 33

R.

Railway Station at Temple Hirst, 246
Ralph the Deacon, 43
Raymond, Count of Tripoli, 32
  ,, Prince of Antioch, 31
Rectory at Haddlesey built, 242
Redman, Lady Elizabeth, 184
Ribstane, 6, 18, 34, 46
Richard I., 32
  ,, II., 130, 131
Richmond, Duke of, 169
Roger de Behal in Hausey, 14
Rohal, Alexander de, 12, 13
  ,, Ralph de, 20, 62
Roos, William, 90, 146
  ,, Edmund, 159
Ros, Robert de, 20, 34
Rosebery, Earl of, 200

Rudstone, Nicholas, 159
Ryther, 4
  ,, Henry, 165

S.

Sadler, Sir Ralph, 177
Salisbury, Earl of, 184
Sandhall, 106, 107
Saville, Sir Henry, 88. 179
Sawyer, Mr. John, 223, 224, 229
Scholey and Spofforth families, 226
Scott's 'Ivanhoe' quoted, 49
  ,, 'Lord of the Isles,' 91-94
Scrope, Lord, 188
Selby, 1, 3
  ,, Abbey, tenants of, at Haddlesey, 39, 43, 141
Sheffield, Earl of, 232
Sherburn, 42, 104, 122
Sherwood Farm, 12, 15
Shirwode, 128
Silkstone, 118
Skipton, 3
Slave, gift of a, 14
  ,, sale of a, 40, 41
Smethall, 63
Snaith, 4, 108, 124, 133
Sokemen described, 37
Somerset, Duke of, 180
Sorsby, Rev., Precentor of York, 205 *note*
Southill, Thomas, 85
Sprotborough, 85, 125
St. Mary's Abbey, York, 18
Stage coaches, last of, 235
Stanford, Robert de, 20
Stanley, Dean, quoted, 25
Stapilton, Christopher, 158
Stapleton, 2nd Baron, 120-131; of Carlton, 183-191
Stapleton, Sir Brian, 184-187
  ,,   ,, Miles, 9, 29, 32, 45, 54, 81, 82, 89, 123-130; of Bedale, 120-123
Stapleton, Lord Robert, 18
  ,, Hon. Brian John, 185
  ,, Sir Nicholas, 45, 95, 102
Stapulton, John, 184
Stapylton-Chetwynd, H. E., 191
Stephen, Earl of Albemarle and Holderness, 29

Stephenson, W. Mill, 146, 147
Stirling, siege of, 91
Stiveton, Robert, 39
Strensall, John, Vicar of Brayton, 86
Stuteville, Nicholas de, 13 *note*
Suffolk, Duke and Duchess of, 211
Swynefleet, 101

T.

Talbot, Lord, 107
Tempest, Nicholas and Dousabella, 165
Templar tenants, 64
    ,,   destruction of, 67, 69
    ,,   benefits of, 69-72
Temple Newsam, 6, 10, 18
Temple Hirst, how situated, etc., 22, 61, 103, 119, 143, 167-171, 189
Tewkesbury, 109, 113, 114
Thoresby's 'Ducatus,' 2
Thorn, 65
Thorntons of Birkin, 233
Thriske, William, 166
Throckmorton, Lady, 190
Tickhill Castle, 13
Tilli, Otto de, 12 *note*
  ,, Ralph de, 9
  ,, Roger de, 8
Torr, James, the Church historian, 80 *note*
Towton, Battle of, 187
Tristram, Dr., quoted, 32
Turnpike from Doncaster to Selby, 235
Tutbury Castle, 104

U.

Umfraville, Sir Gilbert, 107

V.

Vavasour, Sir H., 120
Venella, Thomas de, 14
Verelst, H. W., 181
Vernoil, H., 12, 39, 62
Vesci, Lord, 107
Vilers, 9
Vili de Humphrey, 42
Villain, Hamelscia, 13 *note*, 37, 40

W.

Wadworth, William de, 14
Wake, Lord, 107
Ward, Sir Simon, 104
Weighton (Market), 101
Wentworth, Viscount, 179
Wesel in Holland, 217
West, Sir William, 173
West Haddlesey (see also Haddlesey West)
Westerdale, 18
Wetherby, 18, 104
Wheater, 'History of Cawood' quoted, 103
Whiteley, 18
Whitkirk, Vicar of, 20 *note*
Wighill Stapletons, 120-123
Willegby or Willeby, Robert de, 41, 42
William I., 1, 3
Willoughby de Eresby, Lord, 209
Wills proved at Temple Hirst, 167-170
Wilton Castle 165 *note*
Witewode, 13 *note*
Wolsey, Cardinal, 150
Womersly, William, 167
Woolley, parish of, 118
Wressil, 100
Wycliffe, John, 10, 122, 143, 155
Wykerlay, Robert de, 42
Wynhill, 18

Y.

York, City of, 78, 97, 102-105
Yorkshire Archæological Journal quoted from, 14 *et seq.*
Yorkshire, Archbishops of, 74, 75
    Greenfield, 51, 68, 96
    Gray, 74-78
    Thomson, 243

Z.

Zetland, Earl of, 158

THE END.

OTHER WORKS BY THE REV. J. N. WORSFOLD.

THE VAUDOIS OF PIEDMONT: Visits to their Valleys, with a Sketch of their Remarkable History as a Church and People. Price 3s. 6d. Second edition.

LIFE OF PETER WALDO. Cloth limp, 1s.

WATER MADE WINE. Price 1d.

LECTURE ON JOHN WYCLIFFE. Second edition. Dedicated, by permission, to the Archbishop of York. Price 6d.

SALVATION BY GRACE. Price 2d.

RITUALISM EXPOSED. Price 6d., or 3s. per dozen for distribution.

RIGHT OF INFANTS TO BAPTISM. 2s. per dozen.

PRAYERS AND HYMNS FOR USE OF NATIONAL AND OTHER SCHOOLS. 3d. each; 2s. 6d. per dozen.

BLESSED HOPE SERIES OF TRACTS. 2s. 6d. per 100.

The Wellington Tract Series.

1. 'IS IT WELL WITH THY CHILD?' Fifteenth Thousand. 2s. 6d. per 100.
2. 'THOU SHALT DIE!' Eighty-second Thousand. 1s. 6d. per 100.
3. 'SABBATH BREAKING AND KEEPING.'* Eighty-third Thousand. 2s. per 100.
4. 'WHERE ART THOU?' Eighth Thousand. 2s. 6d. per 100.
5. 'COME TO THE WATERS!' Sixth Thousand. 6s. per 100.
6. 'DOES MASSA LOVE MY JESUS?'* Fifth Thousand. 3s. per 100.
7. 'TRUST IN THE LORD.'* Fifth Thousand. 2s. per 100.
8. 'THE SWEARING MATCH!'* Fifth Thousand. 2s. per 100.
9. 'SPIRITUAL WORSHIP.'* Fifth Thousand. 9d. per 100.
10. 'CLAIMS OF THE TEMPERANCE MOVEMENT.' Second Thousand. 4s. per 100.

Assorted Packets, 3s. per 100.

The Tracts marked thus (*) are Narratives.

☞ The Author will send any of the above post free on receipt of remittance with the order.

www.ingramcontent.com/pod-product-compliance
Lightning Source LLC
Chambersburg PA
CBHW032105230426
43672CB00009B/1651